Creative Accounting

Creative Accounting

The effectiveness of financial
reporting in the UK

Trevor Pijper

150th YEAR
M
MACMILLAN

First published in the United Kingdom by
MACMILLAN PUBLISHERS LTD, 1993
Distributed by Globe Book Services Ltd
Brunel Road, Houndmills,
Basingstoke, Hants RG21 2XS, England

ISBN 0-333-59592-0

A catalogue record for this book
is available from The British Library.

While every care has been taken in compiling the
information contained in this publication, the publishers
and author accept no responsibility for any errors or
omissions.

Typeset and printed in Great Britain

Contents

Acknowledgements

Oh Mary this London's a wonderful sight,
With the people here working by day and by night,
They don't sow potatoes nor barley nor wheat,
But there's gangs of them digging for gold in the street.
At least when I asked them that's what I was told,
So I just took a hand at this digging for gold.
But for all that I found there I might as well be
Where the Mountains of Mourne sweep down to the sea.

Percy French[1]

For giving me an opportunity to search for gold in their city, I am greatly indebted to the London office of the accounting firm, Ernst & Young. That my efforts were unsuccessful should not detract from the considerable assistance I received from the members of the firm's Technical Services Department. My debts are owed to all its many talented members, Ron Paterson, Allister Wilson and Vivian Pereira being among the larger creditors.

I would also like to thank my mentors at the stockbroking firm, Fergusson Bros., Hall, Stewart & Co., in that other city of gold, Johannesburg. William Bowler and Steve Rubenstein deserve special mention.

My good fortune in being able to exchange ideas with all of these people is matched only by the unfailing support and encouragement that I have received from my father, Fredrik; his brother, Jan; and my wife, Anne.

My greatest debt is, however, owed to my late mother, Kathleen Patricia, for reminding me that there is more to life than digging for gold and recording the outcome of that activity.

TJP
Vancouver, B.C.
May 1993

1 *The Words of 100 Irish Songs and Ballads* (1992), (Cork: Bookmark)

Preface

In May 1992, Terry Smith wrote a book titled *Accounting for Growth*.[1] Suspecting that 'much of the growth in profits which had occurred in the 1980s was the result of accounting sleight of hand', he set out 'to expose the main techniques involved, and to give live examples of companies using those techniques.'[2] *Accounting for Growth* contains a table showing the relatively poor share price performances of companies 'using 5 or more of the 11 accounting and financing techniques'[3] identified in a 1991 research report co-authored by Smith and Richard Hannah. By allocating 'blobs' to companies which used these 'techniques', Smith claimed to have unearthed 'an amazingly accurate guide to the companies to avoid.'[4]

My conviction that the matter was unlikely to be that simple has prompted me to explore the effectiveness of the current system of financial reporting in the UK from a broader perspective. What is the purpose of financial reporting? Does the stock-market pay any attention to company financial statements? Do the statements contain useful information? Can the profit and loss account ever be a reliable measure of financial performance? What significance should be attached to the balance sheet? Is there such a thing as 'creative accounting'?

I have attempted to answer these questions in the context of the reforms introduced by the Companies Act 1989. Since the inception of the Financial Reporting Council in May 1990 its operational bodies, the Accounting Standards Board and the Financial Reporting Review Panel, have featured prominently in the financial press. Now is an appropriate time to examine whether the new regime is likely to succeed in its objective of improving financial reporting practices in the UK. What are the problems? Are there any solutions? Whose responsibility is it when the system fails to operate properly? What is the role of the auditor? Will the recommendations of the Cadbury Committee help to restore the public's confidence in financial reporting?

There are no easy answers to any of these questions. The suggestions which follow are based on my work experiences in the audit, review and use of financial statements. I would like the book to be seen as a contribution to the debate about the effectiveness of financial reporting in the UK. It will have achieved its purpose if it gives readers a better understanding of the complexities and limitations of company financial statements.

1   Smith, Terry (1992), *Accounting for Growth* (London: Century Business).
2   *Ibid.*, p.4.
3   *Ibid.*, p.5.
4   *Ibid.*, p.4.

Index of Extracts from Company Financial Statements

Company

1 : Financial Reporting – Serving a Useful Purpose?

> *A rich man had a steward who was reported to him for*
> *squandering his property. He summoned him and said, 'What is*
> *this I hear about you? Prepare a full account of your*
> *stewardship, because you can no longer be my steward.'*
>
> Luke 16: 1–2[1]

BACKGROUND

Difficult problems are sometimes solved when viewed from a different perspective. Whether an examination of the current state of financial reporting in the UK should begin from a point nearly 2000 years ago is open to debate but the Parable of the Dishonest Steward seems a useful place to start. It may not be the earliest known reference to the existence of financial reporting but I can think of few better descriptions of its purpose. Fearing that his property had been squandered, the rich man wanted information about his financial affairs. He therefore asked for a suitable account to be drawn up.

This book seeks to answer basic questions about the current system of financial reporting in the UK. Why are financial statements drawn up at all? What do they seek to achieve? Is there a need for them to be audited? Should their preparers be regulated? What level of knowledge does their user need to have in order to understand them? Is there such a thing as 'creative accounting'? Whose responsibility is it when the system fails to operate properly? To answer these questions, it seems sensible to start by clarifying the purpose of the financial reporting process itself.

PURPOSE OF FINANCIAL REPORTING

The Accounting Standards Board (ASB) has defined the objective of financial statements as being:

> to provide information about the financial position, performance and financial adaptability of an enterprise that is useful to a wide range of users in making economic decisions.[2]

1

I doubt whether the rich man in the parable would have used terms like 'financial position, performance and financial adaptability.' His request for information would probably have been couched in relatively uncomplicated terms. He wanted to know the extent of the damage to his property before considering the appointment of a replacement steward.

His request for information nevertheless puts him in a similar position to today's user of financial statements. Whether this information needs to be about the 'financial position, performance and financial adaptability' of the enterprise concerned is not certain. The use of these terms seems to prejudge the issue. The form and content of the information required should be determined by its relevance to the decision-making process. One of the purposes of this book is to explore the usefulness of today's balance sheets, profit and loss accounts and cash flow statements. These will be examined in the context of the financial reporting process, which can be summarized as follows:

- financial reporting is essentially concerned with the provision of information;
- users of financial statements need this information in order to make economic decisions;
- its usefulness is a function of its relevance to the decision-making process;
- responsibility for the decisions lies with the user. It seems logical for the user to specify the form, content and extent of the information required and to object if the information provided is considered to be inadequate.

I should stress that this book is concerned with the financial reporting process taken as a whole. The drawing up of financial statements is a critical part of the process but it is equally important to consider the role of the auditor and the regulatory body currently responsible for the effectiveness of the financial reporting process in the UK. The book is, however, primarily and ultimately concerned with the user. Does the current system provide the information needed to make sensible economic decisions? Is the information reliable? Can users make sense of it? Is there scope for improving the effectiveness of the decision-making process by enhancing the quality of the information?

Although there is a wide range of potential users of financial statements, the book has been written from the perspective of the providers of finance: existing and potential shareholders, bankers, financiers and other creditors. This 'investor' category is commonly used as a proxy for other users like employees, customers, taxation and other governmental authorities, all of whom have an interest in financial information about the reporting entity.

Having clarified the purpose of financial reporting, it is instructive to consider the behaviour of the rich man's steward 2000 years ago. His dismissal for dishonesty or incompetence being imminent:

> He called in his master's debtors one by one. To the first he said, 'How much do you owe my master?' He replied, 'One hundred measures of olive oil.' He said to him, 'Here is

your promissory note. Sit down and quickly write one for fifty.' Then to another he said, 'And you, how much do you owe?' He replied, 'One hundred kors of wheat.' He said to him, 'Here is your promissory note; write one for eighty.' [3]

It seems inevitable that he should behave in this manner. One would expect him to produce a fraudulent account of his stewardship. He had nothing to lose. There was no requirement for his account to be audited and there would have been no accounting standards to guide the auditor. The rich man in the parable seems certain to suffer the consequences of this lack of regulation. His financial loss magnified, there would appear to be no recourse to a negligent third party. The case for detailed and effective regulation appears to be compelling.

LEGISLATIVE REQUIREMENTS AND ACCOUNTING STANDARDS

Although the purpose of financial reporting has changed little since the days of the rich man, today's steward would have to cope with a significant body of legislation. The rich man's business would almost certainly be conducted through the mechanism of a legally separate entity. That would bring it under the protection of the Companies Act 1985. Section 226(1) of the Act requires that:

> The directors of every company shall prepare for each financial year of the company –
> (a) a balance sheet as at the last day of the year, and
> (b) a profit and loss account.

This is not dissimilar to what the rich man wanted. His equivalent today would, however, appear to be significantly better off. Section 226(2) of the Act stipulates that:

> The balance sheet shall give a true and fair view of the state of affairs of the company as at the end of the financial year; and the profit and loss account shall give a true and fair view of the profit or loss of the company for the financial year.

This requirement seems designed to ensure that the financial statements are of a satisfactory standard. They have to give a 'true and fair' view. It should ensure that they provide a sound basis for making sensible economic decisions about the reporting entity.

The 'true and fair' concept is relatively new, particularly when viewed from the 2000 year perspective of the rich man and his steward. It first appeared in the Companies Act 1947.[4] Prior to 1947, financial statements had to be 'true and correct'. Confusion about the meaning of this requirement eventually led to its replacement. Could financial statements be 'true' but not 'correct', or 'correct' but not 'true'?

In an attempt to overcome confusion of this kind, 'true and correct' became 'true and fair'. Yet the concept remains difficult to grasp. What does 'true and fair' really mean? How does the preparer set about achieving this happy state of affairs? It is important to note that the 'true and fair' concept is an overriding requirement. Strict compliance with the letter of the Companies Act 1985 may not be sufficient to achieve the 'true and fair' objective. Section 226 also contains the following requirements:

(3) A company's individual accounts shall comply with the provisions of Schedule 4 as to the form and content of the balance sheet and profit and loss account and additional information to be provided by way of notes to the accounts.

(4) Where compliance with the provisions of that Schedule, and the other provisions of this Act as to the matters to be included in a company's individual accounts or in notes to those accounts, would not be sufficient to give a true and fair view, the necessary additional information shall be given in the accounts or in a note to them.

(5) If in special circumstances compliance with any of those provisions is inconsistent with the requirement to give a true and fair view, the directors shall depart from that provision to the extent necessary to give a true and fair view.

Particulars of any such departure, the reasons for it and its effect shall be given in a note to the accounts.

Section 226 is concerned with the financial statements of individual companies. There are identical requirements in section 227 governing the preparation of consolidated financial statements where the reporting entity is a parent company.

The sections recognize two rather alarming possibilities. First, mere compliance with the legislation contained in the Companies Act 1985 will not ensure that the financial statements give a true and fair view. Secondly, some of the provisions contained in the legislation may even be inconsistent with the achievement of that objective. The 'true and fair' requirement is paramount. Yet what does it mean? Being a legal concept its meaning might one day be explained by the courts. Until then, the rich man's steward is unlikely to receive a satisfactory explanation as to what he is expected to achieve when drawing up his financial statements. He will, though, be aware that they need to be of a reasonably satisfactory standard. The total of the promissory notes has to bear some relation to the real amounts owed by his master's debtors.

The task of today's steward is further complicated by the existence of accounting standards. He will not be pleased to learn that there is more to preparing financial statements than mere compliance with the Companies Act 1985. This development is also a relatively new one. Prior to the Companies Act 1989 (which amended the 1985 legislation), there were no references to accounting standards in the legislation. Until as recently as 1970 there were no mandatory accounting standards at all. The company law provisions were relatively basic and accounting practices were varied. Only in 1970 did the Institute of Chartered Accountants in England and Wales (ICAEW) decide to set up the Accounting Standards Steering Committee to develop definitive standards for financial reporting. That body became the Accounting Standards Committee (ASC). By the time of its demise in 1990, it had recommended thirty-four Statements of Standard Accounting Practice (SSAPs) or revised SSAPs for final approval by the six major accountancy bodies in the UK and Ireland.

These standards were 'developed in the public interest ... as being authoritative statements on accounting practice. Their primary aim is to narrow the areas of difference and variety in the accounting treatment of the matters with which they deal.'[5] Given the burden they impose on the preparer, today's steward will probably want to hear a more convincing case for their desirability. The following summary by David Solomons[6] is worth examining further:

> The first argument is that the market cannot be depended on to discipline promptly corporations that are left free to choose what to report and how to report to their investors and creditors. Even if good accounting can be relied on to drive out bad in the long run, too much damage may be inflicted on investors in the short run to make freedom from regulation in this field an acceptable policy.
>
> The second argument rests on the need for comparability of the financial information published by business enterprises. The value of information provided by each enterprise to its stockholders is greatly enhanced if it can be compared easily with information from other enterprises.
>
> The third argument appeals to the limited capacity of receivers of information to interpret and use it.
>
> The fourth argument appeals to the credibility of financial reporting in the eyes of the public.

Of these four arguments, the first and third are of particular interest. The first is based on what Solomons has termed the 'peculiarities of information as a commodity'. He explains that 'its consumption or enjoyment by one individual or group does not reduce its availability to others. It is difficult to exclude "free riders" when information is made available to those who initially might be willing to pay for it, and this fact may be expected to depress the effective demand for it in a free market. On the supply side, there may be greater gains to managers who have information from withholding it than from disclosing it; so supply may likewise be depressed.' Solomons concludes that 'regulation is needed to correct these market imperfections'. The third argument stresses the advantages which result from having standard accounting practices that the user can take for granted. Closer examination of these arguments is beyond the scope of this book. It is sufficient to note that both seem to imply an inability on the part of users to determine what information they need to make sensible economic decisions. Whether regulation can be an effective substitute for user ignorance of this kind, is an issue that lies at the heart of much of the discussion in this book.

Regardless of whether today's steward finds the case for accounting standards to be particularly compelling, would he be required to comply with them? It should be remembered that, prior to the Companies Act 1989, there were no references to accounting standards in the legislation. Instead there was, and still is, a rather confusing reference to certain accounting *principles* that have to be followed in the preparation of financial statements. These principles are contained in paragraphs 10 to 14 of Schedule 4 to the Companies Act 1985:

10   The company shall be presumed to be carrying on business as a going concern.

11   Accounting policies shall be applied consistently within the same accounts and from one financial year to the next.

12   The amount of any item shall be determined on a prudent basis, and in particular –
    (a)   only profits realised at the balance sheet date shall be included in the profit and loss account; and
    (b)   all liabilities and losses which have arisen or are likely to arise in respect of the financial year to which the accounts relate or a previous financial year shall be taken into account, including those which only become apparent between the balance sheet date and the date on which it is signed on behalf of the board of directors in pursuance of section 233 of this Act.

13   All income and charges relating to the financial year to which the accounts relate shall be taken into account, without regard to the date of receipt or payment.

14   In determining the aggregate amount of any item the amount of each individual asset or liability that falls to be taken into account shall be determined separately.

The significance of these principles will become evident later in the book. Compliance with them is subject to the overriding requirement that the financial statements should give a 'true and fair' view. Particulars of, and reasons for, any departures would have to be disclosed in the financial statements.

Although these principles are not accounting standards as such, they are very similar to the fundamental accounting concepts contained in SSAP 2 *Disclosure of accounting policies*. To that extent, compliance with accounting standards is mandatory under the law. The Companies Act 1989 contained the first reference to accounting standards in the legislation. It requires large companies to comply with the following requirement:

> It shall be stated whether the accounts have been prepared in accordance with applicable accounting standards and particulars of any material departure from those standards and the reasons for it shall be given.[7]

Applicable accounting standards are those issued by the Accounting Standards Board (ASB), which has formally adopted the SSAPs issued by its predecessor body, the ASC. It should be noted that the law does not require companies to comply with these accounting standards. It merely requires large companies to state whether their accounts have been prepared in accordance with them. The primary legal requirement is that the accounts should give a 'true and fair' view.

The obligation to comply with accounting standards is derived from the standards themselves. The *Explanatory Foreword* to accounting standards issued by the ASC in 1975 and revised in 1986, explains that the standards 'are applicable to all financial statements whose purpose is to give a true and fair view of financial position and of profit or loss for the period'.[8] However, the Foreword also notes that:

> They are not intended to be a comprehensive code of rigid rules. They do not supersede the exercise of an informed judgement in determining what constitutes a true and fair view in each circumstance. It would be impracticable to establish a code sufficiently elaborate to cater for all business situations and innovations and for every exceptional or marginal case. A justifiable reason may therefore exist why an accounting standard may not be applicable in a given situation, namely when application would conflict with the giving of

a true and fair view. In such cases, modified or alternative treatments will require to be adopted.[9]

The ASB has adopted a slightly different approach. Its draft *Foreword to Accounting Standards*, issued in 1991 states that:

because accounting standards are formulated with the objective of ensuring that the information resulting from their application faithfully represents the underlying commercial activity, the Board envisages that only in exceptional circumstances will departure from the requirements of an accounting standard be necessary in order for financial statements to give a true and fair view.[10]

It seems that the ASB has more confidence in its ability to formulate accounting standards that give a 'true and fair' view. The important point to note, however, is that both the ASC and the ASB have had to work within the constraint of the 'true and fair' requirement which has been granted paramount status by the legislature.

The position faced by today's steward can therefore be summarized as follows:

- His financial statements have to be prepared in accordance with the Companies Act 1985, as amended by the Companies Act 1989.
- The statements are required to give a 'true and fair' view of the company's state of affairs at the end of its financial year and of its profit or loss for the period then ended.
- The financial statements should comply with the accounting principles and disclosure requirements contained in the Companies Act 1985. Compliance with these provisions is, however, subject to the overriding 'true and fair' requirement.
- If the reporting entity is a large company, the financial statements should state whether or not they have been prepared in accordance with applicable accounting standards.
- The body responsible for issuing the applicable accounting standards envisages that compliance with them 'will normally be necessary for the financial statements to give a true and fair view'.[11] Departures are, however, allowed in exceptional circumstances to ensure that the 'true and fair' requirement contained in the legislation can be met.

It is clear that today's steward has been given a great deal of authoritative, well researched and fairly detailed guidance. The suspicion remains, though, that he is ultimately pursuing a vague and poorly defined objective.

THE ROLE OF THE AUDITOR

The possibility that today's steward might adopt the same course of action as his dishonest predecessor 2000 years ago has not been overlooked by the legislature. Accordingly, section 235 of the Companies Act 1985 requires that:

(1) A company's auditors shall make a report to the company's members on all annual accounts of the company of which copies are to be laid before the company in general meeting during their tenure of office.

(2) The auditors' report shall state whether in the auditors' opinion the annual accounts have been properly prepared in accordance with this Act, and in particular whether a true and fair view is given –

  (a) in the case of an individual balance sheet, of the state of affairs of the company as at the end of the financial year,

  (b) in the case of an individual profit and loss account, of the profit or loss of the company for the financial year,

  (c) in the case of group accounts, of the state of affairs as at the end of the financial year, and the profit or loss for the financial year, of the undertakings included in the consolidation as a whole, so far as concerns members of the company.

The auditors' report is usually similar to the one in the following example:

Illustration 1.1: Polly Peck International PLC (1989)

REPORT OF THE AUDITORS
to the members of Polly Peck International PLC

We have audited the Financial Statements set out on pages 31 to 55 in accordance with Auditing Standards.

In our opinion the Financial Statements give a true and fair view of the state of affairs of the Company and the Group at 31st December 1989 and of the profit and source and application of funds of the Group for the year ended on that date and have been properly prepared in accordance with the Companies Act 1985.

Stoy Hayward *Chartered Accountants*

8 Baker Street
London W1M 1DA
17th April 1990

The auditors' report is a brief document. It confirms that the auditors have discharged the duties required of them by the Companies Act 1985. Its wording closely mirrors the contents of section 235 reproduced above. It is not an extensive report, but it is clear and unambiguous. It confirms that the financial statements are of the standard required by the legislature.

EXPECTATIONS OF THE USER

In the 2000 years since The Parable of the Dishonest Steward, a great deal has been done to improve the lot of the user of financial statements. This chapter has outlined the legislative requirements affecting the preparation of financial statements. They are designed to ensure that the statements contain relevant information, that they are comparable, that they are credible in the eyes of the public and that their reliability can be taken for granted.

The chapter has also noted that the requirements seem to have been developed on the basis that most users have a limited ability to understand financial information. It would even appear that they are collectively unable to determine exactly what information they need for their decision making. Being unable to discipline errant preparers themselves, legislation has been introduced to do it for them. Has it succeeded? Are today's users better off than the rich man in the parable?

The spate of legislation put together in the public interest in the last 20 years or so has almost certainly created an expectation that today's users should be better off. After all, a great deal has been done on their behalf by many clever and dedicated people. Despite these efforts, today's users seem to be dissatisfied.

In May 1991, the Financial Reporting Council (which will be discussed in more detail in Chapter 2), the London Stock Exchange and the accountancy profession set up a committee (the 'Cadbury Committee') to address 'The Financial Aspects of Corporate Governance'. The Committee's report was published on 1 December 1992. The reasons for its establishment were explained as follows:

> Its sponsors were concerned at the perceived low level of confidence both in financial reporting and in the ability of auditors to provide the safeguards which the users of company reports sought and expected. The underlying factors were seen as the looseness of accounting standards, the absence of a clear framework for ensuring that directors kept under review the controls in their business, and competitive pressures both on companies and on auditors which made it difficult for auditors to stand up to demanding boards.[12]

The Committee also referred to a so-called 'Expectations Gap'. In the context of recommendations on ways to increase the effectiveness and value of the audit, it noted that:

> An essential first step is to be clear about the respective responsibilities of directors and auditors for preparing and reporting on the financial statements of companies, in order to begin to narrow the 'expectations gap'.
>
> The auditors' role is to report whether the financial statements give a true and fair view, and the audit is designed to provide a reasonable assurance that the financial statements are free of material misstatements. The auditors' role is **not** (to cite a few of the misunderstandings) to prepare the financial statements, nor to provide absolute assurance that the figures in the financial statements are correct, nor to provide a guarantee that the company will continue in existence. The Auditing Practices Board is at present developing proposals for an expanded report which would describe the key features of the audit process. The Committee supports this initiative. Auditors' reports should state clearly the auditors' responsibilities for reporting on the financial statements, as a counterpart to a statement of directors' responsibilities for preparing the financial statements.[13]

These proposals are quite extraordinary. They suggest a staggering lack of knowledge on the part of most users of financial statements. Looking at the auditors' report contained in Illustration 1.1, it seems obvious that:

- the auditor has audited but not prepared the financial statements;
- the report is neither a guarantee nor a certificate of fact;
- the auditor is simply expressing an opinion as to whether the financial statements give a 'true and fair' view, and whether they have been properly prepared in accordance with the Companies Act.
- the auditor has not provided a guarantee that the company will continue to exist in the future.

Having demonstrated their inability to understand a report comprised of 77 words, shareholders of companies will soon receive a replacement containing 273. In May 1993, the Auditing Practices Board issued a new auditing standard titled *Auditors' Reports on Financial Statements*. It contains the following example of the audit report most likely to be appended to financial statements in the UK:

Illustration 1.2: *Auditors' Reports on Financial Statements*[14]

Example of an unqualified opinion: company incorporated in Great Britain.

Auditors' Report to the Shareholders of XYZ PLC

We have audited the financial statements on pages ... to ... which have been prepared under the historical cost convention [as modified by the revaluation of certain fixed assets] and the accounting policies set out on page ...

Respective responsibilities of directors and auditors
As described on page ... the company's directors are responsible for the preparation of financial statements. It is our responsibility to form an independent opinion, based on our audit, on those statements and to report our opinion to you.

Basis of opinion
We conducted our audit in accordance with Auditing Standards issued by the Auditing Practices Board. An audit includes examination, on a test basis, of evidence relevant to the amounts and disclosures in the financial statements. It also includes an assessment of the significant estimates and judgments made by the directors in the preparation of the financial statements, and of whether the accounting policies are appropriate to the company's circumstances, consistently applied and adequately disclosed.

We planned and performed our audit so as to obtain all the information and explanations which we considered necessary in order to provide us with sufficient evidence to give reasonable assurance that the financial statements are free from material misstatement, whether caused by fraud or other irregularity or error. In forming our opinion we also evaluated the overall adequacy of the presentation of information in the financial statements.

Opinion
In our opinion the financial statements give a true and fair view of the state of the company's affairs as at 31 December 19.. and of its profit [loss] for the year then ended and have been properly prepared in accordance with the Companies Act 1985.

Registered auditors   *Address*
Date

The new auditors' report contains a paragraph dealing with the respective responsibilities of directors and auditors. The Cadbury Committee envisages that their statement of directors' responsibilities will be included immediately before the auditors' report. As the latter includes a statement of the auditors' responsibilities, the two statements are expected to be complementary. The Committee has recommended that the directors' statement should cover the following matters:

- the legal requirement for directors to prepare financial statements for each financial year which give a true and fair view of the state of affairs of the company (or group) as at the end of the financial year and of the profit and loss for that period;
- the responsibility of the directors for maintaining adequate accounting records, for safeguarding the assets of the company (or group), and for preventing and detecting fraud and other irregularities;
- confirmation that suitable accounting policies, consistently applied and supported by reasonable and prudent judgements and estimates, have been used in the preparation of the financial statements;
- confirmation that applicable accounting standards have been followed, subject to any material departures disclosed and explained in the notes to the accounts.[15]

It is ironic that the legislature's attempt to look after the interests of users of financial statements has progressed to a point where it is now necessary to repeat much of the legislation in the financial statements themselves. Having failed to study it in its original form, will users bother to read it when it is repeated to them every year?

Of greater significance, however, is the possibility that the legislation might be incapable of achieving what users expect of it. It is up to the users themselves to determine what information they need in order to make economic decisions about the reporting entity. That is their responsibility. Relying on accounting standards and the Companies Act to do it for them may prove to be a poor substitute.

CONCLUSION

Financial reporting can be said to serve a useful purpose when it supplies the information users need to make economic decisions. This would appear to be an eternal truth, or one that dates back at least 2000 years. The questions that need to be addressed are how to communicate the information and how to safeguard its reliability.

This chapter has outlined some of the steps taken in the last 20 years to address these issues. Most of the effort reflects a desire to solve the problem by regulating the preparation and audit of the financial statements. The burden imposed on the preparer has increased dramatically. A great deal of emphasis has been placed on the responsibilities of directors and auditors. The expectation has undoubtedly been created that users should be able to take the integrity and reliability of the financial statements for granted. Worryingly, however, there now appear to be grounds for believing that the financial reporting process is not delivering a product of the quality expected by those charged with regulating it.

Whether financial statements are capable of supplying valuable information about the reporting entity is an issue which will be examined in other chapters of this book. Whether this information should be focused on the financial position, performance and financial adaptability of the entity will also be addressed. It is, however, important not to lose sight of the role of the user in the financial reporting process.

It was common practice in the Palestine of the rich man and the dishonest steward for agents to exploit their master's debtors by inflating their indebtedness.[16] By reducing the outstanding amounts, the steward was, in fact, not guilty of preparing a false account of his stewardship. He was simply reflecting the real debts owed to his master. His dishonesty had nothing to do with his accounting. It related instead to the squandering of his master's property. The rich man might have had the benefit of divine inspiration but he was nevertheless acutely aware of the context in which the stewardship accounts were to be prepared. He expected his steward to exploit his debtors by inflating their indebtedness. The point is equally valid today. The effectiveness of any system of financial reporting depends heavily on the knowledge, skills and abilities of the user of the financial statements. Legislation and regulation are unlikely to be effective substitutes.

1   *New American Bible* (1986) (Nashville, Tennessee: Thomas Nelson). Copyright © 1986 by the Confraternity of Christian Doctrine.
2   Accounting Standards Board (1991) 'The objective of financial statements', Exposure Draft of Chapter 1, *Statement of Principles* (London: ASB), July, para. 12.
3   *New American Bible*, Luke 16: 5–7.
4   Companies Act 1947, s 13(1).
5   *Explanatory Foreword* (Revised August 1986), ASC, para. 1.
6   *The Political Implications of Accounting and Accounting Standard Setting*, Accounting & Business Research, Spring 1983.
7   Companies Act 1985, Sch. 4 , para. 36A.
8   *Explanatory Foreword* (Revised August 1986), para. 2.
9   *Ibid.*, para. 5.
10 *Foreword to Accounting Standards*, ASB, 1991, para. 16.
11 *Ibid.*, para. 15.
12 The Committee on the Financial Aspects of Corporate Governance (1992), *Report of the Committee on the Financial Aspects of Corporate Governance* (London: Gee and Co. Ltd), para. 2.1.
13 *Ibid.*, paras. 5.13–5.14.
14 Auditing Practices Board (1993), *Statement of Auditing Standards, 600 – Auditors' Reports on Financial Statements*, May, Appendix 2, Example 1.
15 *Report of the Committee on the Financial Aspects of Corporate Governance*, Appendix 3, para. 2.
16 *New American Bible* (1986) p. 1171.

2: The New Financial Reporting Regime in the UK

We put too much faith in systems and too little in men
Disraeli

BACKGROUND

In November 1987, the Consultative Committee of Accountancy Bodies (CCAB) appointed a committee to review and make recommendations on the process of setting accounting standards in the UK and Ireland. Chaired by Sir Ronald Dearing, it presented its report in September 1988. The Committee's recommendations have led to radical changes in the financial reporting environment. They represent an attempt to improve the quality of financial reporting by increasing the level of regulation. The chairman of the Financial Reporting Council (FRC) was able to describe the process rather more elegantly in the FRC's Second Annual Review, dated November 1992:

> The effective working of the financial aspects of a market economy rests on the validity of the underlying premises of integrity in the conduct of business and reliability in the provision of information. Even though in the great majority of cases that presumption is wholly justified, there needs to be strong institutional underpinning.
>
> That institutional framework had been shown to be inadequate. The last two to three years have accordingly seen a series of measures by the financial and business community to strengthen it.[1]

The measures originate to a very significant extent from the recommendations contained in the Dearing Report. They are worth examining in detail because they reveal a great deal about the perceived effectiveness of regulation in securing an improvement in financial reporting practices.

The Dearing Committee owes its appointment to dissatisfaction with the body previously responsible for setting accounting standards in the UK, the Accounting Standards Committee (ASC). As noted in the previous chapter, the ASC's origins can be traced to 1970, when the desire to regulate preparers of financial statements first began to gain momentum. Davies, Paterson and Wilson summarized the background to the establishment of the ASC in *UK GAAP – Generally Accepted Accounting Practice in the United Kingdom*, in the following terms:

> Prior to 1970, there were no mandatory requirements in the UK outside company law governing the presentation of financial statements of companies; and even those company law provisions which did exist comprised only the basic minimum, which was inadequate for the purpose of achieving a satisfactory standard of financial reporting. Consequently, accounting practices were varied, inconsistent and sometimes inappropriate; inter-firm and inter-period comparisons were difficult as companies altered accounting treatments and resorted to such practices as 'window-dressing' and 'reserve accounting' to achieve desired results in order to present a picture of profitability and growth.[2]

It is interesting to speculate whether this observation would still be valid at the time of the ASC's demise, 20 years later in July 1990.

The ASC was a voluntary, part-time, 21-member Committee drawn from the accounting profession, industry and commerce. It established working parties to develop accounting standards, issued exposure drafts for public comment and submitted Statements of Standard Accounting Practice (SSAPs) for approval by the six major accountancy bodies that comprise the CCAB. The CCAB approved 34 SSAPs or revised SSAPs of which 21 were in existence at the time of the ASC's demise. Although these standards were issued under the authority of the accountancy bodies, their development included close consultation with representatives of the stock exchange, commerce, industry and government. The ASC also issued 55 exposure drafts, 2 Statements of Recommended Practice, 28 discussion papers and other documents, and 65 technical releases.

Despite a flurry of activity by the ASC in its later years, the pressure for change intensified. The authors of *UK GAAP* observed that 'as the complexities of accounting issues and requirements for more sophisticated levels of financial reporting mounted, the increased demands placed on the ASC clearly indicated that it was unable to fulfil satisfactorily the standard setting role that it was expected to perform. The ASC had to endure mounting criticism for being unable either to respond quickly to changing needs or to deal adequately with fundamental issues such as inflation accounting, off-balance sheet transactions and goodwill.'[3] The Dearing Committee was therefore appointed to review and recommend improvements to the process of setting accounting standards. It made numerous recommendations. Those relevant to the issues in this chapter are summarized below:

- Accounting standards should remain, as far as possible, the responsibility of auditors, preparers and users of accounts and there should not be a general move towards incorporating them into law.
- A Financial Reporting Council should be created covering at high level a wide constituency of interests, whose Chairman would be appointed jointly by the Secretary of State for Trade and Industry and the Governor of the Bank of England, to guide the standard-setting body on work programmes and issues of public

concern; to see that the work on accounting standards is properly financed; and to act as a powerful proactive public influence for securing good accounting practice.

- The task of devising accounting standards should be discharged by a newly constituted, expert Accounting Standards Board, with a full-time Chairman and Technical Director. Its total membership would not exceed nine. The Board would issue standards on its own authority. In the interests of clearly drawn standards avoiding compromise decisions, a majority of two thirds of the Board would suffice for approval of a standard. Government would have observer status.
- The Accounting Standards Board should establish a capability of high standing to publish authoritative, though non-mandatory, guidance on emerging issues.
- A Review Panel should be established to examine contentious departures from accounting standards by large companies.[4]

The recommendations were well received and have now been implemented. The activities of the supervisory body as well as the independent board charged with the development of accounting standards and the review panel responsible for enforcing them, are discussed in the sections which follow.

THE FINANCIAL REPORTING COUNCIL

The British government announced the establishment of the Financial Reporting Council (FRC) in February 1990. Sir Ronald Dearing was appointed as its first chairman. The primary role of the Council is to promote good financial reporting and to publicise its views on reporting standards. It is also responsible for the staffing and funding of its two operational bodies, the Accounting Standards Board (ASB) and the Financial Reporting Review Panel (the Review Panel). By December 1992, the FRC had released two Annual Reviews of The State of Financial Reporting. The chairman's statement in the first Review, dated November 1991, makes for instructive reading:

> The corporate confidence developed during the 1980s boom, the associated readiness by banks to lend and by companies to borrow, the growth of innovative accounting practices (e.g. off balance sheet financing and the development of hybrid financial instruments) sometimes designed solely to avoid an increase in reported company gearing, coupled with a framework of accounting standards that was being outpaced by such developments, have made the recession which followed a correspondingly more chastening experience for bankers, creditors and shareholders, as well as for financial reporting itself.
> The existence of weaknesses in the arrangements for formulating and securing compliance with accounting standards was well recognised long before the boom declined into recession.[5]

Its chairman's frank assessment of the state of financial reporting in the early 1990s provides a clue as to how the FRC intends to tackle the task of improving the existing framework. The need to tighten accounting standards and to strengthen the position of the auditor is stressed throughout the Review. By contrast, references to the role played by the user in the financial reporting process are fleeting:

> While the responsibility of directors is paramount, and while auditors too have a key part to play, others involved in financial reporting can and often do make a positive contribution to change. I have particularly in mind here the major influence that the institutional investors, investment analysts and financial journalists are able to wield. Lawyers and merchant bankers, in the advice they give to clients, have a contribution to make, especially in gaining recognition that the best long-term interests of a company lie in financially prudent practices rather than in resort to technical devices that, while not in conflict with the letter of accounting standards, impair the effectiveness of the system.[6]

There is nothing in the first Annual Review about users having to understand the context in which financial statements are prepared. The need to analyse and interpret them in the light of their many and significant limitations is not mentioned either. Instead of stressing the need for sophisticated analysis, there is the optimistic hope that it could be dispensed with altogether:

> I would also like to see attention given in this period to the needs of the ordinary shareholder and small trader, and also those of employees, who cannot be expected to make a reliable interpretation of full accounts in all their complexity. I should like to see greater recognition that the figures, which form the essence of accounts, need to be supported by commentaries which interpret them, perhaps by borrowing some elements of the US management discussion and analysis.[7]

The chairman of the FRC is confident that the way to improve financial reporting practices is to be found in better accounting standards, a responsible board of directors and a stronger audit function. This view is repeated in the second Annual Review, dated November 1992. It too is silent about the need for sophisticated analysis to overcome the limitations inherent in any system of financial reporting. On the subject of institutional shareholders, the Review simply notes that their 'influence in support of tighter accounting standards and good reporting is important to the whole shareholding community and to creditors'.[8]

The FRC is principally concerned with company financial statements. It is appropriate that its chairman should be confident about improving the usefulness of these documents. It remains to be seen, however, whether this can be achieved by tightening accounting standards and strengthening the procedures for ensuring that they are complied with. Future chapters will highlight the difficulties in developing a system of accounting standards capable of dealing with the complexities and uncertainties which underlie many business transactions.

THE COMPANIES ACT 1989 AND THE DEARING REPORT

Before examining the role and work of the ASB, it is necessary to consider the legislative changes brought about by the Companies Act 1989 in so far as they impact on the legal status of accounting standards. As noted in Chapter 1, the 1989 Act amends the Companies Act 1985 in a number of important respects. It provided the legislature with an opportunity to implement the recommendations of the Dearing Committee. Consequently two important proposals were incorporated into the law. The failure to implement another might, however, prove to be more significant. The two recommendations implemented by the legislature mean that:

- the financial statements of large companies have to state whether they have been prepared in accordance with applicable accounting standards. Particulars of, and reasons for, any material departure must be disclosed;[9] and
- the Secretary of State or other authorised persons are able to apply to court for an order requiring the revision of financial statements which do not comply with the requirements of the Companies Act 1985. Directors party to the approval of the defective statements could be ordered to bear the costs of the revision. Provision also exists for the directors to be notified of apparent defects, to give them the opportunity to revise the financial statements voluntarily.[10]

These changes are significant. They substantially upgrade the importance of accounting standards, giving them statutory recognition for the first time. They also provide a mechanism for the Financial Reporting Review Panel to take effective steps against errant preparers. They stop short of incorporating accounting standards into the law, which was the approach preferred by the Dearing Review Committee.

Importantly, however, another of that Committee's recommendations was not implemented. In his 1991 Review, the chairman of the FRC noted that:

> Parliament did not give the Panel the stronger hand recommended in the report of the Accounting Standards Review Committee in 1988, i.e. that there shall be a statutory rebuttable presumption in legal proceedings that accounting standards should be followed, and that when there was a material departure the onus of satisfying the court that the accounts nevertheless gave a true and fair view should lie upon the company concerned. The presumption would be to the contrary.[11]

The significance of this omission has yet to be determined. It is, however, worth noting that the FRC's 1992 Review concluded with the following, rather ominous, warning:

> One [alternative] is to give stronger teeth to the present arrangements. As may be recalled, the original Dearing Committee recommended that if the Review Panel took a case to the Courts following a departure from an accounting standard, the onus should rest with the company (and its auditors if the accounts were not qualified) to show that its accounts nevertheless gave a true and fair view. A more drastic possibility would be to create a body with powers analogous to those of the United States' Securities and Exchange Commission.

A second approach would be to make accounting standards a matter for prescription by government through statutory instruments, with enforcement by an administrative tribunal appointed by the Government.

The profession's concern to strengthen accounting standards led to the appointment of the Dearing Committee and the adoption of the present arrangements. The other alternatives are all feasible and the Financial Reporting Council will not hesitate from urging the Government to provide a stronger framework than the present one if it proves unable to bear the strains put upon it by companies determined to contest new accounting standards or by auditors who are not prepared to uphold standards in the face of company pressure.[12]

The threat to resort to more legislation contrasts sharply with concern about the ineffectiveness of the existing legislation. The chairman of the FRC's enforcement arm, the Financial Reporting Review Panel, commented in the same Annual Review that:

I also entertain serious doubts as to the appropriateness of litigation as a method of resolving some of the 'grey areas' which inevitably arise between the Accounting Standards Board's careful and sophisticated accounting standards on the one hand and the statute's disarmingly simple requirements of truth and fairness on the other.[13]

The Chairman of the FRC is confident that a 'strengthening of the inherited system of accounting standards' can be achieved.[14] It is possible that changes to the existing legislation might be made to ensure that the improved accounting standards are complied with. The 1992 Annual Review expressed concern about 'a number of issues coming before the Panel which may not conflict with the requirements of the law but which do not best serve the interests of informing shareholders and creditors on the financial affairs of companies.'[15]

THE ACCOUNTING STANDARDS BOARD

In August 1990, the ASB took over responsibility for developing, issuing and withdrawing accounting standards from the ASC. The ASB is an independent body funded by the accountancy profession, the financial community and the government. It issues standards on its own authority. The approval of the six accountancy bodies making up the CCAB is no longer required. As noted in the previous section, the accounting standards issued by the ASB have statutory recognition under the Companies Act. They could form the basis of an application to court by the Review Panel for an order requiring amendment of financial statements found to be defective. After his appointment, the chairman of the ASB commented that:

The Board has many detailed tasks to tackle, but perhaps its most important task – and that for the new system more generally – is to encourage and secure a change of climate in financial reporting, away from the tendency of a minority to use creative accounting and toward financial reporting that is genuinely balanced, helpful and informative. I believe that this change of climate is well on the way; our task now is to ensure that good progress is maintained.[16]

In November 1992, he was able to look back on 'a busy and productive year. Some key statements have been issued, and the foundations have been laid for those that follow.'[17] By that date, the ASB had:

- adopted the 22 extant SSAPs, effectively conferring on them the status of 'accounting standards' within the meaning of the amended Companies Act 1985;
- commissioned the CCAB bodies to investigate problems associated with these SSAPs;
- issued three of its own accounting standards, termed Financial Reporting Standards (FRSs) to distinguish them from the ASC's work. The first, in September 1991, replaced the ASC's SSAP 10 *Statements of source and application of funds* with a new requirement to produce a cash flow statement. The second, in July 1992, amended the accounting for subsidiary undertakings, the ASC's SSAP 14 *Group accounts* having been overtaken by changes introduced by the Companies Act 1989. The third, in October 1992, introduced radical changes to the profit and loss account. The publication of a fourth standard, to amend the ASC's SSAP 15 *Accounting for deferred tax* was imminent;
- published five of the seven chapters of its proposed Statement of Principles, intended to be the framework which underpins the accounting standards;
- continued its work on producing a standard on off-balance sheet finance, the starting point of which was an exposure draft issued by the ASC;
- published proposals on Accounting for Capital Instruments which would affect the balance sheet presentation of certain forms of financing;
- commenced work on a possible standard on the valuation of assets;
- published a discussion paper on the inclusion in annual reports of an Operating and Financial Review, a proposal that financial statements should be supported by detailed commentaries of an interpretive nature.

The above list is not a comprehensive one. It nevertheless reveals the sheer scale of the changes the ASB intends to introduce. The profit and loss account has been revamped, the source and application of funds statement scrapped and the balance sheet seems likely to be affected by changes to the presentation of certain capital instruments. More work lies ahead. Acquisition accounting, merger accounting, goodwill and other intangibles, related party transactions and accounting for associated companies and joint ventures are on the agenda for 1993. Indeed, the chairman of the FRC has warned that:

...the year ahead will severely test the whole system. The Accounting Standards Board will be dealing with a number of issues of formidable difficulty and for some of them there is no uniquely right answer. But these issues have to be faced. For example, goodwill is an increasingly important part of the assets of companies, and financial reporting has to recognise that. Similarly, the issues arising from off-balance sheet financing have to be faced and the limits of legitimacy defined. Definition in this area is bound to be controversial, but unless boundaries are set huge liabilities will progressively disappear from the balance sheet. Difficulties also arise in the area of merger and acquisition accounting.

It follows that whatever course the Board decides to adopt it will find itself the subject of well-argued, well-based criticism, as well as less principled attack from those who will be disadvantaged by its proposals.[18]

That the ASB has tackled its task with enthusiasm is beyond doubt. Whether it will be successful in 'providing shareholders and creditors with an adequate basis for understanding a company's accounts and its financial position'[19] is less certain. Some of the major difficulties facing the ASB will be examined in Chapters 4 and 5. An indication of the complexity of many of the underlying issues is provided in the next section.

THE URGENT ISSUES TASK FORCE

In March 1991, the ASB created the Urgent Issues Task Force (UITF) to provide authoritative guidance where unsatisfactory or conflicting interpretations of accounting standards or legislative requirements are found to exist. The UITF consists of 16 members who attempt to reach a consensus on the recommended accounting treatment for the issue under consideration. When this is achieved, an abstract is published. These abstracts are not accounting standards within the meaning of the law. Instead, they 'should be considered to be part of the corpus of practices forming the basis for what determines a true and fair view.'[20] Companies ignoring the abstracts run the risk of having to explain their accounting treatment to the Review Panel. The establishment of the UITF gives the new financial reporting regime the ability to act relatively quickly, compared with the time taken to develop and issue an accounting standard. Although it was intended that the UITF would be proactive as well as reactive, this has not proved to be the case. The chairman of the FRC deemed it necessary to comment that:

...we have been disappointed that issues have not been coming forward to that committee from the profession or from companies for a ruling before positions have been taken. It was principally for that purpose the Task Force was conceived. We invite auditors and companies to refer substantial new issues to the Task Force where there is real doubt about the most appropriate accounting treatment leading to a true and fair view.[21]

By February 1993, the UITF had published seven abstracts, largely in response to perceived inadequacies in existing reporting practices. They covered the following topics:

(1) Accounting for backdated supplemental interest on convertible bonds.
(2) Accounting for restructuring costs.
(3) The treatment of goodwill on disposal of a business.

(4) The presentation of long-term debtors in current assets.
(5) Transfers from current assets to fixed assets.
(6) Accounting for post-retirement benefits other than pensions.
(7) Disclosure of the true and fair override.

Some of the abstracts will be discussed in more detail in other chapters. At this point, it is sufficient simply to take a closer look at how the respective issues originated.

The first abstract resulted from uncertainty about the true cost of convertible bonds in the period prior to their conversion or redemption. Their conversion into equity would make payment of backdated supplemental interest unnecessary. Authoritative guidance was lacking on how to account for the possibility of a higher interest cost in the future and on how to deal with the backlog interest when a change in circumstances made redemption of the bonds more likely than conversion. The second abstract was a function of conflicting interpretations of the SSAP 6 definition of extraordinary items. The third was a consequence of the SSAP 22 option which allowed purchased goodwill to be eliminated from the balance sheet via a charge to reserves. The fourth arose from a lack of flexibility and consistency in the legally prescribed balance sheet formats. The fifth was a function of the different rules for accounting for diminutions in the value of current and fixed assets. The sixth resulted from confusion about the applicability of the accruals concept and the accounting principles contained in SSAP 24, to accounting for post-retirement benefits. The seventh was prompted by unsatisfactory disclosure in instances where a departure from the statutory rules was required for financial statements to give a 'true and fair' view.

The seven abstracts illustrate the difficulty in formulating a system of rules designed to govern the preparation of financial statements. Rule makers are never able to anticipate all the circumstances they would like to cover. Their rules inevitably suffer from difficulties of definition and they often have unforeseen consequences. Their scope and applicability is sometimes unclear. Not surprisingly, those most likely to be adversely affected by rules display considerable ingenuity in finding suitable ways of avoiding them. These difficulties do not, of course, negate the need for rules in the first place. They should, however, remind the user that accounting rules, like those of the road, do not guarantee the quality of the end product. Although the UITF is intended to be a proactive body, it is worth remembering that bad drivers seldom approach the traffic authorities for clarification of the rules before setting out on their journeys.

THE FINANCIAL REPORTING REVIEW PANEL

Since 1 February 1991, the Review Panel has been empowered to make applications to court for orders requiring the compulsory revision of company financial statements. Its principal role is to act as an instrument for securing good reporting practice. It was created to examine apparent departures from the accounting require-ments of the Companies Act 1985. It would concentrate on public and large private companies. It deals with individual cases by means of small groups drawn from a total membership of 24, with a further increase envisaged in the near future. Its purpose is simply to investigate those cases referred to it, whether the reference is made directly or indirectly. The latter category could include adverse press comment. It does not initiate investigations of its own accord. Its procedure is not to disclose details of cases under investigation until they are resolved, either voluntarily or by application to court.

Being a radically new and powerful body, the Review Panel's rulings were awaited with considerable interest. By late November 1992, 78 cases had been referred to it, sourced from:[22]

Recorded non-compliance with accounting standards and other requirements	25
References from individuals and corporate bodies	30
Press comment	23

These had been dealt with as follows:

Not pursued, immaterial or beyond the scope of the legislation	28
Investigated and concluded	31
Still under consideration	19

Public statements were issued in respect of 10 of the 31 concluded cases:[23]

Public Company	Matters investigated
Ultramar	Recorded non-compliance with SSAP 8.
Williams Holdings	Recorded non-compliance with SSAP 3; failure to disclose fully the names of undertakings acquired and sold.
The Shield Group	Recorded non-compliance with SSAP 6.
Forte	Accounting policies for the capitalisation of interest; the accounting treatment of expenses on major information technology projects; the absence of depreciation on freehold and long leasehold properties; the variance between the date of signing the balance sheet and the auditors' report.
Williamson Tea Holdings	Disclosure and explanation of the accounting treatment of certain items relating to overseas assets.
Associated Nursing Services	Accounting treatment of start-up costs and the adequacy of the explanation given for a change in accounting policy.
GPG	Recorded non-compliance with SSAP 6 and SSAP 3.
Trafalgar House	The reclassification of certain properties from current assets to fixed assets and the amount of Advance Corporation Tax carried forward in the balance sheet; also the accounting treatment of other matters including the disclosure in respect of the company's investment in BREL and compliance with the statutory format required for the profit and loss account.

British Gas	Presentation of the change in financial year end.
S.E.P. Industrial Holdings	The treatment as a prior year item of an amount in respect of stock provisions and the recorded non-compliance with SSAP 12.

Note: By 'recorded non-compliance' is meant that the departure from the relevant accounting requirement was disclosed in the financial statements themselves or in the auditors' report thereon or in both the financial statements and the auditors' report.

It is beyond the scope of this chapter to examine in detail the Review Panel's findings in all of these cases. Of greater relevance is the need to consider its workings and overall effectiveness. The first point of interest is that the majority of the 78 cases were insignificant, beyond its scope or clearly recorded departures from accounting standards and other legal requirements. The Review Panel's findings in respect of the accounts of GPG plc for the year ended 30 September 1991 are an example of the last category. The auditor's report provides an accurate summary of the issue under investigation.

Illustration 2.1: GPG plc (1991)

AUDITOR'S REPORT

To the members of GPG plc

1. We have audited the accounts on pages 8 to 30 in accordance with Auditing Standards.

2. As stated in note 1 to the accounts, the accounts have been prepared in compliance with Financial Reporting Exposure Draft No. 1. The principal effect of this is to reclassify certain items as exceptional which would be classified as extraordinary under Statement of Standard Accounting Practice No. 6 ("SSAP 6") and, as a consequence, to show earnings per share on a different basis from that required by Statement of Standard Accounting Practice No. 3 ("SSAP 3"). The impact of these departures is disclosed in Note 17 to the accounts.

3. Except for the effects of the departures from SSAP 6 and SSAP 3 referred to in the preceding paragraph, in our opinion the accounts give a true and fair view of the state of affairs of the Company and the Group at 30 September 1991 and of the profit and source and application of funds of the Group for the year then ended and have been properly prepared in accordance with the Companies Act 1985.

Coopers & Lybrand Deloitte
CHARTERED ACCOUNTANTS AND
REGISTERED AUDITOR
London
3 February 1992

Note 17 to the accounts explained the impact of the departures as follows:

Illustration 2.2: *GPG plc (1991)*

17 FINANCIAL REPORTING EXPOSURE DRAFT NO. 1 (extract)

The adoption of FRED 1 has reclassified certain extraordinary items in the profit and loss account as exceptional. The following restates certain key amounts on the assumption that FRED 1 had not been adopted and the accounts had been prepared in accordance with SSAP 3 and SSAP 6.

	1991 £000	1990 £000
Profit on ordinary activities before tax	4,992	5,881
Profit on ordinary activities after tax	5,122	6,044
Extraordinary items	5,802	(1,223)
Earnings per share (pence)	1.58	1.87

The GPG group profit and loss account for 1991 showed pre-tax profit of £10.794 million, being the £4.992 million shown above increased by the extraordinary items of £5.802 million. Earnings per share were shown as 3.38 pence, compared with the 1.58 pence disclosed in Illustration 2.2.

The issue referred to the Review Panel is relatively straightforward. It arises from the different treatment of extraordinary items under existing accounting standards and the proposed amendment to those standards. All the relevant facts were disclosed to the user of the financial statements and the auditor's report highlighted the unusual presentation adopted by the company. After an investigation, the Review Panel announced that:

> The Panel has informed the company that the substitution of the proposed requirements of an exposure draft for those of an existing accounting standard is not acceptable. The Panel noted that the Accounts of GPG clearly identified the departures from accounting standards and disclosed the effect, but does not regard such action as fulfilling the requirement to comply with current accounting standards. In normal circumstances therefore the Panel would be likely to seek revision of the accounts in question. However, as it is understood that an accounting standard incorporating the most significant of the proposals of FRED 1 is now close to issue, the Panel has concluded that on this occasion it should take no further action.[24]

The Review Panel's intervention in this case has merely reinforced the qualification in the auditor's report. Its findings seem to be of little benefit to users of financial statements. They also took considerable time to process. The press release announcing the outcome of the GPG plc investigation was dated 7 October 1992, more than a year after the end of the financial period concerned. It should be borne in mind, however, that a substantial portion of the Panel's time will necessarily be spent upholding the accounting standards by which it seeks to judge the behaviour of other companies. Those users who expect it to have a direct and immediate impact on the quality of information provided to them, are likely to be disappointed. The Panel is more likely to have an indirect effect on reporting practices. The knowledge of its existence should act as a spur to both preparers and auditors.

The second important point about the operation of the Panel is that an external body is unlikely to be able to get to the heart of many of the accounting issues involved. Whether financial statements give a 'true and fair' view depends as much on the reliability of the directors' judgement as on the adequacy of the disclosures given. The activities of the Panel will necessarily have to focus on the latter issue. It appears to be doing a sound job in requesting companies to clarify inadequacies in the disclosure of their accounting policies. Whether it is able to confirm the correct application of the policies is another matter altogether.

The ability of the Review Panel to be a powerful influence in improving the clarity of disclosure in company financial statements should nevertheless not be discounted. This is best illustrated by its findings in the Trafalgar House case. The issue is worth examining in more detail. Trafalgar House's 1991 profit and loss account revealed the following picture to users of its financial statements:

Illustration 2.3: *Trafalgar House Public Limited Company (1991)*

CONSOLIDATED PROFIT AND LOSS ACCOUNT (extract)

	Year ended 30th September 1991	Year ended 30th September 1990 restated
	£m	£m
Construction and engineering	82.3	68.4
Property and investment	29.8	77.4
Shipping and hotels	36.8	60.5
Operating profit	148.9	206.3
Interest and finance charges	32.5	62.4
Operating profit after interest and finance charges	116.4	143.9
Profits less losses of associated companies	6.0	7.6
Profit on ordinary activities before taxation	122.4	151.5

Although the profit and loss account reflects a lower level of pre-tax profit for 1991, the decline appears to have been limited to 19.2 per cent. Closer examination of the notes to the accounts would, however, reveal that there had been a significant change in the classification of certain properties owned by the group:

Illustration 2.4: Trafalgar House Public Limited Company (1991)

14 Developments for sale (extract)	1991	1990
		restated
	£m	£m
Commercial Property:		
United Kingdom	84.5	217.7
United States	25.0	19.7
	109.5	237.4

On 1st October 1990 certain commercial properties in the UK were transferred to tangible fixed assets (Note 12).

The reclassification of the commercial properties from 'Developments for Sale' under current assets to fixed assets was recorded in note 12 to the accounts.

Illustration 2.5: Trafalgar House Public Limited Company (1991)

12 Tangible fixed assets (extract)	Freehold Properties	Long Leasehold Properties
	£m	£m
Cost or valuation		
As at 30 September 1990	47.0	16.5
Exchange adjustments	1.1	.1
Reclassification from current assets	111.4	44.0
Owned by companies acquired	41.5	10.6
Expenditure	1.3	.7
Disposals	(3.7)	-
Deficit on valuation	(50.5)	(17.5)
As at 30 September 1991	148.1	54.4

Properties reclassified from current assets were valued on 30 September 1991 on the basis of open market value by independent firms of chartered surveyors (£78.1m), and by internal qualified surveyors (£9.3m).

Note 12 reveals that the book value of the commercial properties transferred from current assets on 1 October 1990 was £155.4 million (111.4 + 44.0). These properties were valued at £87.4 million on 30 September 1991, resulting in a deficit of £68.0 million.

The fixed asset revaluation rules contained in the Companies Act 1985 allow deficits of this kind to be charged to the revaluation reserve, provided that certain conditions are met:

Illustration 2.6: *Trafalgar House Public Limited Company (1991)*

24 Reserves (extract)

	Revaluation Reserve £m
As at 30 September 1990	
As previously reported	84.0
Adjustment to prior years	-
As restated	84.0
Revaluation of fixed asset properties (Note 12)	(68.0)
Revaluation of property associates (Note 13)	(34.7)
As at 30 September 1991	(18.7)

The additional deficit of £34.7 million shown in note 24 arose in similar circumstances to those which gave rise to the £68.0 million shortfall. Properties owned by associates are not permitted to be included with those shown in notes 12 and 14. The group is nevertheless exposed to its share of any deficits arising on their valuation.

Note 24 in Illustration 2.6 reveals that the group suffered a loss of £102.7 million on the valuation of properties previously classified as current assets. Had their classification remained unchanged, this loss would have been charged in the profit and loss account. It would have reduced the 1991 pre-tax profit from £122.4 million to £19.7 million. The classification of assets as 'fixed' or 'current' depends on whether they are 'intended for use on a continuing basis in the company's activities.'[25] If not intended for such use, they are current assets. Trafalgar House presumably concluded that a change of intention warranted reclassification of the properties concerned.

The company's accounting treatment attracted considerable interest. The pre-tax profit figure appeared to have benefited from the timing of the reclassification and the value at which it had been done. In order to prevent further confusion about the appropriate accounting treatment in similar circumstances, the Urgent Issues Task Force issued Abstract No. 5 in July 1992. It stipulated that:

> ...where assets are transferred from current to fixed, the current asset accounting rules should be applied up to the effective date of transfer, which is the date of management's change of intent. Consequently the transfer should be made at the lower of cost and net realisable value, and accordingly an assessment should be made of the net realisable value at the date of transfer and if this is less than its previous carrying value the diminution should be charged in the profit and loss account, reflecting the loss to the company while the asset was held as a current asset.[26]

The Abstract became effective for accounting periods ending on or after 23 December 1992. It was not in existence when Trafalgar House's financial statements for the year to 30 September 1991 were being prepared. The Review Panel's investigation of the financial statements was therefore of special interest. The *Financial Times* of 6 October 1992 contained the following report (by Roland Rudd):

Trafalgar House stands ground over 1991 results

TRAFALGAR HOUSE, the property, construction and engineering group, is determined not to restate its 1991 financial results following an investigation by the Financial Reporting Review Panel, the new accounting standards watchdog.

Trafalgar, which is under siege from Hongkong Land, has told the panel that it is willing to change its accounting policies by transferring property developments from fixed to current assets.

But according to one of its financial advisers it is adamant that it should not have to restate last year's figures.

If Trafalgar's write-downs of wholly-owned properties and associates had been deducted from the profit and loss account they would have severely reduced last year's £122.4m pre-tax profits.[27]

A potentially troublesome issue was resolved nine days later, on 15 October, when press releases were issued by both the Review Panel and Trafalgar House. The Review Panel's release contained the following paragraph:

On the basis of independent legal and accounting advice the directors of Trafalgar House have hitherto not accepted the Review Panel's view on the two principal matters in contention. The Review Panel has therefore been minded to make an application to the court under section 245B of the Companies Act 1985 for an order requiring the directors of the company to prepare revised accounts. However the directors of the company have now undertaken to make appropriate changes and adjustments in the accounts of the company for the year ended 30 September 1992 to meet the Review Panel's concerns, and on this undertaking the Review Panel will not be proceeding with the section 245B court application.[28]

The Trafalgar House press release explained the adjustments in more detail:

As a consequence of the agreement the Company will restate the 1991 comparative figures in its 1992 accounts to comply with the requirements of Urgent Issue Task Force Abstract No. 5 issued on 22nd July, 1992. As a result the 1991 comparative figures will show deficits on revaluation of properties of £102.7 million as a charge to the profit and loss account rather than to reserves.

In addition the Company will revise its policy on Advance Corporation Tax which is expected to result in an increase of £20 million in the tax charge included in the 1991 comparative figures and an increase in the write off in the 1992 accounts.[29]

The Review Panel investigation was significant for two reasons. First, unlike many of the cases referred to earlier in this chapter, the 1991 financial statements of Trafalgar House received an unqualified audit report. Secondly, application of UITF Abstract No. 5 would not have been mandatory when the 1992 financial statements came to be prepared later in that year. Without the intervention of the Review Panel, it is not clear whether the 1991 comparative figures would have been restated.

The Trafalgar House investigation demonstrates the potential effectiveness of two of the new bodies created as a consequence of the Dearing Report. It is again worth noting that the process is a slow-moving one. The agreement with the directors of Trafalgar House was reached more than a year after the end of the financial period concerned. Furthermore, the information about the valuation deficits was clearly disclosed in the 1991 financial statements. The Review Panel and the UITF merely clarified its presentation. They were obviously not in a position to comment on the appropriateness of the valuations adopted. The limitations of their involvement in safeguarding the quality of information provided to users should therefore not be overlooked. The need for users to analyse that information in a sensible manner is also apparent. Whether they were able to do so in the Trafalgar House case, will be examined in Chapter 6.

AN EFFECTIVE SOLUTION?

In November 1992, the FRC concluded its Second Annual Review by noting that 'the instruments are now in place to strengthen financial reporting'.[30] The determination of the new bodies created as a consequence of the Dearing Report to achieve this objective is not in doubt. It is worth remembering, however, that the Accounting Standards Steering Committee probably set out with similar enthusiasm and optimism in 1970. Serious problems needed to be tackled. 'Accounting practices were varied, inconsistent and sometimes inappropriate; inter-firm and inter-period comparisons were difficult as companies altered accounting treatments and resorted to such practices as "window-dressing" and "reserve accounting" to achieve desired results in order to present a picture of profitability and growth.'[31]

The Accounting Standards Steering Committee became the Accounting Standards Committee (ASC). The ASC developed 34 Statements of Standard Accounting Practice, or revised Statements and 21 of these were in existence at the time of its demise 20 years later, in July 1990. Of these standards, five (statements of source and application of funds, group accounts, extraordinary items and prior year adjustments, earnings per share and deferred tax) have already been completely or partially revised by the ASC's successor body, the Accounting Standards Board (ASB). The latter body has announced its intention to consider the revision of another six of the ASC's standards (accounting for associated companies, depreciation, investment properties, leasing, foreign currency and pension costs). Exposure drafts proposing the amendment of another two standards (accounting for goodwill and acquisitions and mergers) will be considered in 1993.

The ASB is understandably confident about producing a superior product. Its first accounting standard on cash flow statements was issued in September 1991. However, 14 months later its chairman deemed it necessary to comment that:

The Board will keep all its published standards under review, but is firmly of the view that they need to be fully and widely tested in operation before any changes or modifications can be contemplated. The Board would not normally expect to consider any case for modification until at least two years' experience of the practical operation of a standard had been gained. To remove any uncertainty, since there has been some Press speculation to the contrary, I should record that this is the policy that the Board has adopted in respect of FRS 1 *Cash Flow Statements.*[32]

To secure an improvement in reporting practices by regulation is extremely difficult. The review and amendment of accounting standards is a never-ending process. There always seems to be a need for more standards. Those already in existence are never entirely satisfactory. They are continually having to be revised. Some have to be withdrawn. It is doubtful whether the ASC was able to overcome successfully the problems prevalent at the time of its establishment in 1970. In 1990, companies were arguably still resorting to 'such practices as "window-dressing" and "reserve accounting" to achieve desired results in order to present a picture of profitability and growth'.

The desire to secure improvements in financial reporting practices by increased regulation remains undiminished. It is matched by an equally strong wish on the part of users of those statements to place unquestioning reliance on their integrity. The new financial reporting regime has many impressive features. The limitations of relying on any system of financial reporting to safeguard the quality of the information produced by it are, however, likely to be ever present. There is a danger in expecting too much of the new regime.

1   Financial Reporting Council (1992), *The State of Financial Reporting – Second Annual Review*, November, paras. 2.1 and 2.2.
2   Davies, Mike, Paterson, Ron and Wilson, Allister of Ernst & Young (1992), *UK GAAP – Generally Accepted Accounting Practice in the United Kingdom* (London: Macmillan Publishers Ltd), p.10.
3   *Ibid.*, p.12.
4   Extract from 'Report of the Review Committee on the Making of Accounting Standards' as summarised in *Accounting Standards 1991/92* (The Institute of Chartered Accountants in England and Wales: Accountancy Books).
5   Financial Reporting Council (1991), *The State of Financial Reporting – a review*, November, paras. 2.1 and 2.2.
6   *Ibid.*, para. 2.13.
7   *Ibid.*, para. 2.22.
8   *The State of Financial Reporting – Second Annual Review*, para. 2.24.
9   The Companies Act 1985, Sch. 4, para. 36A.
10 *Ibid.*, ss 245B, 245A.
11 *The State of Financial Reporting – a review*, para. 2.7
12 *The State of Financial Reporting – Second Annual Review*, paras. 7.8–7.10.
13 *Ibid.*, para. 4.2.
14 *Ibid.*, para. 2.2.
15 *Ibid.*, para. 2.15.

16   *The State of Financial Reporting – a review*, para. 5.45.
17   *The State of Financial Reporting – Second Annual Review*, para. 3.36.
18   *Ibid.*, paras. 7.2 – 7.3.
19   *Ibid.*, para. 7.4.
20   *The State of Financial Reporting – a review*, appendix b, para. 3.
21   *The State of Financial Reporting – Second Annual Review*, para. 2.14.
22   *Ibid.*, paras. 4.4–4.6.
23   The Financial Reporting Review Panel (1992), *FRRP PN 4*, 28 January; *FRRP PN 5* (1992),
     28 January; *FRRP PN 6* (1992), 31 January; *FRRP PN 7* (1992), 4 February; *FRRP PN 10*
     (1992), 10 August; *FRRP PN 11* (1992), 10 August; *FRRP PN 12* (1992), 7 October; *FRRP
     PN 13* (1992), 15 October; *FRRP PN 14* (1992), 26 October; *FRRP PN 15* (1992), 26 October.
24   The Financial Reporting Review Panel, *FRRP PN 12* (1992), 7 October.
25   Companies Act 1985, s 262.
26   Urgent Issues Task Force Abstract 5 (1992), *Transfers from Current Assets to Fixed Assets*,
     July, para. 5.
27   *Financial Times* (1992), 6 October, p.24.
28   The Financial Reporting Review Panel (1992), *FRRP PN 13*, 15 October.
29   Trafalgar House Press Release (1992), 15 October.
30   *The State of Financial Reporting – Second Annual Review*, para. 7.1.
31   *UK GAAP – Generally Accepted Accounting Practice in the United Kingdom*, p.10.
32   *The State of Financial Reporting – Second Annual Review*, para. 3.10.

3:   What is 'Creative Accounting'?

There are many theories, but to me, it always comes
down to earnings and assets. Especially earnings.

Peter Lynch[1]

INTRODUCTION

On 16 May 1991, an article in the *Financial Times* by David Waller observed that:

> Ever since Coopers & Lybrand attacked BTR's profit record during the middle of the
> conglomerate's battle for Pilkington in January 1987, it has been customary for those
> engaged in takeover battles to attack each other's accounting. Given the subjectivity
> inherent in all accounting, and the ease with which ingenious finance directors and
> merchant bankers can manipulate the numbers to demonstrate the irrefutable logic of
> whatever case they are trying to prove, this is not surprising.[2]

The implication that accounting could be used as a tool to achieve certain objectives
of the preparer is significant. The article also reveals the perceived need to expose
deception, lest shareholders be misled into making economic decisions they might
later regret. The proposition that accounting could be 'creative' in its ability to
portray a picture vastly different to the underlying reality, formed the subject of
Terry Smith's book *Accounting for Growth*. Its introduction explained that:

> The title *Accounting for Growth* was a deliberate pun. We felt that much of the apparent
> growth in profits which had occurred in the 1980s was the result of accounting sleight of
> hand rather than genuine economic growth, and we set out to expose the main techniques
> involved, and to give live examples of companies using those techniques.[3]

Smith accordingly set out to prevent his readers from losing money by showing them
'where to find the information and how to perform the calculations needed to spot
creative accounting techniques.'[4] That accounting could be used as a tool to distort
the user's view of the underlying reality is a concept far removed from the purpose of
financial reporting as previously defined. It suggests that the ASB may have
overlooked the possibility that the preparer of financial statements probably has a
different objective to the statements themselves. The purpose of the latter might be
'to provide information about the financial position, performance and financial

adaptability of an enterprise that is useful to a wide range of users in making economic decisions'[5] but the former may well have another goal in mind. One commentator has suggested that:

> Corporate reporting is a variable to be adjusted or manipulated by management in support of its strategies and goals, subject to whatever statutory disclosure constraints exist.[6]

The possibility that financial reporting might be used in a 'creative' manner has important implications for the user's ability to make economic decisions based on the information provided. This chapter therefore seeks to answer the following questions:

- What are the objectives of the preparer of financial statements?
- Can financial reporting be used in a 'creative' manner to achieve these objectives?
- What are the implications for the user of financial statements?

OBJECTIVES OF THE PREPARER

The FRC's 1991 Annual Review observed that:

> ...while there is much support for action to secure better accounts, we acknowledge that there is concern that, by requiring more disclosure in the service of effective markets and more stringent accounting practices, there could be consequent detriment to the international competitiveness of our companies. This anxiety has been expressed by the CBI and the Hundred Group as a factor which they would want the Accounting Standards Board to weigh.[7]

One view is that the first priority of any preparer of financial statements is to provide as little information as possible. The financial reporting requirement is a costly hindrance to the effective conduct of business. It is tolerated because it provides access to the capital markets.

Another view is that financial reporting provides a valuable opportunity to shape investor and public perceptions of the company's merits. It is usually in the best interests of a company's business to be highly regarded by the public. To be held in favourable regard by the investment community in particular, can have significant financial benefits:

Example 3.1

Two companies of identical size are involved in the same line of business. Their financial results for the year to 31 December 19x1 are as follows:

	Company A	Company B
Net Profit after tax	£1m	£1m
Shares in issue	5m	5m
Earnings per share (EPS)	20p	20p
Share price	400p	200p

For various reasons, company A is held in higher regard by the investment community. Its favourable market rating is evidenced by its higher price earnings (PE) ratio of 20 (share price divided by EPS).

On 1 January 19x2, company A makes a takeover offer for company B. Because the former's shares are worth 400p each, it offers company B's shareholders 1 of its shares for every 2 that they own in company B. Assuming that both companies make unchanged profits of £1m in 19x2, what is the impact on company A's EPS if its offer is accepted by company B's shareholders?

Company A's EPS in 19x2 would be 26.7p, an improvement of approximately 33 per cent on its 19x1 result.

What would the answer be if company A's shares were valued at 200p instead of 400p? Under these circumstances, company A would have to offer 1 of its shares for every 1 of company B's.

Company A's EPS in 19x2 would be 20.0p, an unchanged performance when measured against its 19x1 result.

What would be the impact on company B's EPS if the position were reversed and it made an offer for company A? This would have to be based on 2 of its shares, worth 200p, for every 1 of company A's, worth 400p.

Company B's EPS in 19x2 would be 13.3p, a decline of approximately 33 per cent on its 19x1 result.

This simple example illustrates the advantage of being able to issue highly rated shares when making an acquisition. It enables company A to report a healthy improvement in EPS despite an unchanged trading performance by both companies in the enlarged group. The 33 per cent improvement is due entirely to its higher share price of 400p. Company B's lower share price puts its management at a significant disadvantage, should it decide to make an offer for company A.

The principle applies equally to issues of shares for cash. Company A needs to earn only 5 per cent after tax on an issue priced at 400p in order to maintain its EPS at 20p per share. A higher return on the new funds would result in an improvement in its EPS. Company B would, however, have to earn 10 per cent after tax merely to maintain its EPS after a rights issue priced at 200p. Company B's relatively low share price could significantly constrain its ability to expand. (The calculations have ignored the likelihood that the new shares would have to be issued at a discount to their current market prices but this would impact only on the magnitude of the respective advantages and disadvantages.)

To be held in favourable regard by the investment community can clearly be of considerable benefit to the reporting entity. A negative perception could be catastrophic, denying access to the finance necessary to carry on business. As management is also responsible for preparing the financial statements, there is another advantage to be gained from creating a favourable perception with the investment community.

Illustration 3.1: SmithKline Beecham plc (1991)

32. Directors' emoluments (extract)

The compensation of all Executive Directors is determined by the Remuneration and Nominations Committee of the Board comprised wholly of non-executive Directors. Non-executive Directors receive payments in accordance with the Company's Memorandum and Articles of Association. As a leading transnational healthcare company the Company has to attract, retain and motivate high calibre executives. The Company expects quality leadership, commitment and, most important, results. In return, the Company provides an internationally competitive package of incentives and rewards linked to performance.

Current compensation
The Executive Directors' compensation consists of four components.
a) *Salary:* This reflects an executive's experience and market value. Increases are based on effective management of the Company and on increased responsibility.
b) *Bonus:* This is based on performance by business teams against financial targets and individual accomplishments against objectives.
c) *Pension and other benefits:* These are consistent with those provided by other transnational companies.
d) *Long term incentives:* These comprise share options and stock appreciation rights (SARs) that link reward to added shareholder value.
Share options allow Executives to buy the Company's shares at a future date at a price determined at the date of grant. The SAR plans pay a cash bonus based on the increase in either the Company's A Share or the Equity Unit price since the date of grant.

The remuneration of members of the body responsible for preparing the financial statements is often linked to the performance of the entity's share price. As Illustration 3.1 demonstrates, this is commonly done either by the granting of share options or by a cash payment linked to increases in the share price. The example also illustrates that remuneration is sometimes based on the achievement of financial targets, calculated by reference to the information contained in the financial statements. This introduces another factor influencing the preparer, recognised in the ASB's statement of the objective of financial statements:

> Financial statements also show the results of the stewardship of management, that is, the accountability of management for the resources entrusted to it. Those users who wish to assess the stewardship of management do so in order that they may make economic decisions; these decisions may include, for example, whether to hold or sell their investment in the enterprise or whether to re-appoint or replace the management.[8]

It is clearly in management's interest to produce the best possible account of its stewardship. Its re-appointment probably hinges on convincing the owners of the enterprise that it is worthy of managing the resources entrusted to it.

This section has discussed some of the factors influencing the behaviour of preparers of financial statements. Some regard financial reporting as a costly hindrance. Others adopt a more positive attitude, in recognition of the benefits that may

35

result from creating a favourable perception of the reporting entity. Whichever approach is adopted, the re-appointment and remuneration of the company's management is usually dependent on the information contained in the financial statements. This is bound to have some bearing on the way in which the task of preparing them is likely to be tackled.

USING FINANCIAL REPORTING TO ACHIEVE A DESIRED OUTCOME

The purpose of this section is to examine whether financial reporting can be used as a tool to achieve some of the objectives of the preparer, as discussed in the previous section. At the outset, it is worth considering two pieces of evidence in support of the view that its use for this purpose is relatively widespread.

Contested takeovers

Given the number of issues involved when one company makes an offer to acquire control of another, it is surprising that accounting should enjoy the prominence often accorded to it. The following newspaper article is a case in point:

Macarthy alleges profit distortion

THE battle for control of Macarthy intensified after the retailer and drugs manufacturer issued a hard-hitting defence against a £79 million hostile bid by Grampian Holdings.

Macarthy accused Grampian, the Scottish mini-conglomerate, of employing 'accounting camouflage' to distort profits through last-minute property deals, 'dubious' extraordinary charges and deferred costs.

Bill Hughes, the Grampian chairman, dismissed Macarthy's defence as 'a catalogue of misleading and mischievous assertions'.

Macarthy raised questions about sale and leaseback agreements between Grampian and Brian Dempsey, a builder and property developer. Mr Dempsey said yesterday that he was considering legal action against Macarthy.

Macarthy also criticised Grampian for taking one-off gains above the line while treating one-off costs as extraordinary charges in connection with Patrick, its sporting goods subsidiary. Mr Hughes replied that the charges related to the closure of manufacturing facilities and accorded with accepted accounting practice.

Grampian shares rose 1p to 195p yesterday; Macarthy shares were unchanged at 273p. The offer closes on November 1.[9]

That accounting practices should be regarded as a relevant factor in deciding whether to accept an unwelcome takeover offer, has been a common feature during the last five years. A newspaper article covering Racal Electronics' defence against an offer from Williams Holdings started with the following three paragraphs:

Williams accounts attacked by Racal

RACAL Electronics has attacked the accounting policies of Williams Holdings in its first defence document against the £719 million hostile takeover offer from Nigel Rudd's and Brian McGowan's industrial conglomerate.

The document argues that Williams' all-paper offer is 'of uncertain value' because of the company's accounting treatment. Three aspects of Williams' accounts come under attack: the level of disclosure on acquisition accounting, the 'unusual' inclusion of the pension fund surplus as an asset on the balance sheet, and 'the non-standard' treatment of exceptional items.

Racal shareholders are urged to reject the 'inequitable, uncertain, opportunistic and inadequate' offer from Williams. [10]

These articles reveal something about the perceived ability of financial reporting to obscure the underlying reality. Both of the takeover defence documents in the examples quoted are concerned about the ability of financial reporting to accentuate the good news and to hide the bad. This was presumably considered to be sufficiently important for it to be drawn to the attention of shareholders. The obvious implication is that accounting is capable of being manipulated to achieve the objectives of the preparer of the financial statements.

The 'creative accounting' industry

Further evidence in support of the belief that accounting can be used as a valuable tool, is to be found in the existence of the so-called 'creative accounting' industry. By this term is meant the practice of merchant and other bankers to offer financial instruments to their clients in place of more conventional forms of financing. These instruments are designed to achieve an accounting advantage. They supposedly present a more favourable view of the underlying transaction. A belief that this could be to the advantage of the preparer has led to the existence of an active market. The following example illustrates how a financial instrument might work in practice.

Example 3.2

A company wishes to expand its operations by acquiring new retail premises. One option is to obtain the finance required via a 10-year loan, secured on the new premises. If there is sufficient demand from a number of clients for premises of this kind, a merchant bank is likely to propose the following solution:

- A special-purpose company will be set up with loan finance from various banks to acquire the properties concerned. The loans will be secured on the individual properties.
- Ownership of this company will be spread over the many clients taking part in the scheme.
- The company will lease the selected properties to the clients for an initial period of 10 years.
- The rentals will be used to pay the interest on the loan finance provided by the banks.

37

- At the end of the initial lease period, the clients will have an option to buy the leased premises. The price payable is set at the same amount paid by the special-purpose company when it initially acquired the property concerned.
- If a client decides not to buy the property, it will be sold on the open market. The client will, however, be liable for any shortfall between the sale proceeds and the price originally paid to acquire the property.
- The sale proceeds will be used to repay the bank loans and the special-purpose company, having served its 10-year purpose, will then be wound up.

The merchant bank's proposal is easier to follow when viewed from the perspectives of the banker and his client. It soon becomes clear that its substance is virtually identical to the simple loan arrangement proposed at the start of the example.

From the banker's perspective:
- A 10-year secured loan, equal to the purchase price of the property, is made to the special-purpose company.
- Interest is received on this loan via the rentals paid to the special-purpose company by the client/lessee.
- If the client decides not to buy the property in 10 years' time, it is obliged to make good any loss suffered by the bank on its sale to a third party. The existence of this guarantee means that the bank is effectively loaning the money to the client, rather than to the special purpose company.

From the client's perspective:
- Immediate access is gained to the selected retail premises.
- If the property appreciates in value, the benefit can be accessed by exercising the purchase option after 10 years.
- If the property falls in value, a loss will be suffered. This is, however, no different to the position that would have prevailed had the property been bought outright under the simple loan arrangement.

The proposals are likely to appeal to the merchant bank's client. They appear to have an accounting advantage. Effective ownership of the property is gained without having to borrow a large sum of money from the bank. The commitments assumed are in substance very similar to those under a loan agreement. Their appeal lies in the fact that there would appear to be no need to reflect the existence of a loan in the financial statements. The only disclosure required is to show the rentals actually paid together with those payable in the next twelve months. Disclosure of the guarantee is not necessary if the possibility of loss is considered to be remote.

It should be noted that the proposals in the example are probably too simplistic to achieve the desired accounting outcome in practice. They nevertheless illustrate the relatively widespread practice of altering the legal form of transactions to achieve perceived accounting benefits.

The existence of an active market in financial instruments and the contents of many takeover documents provide solid evidence to support the belief that financial reporting can be manipulated to achieve a desired outcome. The examples are, however, rather specific. What about the annual reporting requirement? Is there evidence to support the view that financial statements are regularly prepared with specific objectives in mind?

Financial reporting and the stockmarket

The potential advantages to be gained from creating a favourable impression with the investment community were noted earlier in this chapter. A high share price can be a powerful boost to expansion plans, as well as an effective way of remunerating key members of the management team. By keeping the owners happy, it is also likely to ensure the re-appointment of the management. How does a company go about winning the confidence of the investment community? Can financial reporting help to achieve this objective?

One way of attempting to answer these questions is to ask a leading fund manager what investors are looking for in deciding whether to invest in a company. Peter Lynch, former manager of the multi-billion dollar Fidelity Magellan Fund, is regarded by many as America's most successful investor:

> What you're asking here is what makes a company valuable, and why it will be more valuable tomorrow than it is today. There are many theories, but to me, it always comes down to earnings and assets. Especially earnings. Sometimes it takes years for the stock price to catch up to a company's value, and the down periods last so long that investors begin to doubt that will ever happen. But value always wins out – or at least in enough cases that it's worthwhile to believe it.[11]

Lynch quotes many examples in support of the link between earnings and share prices, the most spectacular being the case of Masco Corporation. Between 1958 and 1987, Masco's earnings rose 800-fold. During this period, there was a 1,300-fold increase in the company's share price. 'As long as the earnings continued to increase, there was nothing to stop it.'[12] He also notes the reverse effect when earnings fall:

> During the last decade we've seen recessions and inflation, oil prices going up and oil prices going down, and all along, these stocks have followed earnings. Look at the chart of Dow Chemical. When earnings are up the stock is up. That's what happened during the period from 1971 to 1975 and again from 1985 through 1988. In between, from 1975 through 1985, earnings were erratic and so was the stock price.[13]

Lynch also stresses the significance of a steady increase in earnings over time. The benefits of compounding are vividly illustrated by his example of the Manhattan Island transaction:

> Consider the Indians of Manhattan, who in 1626 sold all their real estate to a group of immigrants for $24 in trinkets and beads. For 362 years the Indians have been the subject

of cruel jokes because of it – but it turns out they may have made a better deal than the buyers who got the island.

At 8 percent interest on $24 (note: let's suspend our disbelief and assume they converted the trinkets to cash) compounded over all those years, the Indians would have built up a net worth just short of $30 trillion, while the latest tax records from the Borough of Manhattan show the real estate to be worth only $28.1 billion.[14]

Of course, Lynch also recognizes that investing is essentially concerned with the future.

Future earnings – there's the rub. How do you predict those? The best you can get from current earnings is an educated guess whether a stock is fairly priced. If you do this much, you'll never buy a Polaroid or an Avon at a 40 p/e, nor will you overpay for Bristol-Myers, Coca-Cola, or McDonald's. However, what you'd really like to know is what's going to happen to earnings in the next month, the next year, or the next decade.

Earnings, after all, are supposed to grow, and every stock price carries with it a built-in growth assumption.[15]

Fund managers are clearly interested in the earnings of companies, or rather, their potential to continue to increase their earnings. Is there any evidence to suggest that this has influenced financial reporting practices? A scrutiny of UK company Annual Reports would probably confirm that preparers are certainly aware of what the investment community is looking for. Consider the following example, taken from the 1990 Chairman's Report of Shandwick plc:

Illustration 3.2: *Shandwick plc (1990)*

Chairman's Report (extract)

For the fifth successive year since becoming a public company, I am delighted yet again to report record results.

...Research conducted worldwide by Shandwick during the summer, which is being published with this Report, reveals that public relations consultancy is growing at around 20 per cent per annum with a 1990 global market of approximately £3 billion in fees.

While there is some evidence that high budget consumer-orientated programmes in the United Kingdom may have been cancelled or deferred, the sheer volume and mix of new business available around the world has more than compensated for any cut backs. Indeed, top line research suggests that full service public relations programmes may be counter-cyclical, particularly where corporate and Government clients are concerned. Financial and Hi-Tech PR have recently shown renewed buoyancy and this has added to the generally optimistic outlook.

The desire to provide potential investors with sound reasons for investing in the company is common to many Annual Reports. Investors are clearly also looking to see whether the growth predictions are being achieved. This would help to explain why so much importance is attached to the earnings per share figure, shown at the foot of the profit and loss account.

There is another indication that companies have responded to the investment community's desire to see steady increases in earnings over time. Tesco PLC has gone so far as to link a substantial portion of its management's remuneration to the growth in the company's earnings. The justification must be that this achieves commonality with the objectives of its shareholders.

Illustration 3.3: Tesco PLC (1992)

2. Employment costs (extract)

c) Directors' emoluments

Aggregate emoluments of the directors of the parent company were as follows:

	1992 £000	1991 £000
Directors' emoluments	3,639	2,414
Performance related incentive payments	1,779	4,326
	5,418	6,740

The executive directors' salaries and performance-related incentive scheme are determined by the Remuneration Committee, which does not include any directors participating in the scheme.

Directors' salaries have been increased during the year, with a corresponding reduction in the level of incentive payments.

The group operates a performance-related incentive scheme for seven executive directors, payments under which are related to the cumulative growth in fully diluted earnings per share (excluding extraordinary items and net surplus on sales of properties and after tax) over three year cycles.

The performance related incentive schemes of £1.8m in the year represent the entitlement vesting in 1991–92 in respect of the second three year cycle from 1988–89 to 1990–91. Over this three year period earnings per share increased by 77 %. The aggregate amount of £1.8m was charged against profits in those three years.

The amount due in respect of the performance for the third three year cycle from 1989–90 to 1991–92 has now been finalised at £2.1m. Over this three year period, earnings per share increased by 82%. The amount of £2.1m is not included in directors' emoluments in the 1991–92 financial year, since the compensation is dependent upon the performance over a three year period and this entitlement will not vest until the 1992–93 financial year.

The preoccupation with earnings as the best guide to a company's value would also help to explain why accounting features so prominently in takeover documents. Success or failure often hinges on convincing the investment community of the company's so-called 'true earnings', so that its value can be more reliably assessed. Other advice from Peter Lynch provides a clue as to why demand exists for the financial instruments referred to earlier in this section:

Among turnarounds and troubled companies, I pay special attention to the debt factor. More than anything else, it's debt that determines which companies will survive and which will go bankrupt in a crisis. Young companies with heavy debts are always at risk.[16]

IMPLICATIONS FOR THE USER

The first chapter of this book focused on the purpose of the financial reporting process. The need was stressed for the user to be aware of the context in which the financial statements had been prepared. The discussion in this chapter suggests that their context is best understood by examining the goals of their preparer. These are probably more important than any definition of the objective or purpose of the statements themselves. What does this chapter reveal about the objectives of the preparer?

The first point is that some preparers will be unwilling to provide any more information than the statutory minimum. For them, the financial reporting process is a costly hindrance to the effective conduct of their business. In these circumstances, users will need to decide whether the information provided is adequate for their needs.

The second point is that other preparers will approach the preparation of their financial statements in a more positive manner. It is reasonable to expect them to present financial information in a way that shows the reporting entity in the best possible light. They will be acutely aware of the investment community's desire to see a solid record of steadily increasing earnings, with the prospect of more of the same to come. They will also be conscious of the need to show that debt is being managed prudently and that it is at a comfortable level.

Whether financial reporting can be used as a tool to achieve these objectives when the underlying reality suggests otherwise, is a question that requires further investigation. This will be attempted in the ensuing chapters. At this point, it is sufficient to note the existence of a perception that it is capable of being used in a 'creative' manner. It provides a strong clue as to the way in which certain preparers are likely to tackle the task of reporting financial information.

1   Lynch, Peter and Rothchild, John (1989), *One Up on Wall Street* (New York: Simon & Schuster), pp.155–6. Copyright © 1986 by Peter Lynch.
2   Waller, David (1991), 'Taking account of the prize', *Financial Times*, 16 May, p. 31.
3   Smith, Terry (1992), *Accounting for Growth* (London: Century Business), p. 4.
4   *Ibid.*
5   Accounting Standards Board (1991), 'The objective of financial statements', Exposure Draft of Chapter 1, *Statement of Principles* (London: ASB), July, para. 12.
6   Standish, P. M. (1975), 'Winds of Change in British Financial Reporting', *The Australian Accountant*, December.

7 Financial Reporting Council (1991), *The State of Financial Reporting – a review*, November, para. 12.12.

8 *The objective of financial statements*, para. 14.

9 Barrow, Martin (1991), 'Macarthy alleges profit distortion', *The Times*, Thursday 24 October.

10 Prynn, Jonathan (1991), 'Williams accounts attacked by Racal', *The Times*, Saturday 5 October.

11 *One Up on Wall Street*, pp. 155–6.

12 *Ibid.*, p. 159.

13 *Ibid.*

14 *Ibid.*, p. 54.

15 *Ibid.*, p. 168.

16 *Ibid.*, p. 201.

4:   Profit and the Profit and Loss Account

He thought he saw an Elephant,
That practised on a fife:
He looked again, and found it was
A letter from his wife.
'At length I realize,' he said,
'The bitterness of Life!'

Lewis Carroll[1]

INTRODUCTION

According to the Accounting Standards Board (ASB), the objective of financial statements is to provide financial information about three aspects of the reporting entity. The second of these is information about its financial performance.[2] To most users, this means a statement showing whether it has made a profit or a loss. Their understanding of the profit concept is probably similar to the Concise Oxford Dictionary's definition of the term:

> **profit** *n.* **1.** advantage, benefit, (*have studied it to my profit; no profit in such pursuits*).
> **2.** pecuniary gain, excess of returns over outlay, (*sold* **at a ~**, for more than one paid to get it);

The purpose of this chapter is to examine whether the existing accounting rules provide useful information about the financial performance of the reporting entity. At first glance, the Companies Act 1985 appears to be supportive of the user's desire to find out whether the reporting entity has made a profit or a loss. It requires companies to draw up a profit and loss account using one of four prescribed formats. Format 1, the most commonly used format, specifies that the profit and loss account should consist of the following items (unless special circumstances require them to be adapted):[3]

1. Turnover
2. Cost of sales
3. Gross profit or loss
4. Distribution costs
5. Administrative expenses

6. Other operating income
7. Income from shares in group undertakings
8. Income from participating interests
9. Income from other fixed asset investments
10. Other interest receivable and similar income
11. Amounts written off investments
12. Interest payable and similar charges
13. Tax on profit or loss on ordinary activities
14. Profit or loss on ordinary activities after taxation
15. Extraordinary income
16. Extraordinary charges
17. Extraordinary profit or loss
18. Tax on extraordinary profit or loss
19. Other taxes not shown under the above items
20. Profit or loss for the financial year

The list looks comfortingly similar to the dictionary definition. It starts with the return provided by the entity's sales during the period. It ends with the outcome for the year. It tells the user whether, in aggregate, the returns have exceeded the outlays (thereby producing a profit) or whether the opposite is true (resulting in a loss). Closer examination of the list reveals, however, that the legislature had another objective in mind. The profit and loss account is intended to be more than a simple deduction of debits (representing outlays) from credits (representing returns).

WHICH PROFIT?

Although the prescribed formats for the profit and loss account contain only one item titled 'profit or loss for the financial year', provision is made for this total to be split into two parts. The first consists of items 1 to 14 on the list shown above. It shows the profit or loss on 'ordinary' activities after taxation. 'Extraordinary' income, charges, profits, losses and their related taxes are deliberately excluded from this section. Their distorting effect is considered to be such that they should rather be shown separately. Deducting the aggregate of the debits from the aggregate of the credits was presumably thought to produce a less meaningful measure of financial performance.

The current position

To improve the usefulness of the information contained in the profit and loss account, the Accounting Standards Committee (ASC) decided that 'extraordinary' items should be treated separately. SSAP 6 *Extraordinary items and prior year adjustments* defined the concept as follows:

45

Extraordinary items are material items which derive from events or transactions that fall outside the ordinary activities of the company and which are therefore expected not to recur frequently or regularly. They do not include exceptional items nor do they include prior year items merely because they relate to a prior year.[4]

The important part of the definition is contained in the first sentence. This distinguishes 'extraordinary' items from 'exceptional' items, which the ASC defined as follows:

Exceptional items are material items which derive from events or transactions that fall within the ordinary activities of the company, and which need to be disclosed separately by virtue of their size or incidence if the financial statements are to give a true and fair view.[5]

The difference between the two categories hinges on the definition of 'ordinary activities':

Ordinary activities are any activities which are usually, frequently or regularly undertaken by the company and any related activities in which the company engages in furtherance of, incidental to, or arising from those activities. They include, but are not confined to, the trading activities of the company.[6]

The ASC also issued SSAP 3 *Earnings per share*. It was based on the belief that greater importance should be attached to items that fall within the company's ordinary activities. It therefore stipulated that the all-important earnings per share (EPS) figure should exclude 'extraordinary' items. EPS would be based on item 14 of Format 1 with two relatively minor adjustments to deal with preference and minority shareholders. Although the profit and loss account still ended with an item titled 'profit or loss for the financial year', this figure soon lost its significance.

The ASC's attempt to improve the usefulness of financial performance information inevitably resulted in difficulties of definition. The following examples are taken from the early 1990s, when companies began to recognise the need to make structural changes to their business operations. Applying the SSAP 6 definitions in practice proved to be problematic.

Illustration 4.1: *British Telecommunications plc (1990)*

5 Exceptional charge

A provision of £390m was made in the year ended 31 March 1990 to cover the costs of restructuring the group and refocusing its operations.

The directors of the two companies shown in the extracts appear to be pursuing similar objectives. They are both concerned with the 'restructuring', 'refocusing'

Illustration 4.2: *Imperial Chemical Industries PLC (1990)*

7 EXTRAORDINARY ITEMS (extract)

	Group	
	1990	1989
	£m	£m
Gain on disposal of the investment in Enterprise Oil plc (net of charge for taxation of £9m).	520	
Charge for reshaping the ICI Group business portfolio, comprising withdrawals through business divestments, closures and other restructuring measures. The charge is net of estimated disposal proceeds and includes the expense of obtaining substantial cost reductions which are a significant part of the objective (net of tax relief of £50m of which £46m is deferred).	(300)	
Charge for the withdrawal from UK compound fertilizer manufacture and restructuring, with a view to ultimate divestment, of the ammonium nitrate business (net of tax relief of £12m of which £9m is deferred).	(128)	
ICI's share of an extraordinary item in Tioxide Group PLC, whilst an associated undertaking, relating to its fundamental restructuring (net of tax relief of £2m).	(39)	
Disposal of over-the-counter pharmaceuticals business in the USA (net of deferred tax of £83m).		127
	53	127

and 'reshaping' of their businesses. The directors of British Telecommunications plc decided that the costs of their programme should be classified as 'exceptional' items. Imperial Chemical Industries (ICI) PLC's directors considered theirs to be 'extraordinary' items.

Inconsistencies of this kind run counter to two of the objectives of having accounting standards in the first place, as noted in Chapter 1 of this book. They are perceived to undermine the comparability of financial information. They are also considered to detract from its credibility. Those responsible for regulating financial reporting are expected to eliminate them. Accordingly, in October 1991, the Urgent Issues Tasks Force (UITF) issued an abstract on the subject of restructuring costs. It concluded that:

> Restructuring costs, even if they relate to a fundamental restructuring of the business, are usually part of the ordinary activities of a company and should normally be treated as charges in arriving at the profit or loss on ordinary activities, disclosed, if material, as

exceptional items. Where a company presents restructuring costs as extraordinary items, the onus of proof rests with the company to demonstrate that such treatment is appropriate; in these circumstances the financial statements should include a full description both of the nature of the separate event or transaction that it considers to be extraordinary and of the nature of the related restructuring costs.[7]

The Abstract would clearly affect the accounting treatment adopted by ICI in 1990, as shown in Illustration 4.2. The company's 1991 Accounts, the first to be prepared after the publication of the Abstract, contained the following notes:

Illustration 4.3: *Imperial Chemical Industries PLC (1991)*

2 1990 RESTATEMENT

The comparative figures for the Group for 1990 have been restated to reclassify, as an exceptional item, the ICI share (£41m, less tax relief of £2m) of a provision, previously accounted for as extraordinary by Tioxide Group Ltd while it was an associated undertaking. This restatement is in accordance with the clarification of the accounting treatment of restructuring costs issued by the Accounting Standards Board and has the effect of reducing 1990 profit before tax from £977m to £936m and earnings per share from 87.9p to 82.3p.

8 EXTRAORDINARY ITEMS (extract)

	Group	
	1991	1990
	£m	£m
Gain on disposal of the investment in Enterprise Oil plc (net of charge for taxation of £9m).		520
Charge for reshaping the ICI Group business portfolio, comprising withdrawals through business divestments, closures and other restructuring measures. The charge is net of estimated disposal proceeds and includes the expense of obtaining substantial cost reductions which are a significant part of the objective (net of tax relief of £50m of which £46m is deferred).		(300)
Charge for the withdrawal from UK compound fertilizer manufacture and restructuring, with a view to ultimate divestment, of the ammonium nitrate business (net of tax relief of £12m of which £9m is deferred).		(128)
	-	92

It is worth noting that a reclassification of portion of the £300 million charge for reshaping the ICI business portfolio was not deemed to be necessary. The reference to 'other restructuring measures' in that paragraph had led some commentators to expect a more significant adjustment than the £39 million arising from the Tioxide

Group. The extract taken from ICI's 1990 Accounts is indicative of the way the ASC's two-tier profit and loss account tended to work in practice. 'Extraordinary' items frequently consisted of very large asset disposal profits, losses resulting from the discontinuance of unprofitable business segments and other unexpected costs not expected to recur in the future.

The exclusion of the last two categories from the commonly-used EPS measure was naturally a boon to most preparers of financial statements. It provoked the following comment from the chairman of the Financial Reporting Council (FRC), in the FRC's Second Annual Review, dated November 1992:

> ...such practices can obscure the realities of current performance and even lull managers within a company into a false sense of security. It has been all too easy to regard costs carried below the line as somehow not counting: they do nevertheless inevitably involve the expenditure of real resources.[8]

The comment is surprising when it is remembered that all profit and loss accounts have to end with the 'profit or loss for the financial year' item referred to earlier. This includes the effect of any so-called 'extraordinary' items. The FRC chairman's anxiety reveals a great deal about the consequences of splitting the profit and loss account into two, especially when one section is prioritised by making it the basis of the EPS calculation. It also suggests a startling inability on the part of users to understand the information contained in the profit and loss account.

Dissatisfaction with the profit and loss account mounted as inconsistencies in the application of the 'extraordinary' item definition became more apparent. The ASC's successor body, the Accounting Standards Board (ASB), was quick to announce its intention to make radical changes. On 29 October 1992, it issued FRS 3 *Reporting financial performance*, effective for financial periods ending on or after 22 June 1993.

The new proposals

In retrospect, the ASC's relatively modest plan to separate 'ordinary' and 'extraordinary' activities in the profit and loss account was bound to founder on difficulties of definition. An obvious solution would be to combine the two parts. Further analysis of the result could then be left to supplementary notes, like those required by SSAP 25 *Segmental reporting*. The ASB has decided, however, to proceed along the same lines pursued by the ASC. FRS 3 explains the desire to improve the usefulness of the profit and loss account by fragmenting it, as follows:

> The many parts of a reporting entity's activities exhibit features which differ in stability, risk and predictability, indicating a need for the separate disclosure of components of financial performance in the profit and loss account and in the statement of total recognised gains and losses.[9]

FRS 3 accordingly requires a radical revision of the layout of the profit and loss account. A distinction has now to be drawn between 'continuing' and 'discontinued' operations, with the former itself sub-divided into acquisitions and other. Extraordinary items, seen by many as the cause of the ASC's failure to devise a satisfactory profit and loss account, have virtually been abolished. They are replaced by different classes of exceptional items.

The significantly enlarged profit and loss account will, however, not be sufficient to achieve the ASB's objective:

> The range of important components of financial performance which the FRS requires reporting entities to highlight would often be incomplete if it stopped short at the profit and loss account, since certain gains and losses are specifically permitted or required by law or an accounting standard to be taken directly to reserves. ...It is necessary to consider all gains and losses recognised in a period when assessing the financial performance of a reporting entity during that period.[10]

For these reasons, a new primary statement, the *Statement of total recognised gains and losses*, has been introduced. An appendix to the FRS contains examples of the new primary statement and the revised profit and loss account. The latter requires Format 1 of the statutory formats to be presented as follows:[11]

	Continuing operations	Acquisitions	Discontinued operations	Total	Total
	1993	1993	1993	1993	1992 as restated
	£m	£m	£m	£m	£m
Turnover	550	50	175	775	690
Cost of sales	(415)	(40)	(165)	(620)	(555)
Gross profit	135	10	10	155	135
Net operating expenses	(85)	(4)	(25)	(114)	(83)
Less 1992 provision			10	10	
Operating profit	50	6	(5)	51	52
Profit on sale of properties	9			9	6
Provision for loss on operations to be discontinued					(30)
Loss on disposal of discontinued operations			(17)	(17)	
Less 1992 provision			20	20	
Profit on ordinary activities before interest	59	6	(2)	63	28
Interest payable				(18)	(15)
Profit on ordinary activities before taxation				45	13
Tax on profit on ordinary activities				(14)	(4)
Profit on ordinary activities after taxation				31	9
Minority interests				(2)	(2)
[Profit before extraordinary items]				29	7
[Extraordinary items]*				-	-
Profit for the financial year				29	7

*Extraordinary items have been included only to show positioning. The FRS notes that they are 'extremely rare as they relate to highly abnormal events or transactions that fall outside the ordinary activities of a reporting entity and which are not expected to recur. In view of the extreme rarity of such items no examples are provided.'[12]

The profit and loss account shown above would be supplemented by a detailed note showing the composition of the net operating expenses line. The component parts (distribution costs, administrative expenses, and other operating income) have to be analysed as between continuing and discontinued operations. Comparatives figures are required to be given in this note for all these items and for turnover, cost of sales and gross profit.

The profit for the financial year shown in the profit and loss account is a component of the new primary statement, the *Statement of total recognised gains and losses*. According to FRS 3, the latter is expected to look as follows:

	1993	1992 as restated
	£m	£m
Profit for the financial year	29	7
Unrealised surplus on revaluation of properties	4	6
Unrealised (loss)/gain on trade investment	(3)	7
	30	20
Currency translation differences on foreign currency net investments	(2)	5
Total recognised gains and losses relating to the year	28	25
Prior year adjustment (as explained in note x)	(10)	
Total gains and losses recognised since last annual report	18	

Noting that there are 'other changes in shareholders' funds that can also be important in understanding the change in financial position of the entity', the FRS makes provision for the possibility of yet another primary statement.[13] A *Reconciliation of movements in shareholders' funds* is also required. Instead of being shown as a primary statement, this could be included as a note to the financial statements, as shown in the Appendix to FRS 3:

	1993	1992 as restated
	£m	£m
Profit for the financial year	29	7
Dividends	(8)	(1)
	21	6
Other recognised gains and losses relating to the year (net)	(1)	18
New share capital subscribed	20	1
Goodwill written-off	(25)	
Net addition to shareholders' funds	15	25
Opening shareholders' funds (originally £375 million before deducting prior year adjustment of £10 million)	365	340
Closing shareholders' funds	380	365

In addition to the radical changes to the layout of the profit and loss account, the FRS also contains new rules affecting the measurement of certain items. These will be discussed later in this chapter. Recognising that the new rule for calculating profits on disposal of assets could result in a lack of comparability between different entities, the FRS also makes provision for the inclusion of a *Note of historical cost profits and losses*. This must follow the profit and loss account in instances where the former reveals a materially different picture to that shown in the latter. The Appendix to the FRS contains the following example:

	1993	1992 as restated
	£m	£m
Reported profit on ordinary activities before taxation	45	13
Realisation of property revaluation gains of previous years	9	10
Difference between a historical cost depreciation charge and the actual depreciation charge of the year calculated on the revalued amount	5	4
Historical cost profit on ordinary activities before taxation	59	27
Historical cost profit for the year retained after taxation, minority interests, extraordinary items and dividends	35	20

The new requirements introduced by FRS 3 make for exhausting reading. It is tempting to speculate how users are likely to react to them. For example, when examining the 1993 result, should their attention be focused on:

- the profit for the year, shown in the *Profit and loss account* (£29m)?
- its historical cost equivalent, shown in the *Note of historical cost profits and losses* (£35m)?
- the total recognised gains and losses relating to the year, shown in the *Statement of total recognised gains and losses* (£28m)?
- the net addition to shareholders' funds, shown in the *Reconciliation of movements in shareholders' funds* (£15m)?

It would appear that the ASB wants users to focus on a combination of all four of the above figures. Whether this is relevant to their needs will be examined in the next section. There is another important issue which needs to be covered first. What about the impact of new share issues? Is there any way of determining from the new proposals whether these have enhanced the earnings for existing shareholders?

The requirement to calculate an EPS figure still exists, but the method used to calculate it has been changed. The adverse consequences of the ASC's decision to prioritise a section of the profit and loss account by making it the basis of the EPS calculation have already been noted. Determined to avoid these, the ASB has made provision for the calculation of a variety of EPS-like figures, explaining that:

> It is not possible to distil the performance of a complex organisation into a single measure. Undue significance, therefore, should not be placed on any one such measure

which may purport to achieve this aim. To assess the performance of a reporting entity during a period all components of its activities must be considered.[14]

The accounting firm Ernst & Young, has provided the following example of the EPS disclosures that might be expected under FRS 3:[15]

		19X1	19X0
Earnings per share		29p	33p
Continuing operating profit per share	(Note x)	56p	53p

Note x	19X1 Pence	19X0 Pence
Earnings per share	29	33
Trading loss of discontinued operations	10	12
Loss on disposal of discontinued operations	7	-
Interest payable	8	6
Tax	1	1
Minority interests	1	1
Continuing operating profit per share	56	53

The continuing operating profit per share has been calculated in addition to the earnings per share required by SSAP 3 since in the opinion of the directors this will allow shareholders to consider the results of the future operations of the company. The continuing operating profit per share has not, however, been calculated after tax and minority interests.

The last sentence in the example is particularly important. Whether shareholders are able to 'consider the results of the future operations of the company' without being able to determine the impact of taxation and minority interests is doubtful. The example also reveals that FRS 3 is seeking to overcome the dubious significance of many of the EPS-like figures certain to appear in practice. It hopes to do this by forcing them to be reconciled to the 'real' EPS, based on the profit for the year as shown at the foot of the profit and loss account. The legislature and the ASC probably held similar hopes many years ago. Item 20 of the statutory profit and loss account is, after all, intended to reflect the overall performance of the reporting entity, after taking account of both ordinary and extraordinary items. Whether the ASB's 'real' EPS figure will lose its significance in the same way remains to be seen. It must be a significant possibility.

Meeting the needs of users

Having outlined the essence of the new proposals for the layout of the profit and loss account, it is appropriate to ask whether they are relevant to the needs of the user. Is the 'shift of emphasis from a single performance indicator'[16] to an 'information set' approach that 'highlights a range of important components of performance'[17] what they really want?

If the following extract from a recent *Accountancy Age* editorial can be taken as a guide, the ASB is being a little optimistic:

> For comparability, however, there is clearly a demand for a recognised formula to arrive at a single earnings measure, not so much for its own sake but because so many other ratios depend on it. This is what analysts' body the Institute of Investment Management and Research is now working on.
>
> Of course, users will have their own approaches, but an accepted figure for general use will be of great general benefit. And it would also be of benefit, once such a formula is agreed, for the preparers of accounts to include such a figure – with the appropriate reconciliation – in their accounts.[18]

At the start of this chapter, reference was made to the dictionary definition of profit. This was done in an attempt to shed some light on the term most users instinctively associate with financial reporting. It now appears that it is an elusive concept. Over the last 20 years, the bodies responsible for developing accounting standards have amended the format of the profit and loss account with a view to achieving ever more meaningful presentations of financial performance. The profit arising from ordinary activities was initially considered to be of paramount importance. It is now considered appropriate to place greater emphasis on a whole range of profit measures. Some of these require the user to look beyond the profit and loss account itself. For this reason, a new primary statement has been introduced. A major user group, the Institute of Investment Management and Research, has now apparently embarked on the development of yet another 'recognized formula' for calculating the most appropriate profit figure. These efforts are all characterised by an overriding belief that a meaningful profit figure can be calculated. Rather like a hunt for hidden treasure, it is a case of having to find the spot marked 'X'.

The rest of this chapter is devoted to pursuing an alternative view. It questions whether the existing accounting framework lends itself to the calculation of a profit figure that has any meaning at all. Although profit is computed by deducting debits (representing outlays) from credits (representing returns), applying the formula in practice is a different matter altogether. The five sections which follow are designed to illustrate some of the more common difficulties. Whose debits and credits should be taken into account? Which debits should be deducted from which credits? Should all the debits be taken into account? Should all the credits be taken into account? How should the debits and credits be measured?

WHOSE DEBITS AND CREDITS?

FRS 2 *Accounting for subsidiary undertakings* explains the background to this issue as follows:

> For a variety of legal, tax and other reasons undertakings generally choose to conduct their activities not through a single legal entity but through several undertakings under

the ultimate control of the parent undertaking of that group. For this reason the financial statements of a parent undertaking by itself do not present a full picture of its economic activities or financial position. Consolidated financial statements are required in order to reflect the extended business unit that conducts activities under the control of the parent undertaking.[19]

The key word is 'control'. If one undertaking is controlled by another, it seems appropriate to include the former's debits and credits in order to present a complete picture of the latter's activities. In many instances, the ability of one undertaking to control another is beyond dispute. Ownership of the majority of the voting rights is usually the clearest indicator. In other instances, however, the existence of control is harder to determine. The following newspaper article is a recent example:

Deadline set to settle USAir deal[20]

Government to rule by Dec. 24 on British Airways bid

Associated Press
WASHINGTON – The Bush administration is moving to settle a bid by **British Airways PLC** to buy a major stake in **USAir Inc.** before Bill Clinton, who opposes the deal, takes over as U.S. president in January.

The U.S. Transportation Department has set in motion a process under which Transportation Secretary Andrew Card will decide by Dec. 24 whether to approve a controversial deal under which British Airways would pump $750 million (U.S.) into USAir in exchange for 44 per cent ownership and 21 per cent of the voting stock.

The Transportation Depart-

ment said the issue is whether the deal will transfer effective control of USAir, the sixth-largest U.S. airline, to foreign owners despite terms limiting British Airways to a minority stake.

Current law limits foreign ownership to 25 per cent of voting stock. Foreign interests already own 4 per cent of the airline, so BA's share would be limited to 21 per cent

Al Becker, a spokesman for American Airlines, which is allied with United Airlines Inc. and Delta Air Lines Inc. in opposing the USAir–British Airways deal, said the Dec. 24 deadline for a ruling "does not provide enough time for the government to weigh

the costs and benefits."

American Airlines says the deal will give British Airways an unfair competitive edge and will cost the U.S. airline industry $500-million a year and thousands of jobs.

Mr. Becker said he would prefer to have the matter decided by Mr. Clinton. "The president-elect, through statements he has made, shows a real understanding of the issues involved."

Mr. Clinton has argued that the proposed partnership could steer more business toward European aircraft consortium Airbus Industrie and hurt domestic aircraft companies Boeing Co. and McDonnell Douglas Corp.

The possibility that British Airways could exercise effective control over USAir, despite owning only 44 per cent of it and less than 25 per cent of its voting shares, was clearly an issue of concern to USAir's competitors. British Airways subsequently decided not to proceed with this particular transaction. Had it done so, the appropriate accounting treatment of USAir's debits and credits in British Airways' financial statements would have been difficult to determine. At the time of the proposed transaction, USAir was incurring substantial losses.

The Companies Act 1985 was amended by the 1989 Act to deal with the possibility that effective control might be exercised in situations where an ownership interest amounted to less than 50 per cent. The relevant section reads as follows:

(4) An undertaking is also a parent undertaking in relation to another undertaking, a subsidiary undertaking, if it has a participating interest in the undertaking and –

    (a) it actually exercises a dominant influence over it[21]

FRS 2 has attempted to clarify the meaning of this requirement by explaining that:

The actual exercise of dominant influence is the exercise of an influence that achieves the result that the operating and financial policies of the undertaking influenced are set in accordance with the wishes of the holder of the influence and for the holder's benefit whether or not those wishes are explicit. The actual exercise of dominant influence is identified by its effect in practice rather than by the way in which it is exercised.[22]

The difficulty of applying the concept in practice is apparent from the following explanatory paragraph in the FRS:

A parent undertaking may actually exercise its dominant influence in an interventionist or non-interventionist way. For example, a parent undertaking may set directly and in detail the operating and financial policies of its subsidiary undertaking or it may prefer to influence these by setting out in outline the kind of results it wants achieved without being involved regularly or on a day-to-day basis. Because of the variety of ways that dominant influence may be exercised evidence of continuous intervention is not necessary to support the view that dominant influence is actually exercised. Sufficient evidence might be provided by a rare intervention on a critical matter.[23]

Even if 'dominant influence' is not actually being exercised, there is another possibility to consider. Does the undertaking holding the participating interest exercise a 'significant' influence over the other's operating and financial policy? Significant influence is presumed to exist where 20 per cent or more of the voting rights are held. When significant influence is exercised, the investee is deemed to be an associated undertaking. SSAP 1 *Accounting for associated companies* requires the consolidated financial statements of the investor to include its share of the pre-tax profit or loss of the associated undertaking. The results of the associate are not included on a line-by-line basis, but as a separate line in the profit and loss account of the investor. It is only when neither dominant nor significant influence is exercised, that the results of the other entity are excluded.

The inclusion or exclusion of the debits and credits of another entity and the manner in which they are to be included, hinges on an interpretation of the rules briefly outlined in this section. Whether the rules are capable of coping with the complexity of many of the issues involved is uncertain. It is to be expected that the accounting treatment adopted in individual cases will not meet with universal approval. The following extract from an article in the *Financial Times*, covering Coats Viyella's hostile takeover of the Tootal textile group, is a case in point:

...Coats' criticisms focus on the way Tootal accounted for two recent disposals. First, the company concluded a phased sale of its 49.8 per cent stake in Da Gama Textile Company in February 1989, for a total of £25m in five equal tranches. Second, Tootal sold off Sandhurst Marketing for £4.2m, having paid £25.3m for it in December 1986.

    The criticism of the first disposal was that Tootal treated the gain on the sale of the Da Gama stake as if it were an ordinary trading item, and that it took credit for profits arising from Da Gama even after it ceased to have any real financial interest in the company.[24]

Prior to February 1989, Tootal's 49.8 per cent interest in Da Gama Textile Company was accounted for as an associated undertaking. The first stage of the five-tranche disposal would have reduced Tootal's shareholding to 39.8 per cent. Tootal considered this interest large enough to allow it to continue to exercise significant influence. It therefore continued to include its share of Da Gama's profits in its profit and loss account.

The purchaser of the shares, South African Breweries Limited, took a different view. Believing that it was in a position to exercise whatever influence attached to the shares, its financial statements for the year to 31 March 1989 reflect the acquisition of Tootal's entire 49.8 per cent interest in Da Gama.

WHICH DEBITS AND CREDITS?

Once a decision has been made as to which entities to include in the consolidated financial statements, the appropriate treatment of their debits and credits needs to be determined. The accounting process will have recorded the existence of many transactions. Not all of these will find their way into the profit and loss account. For that document to present a meaningful picture, the Companies Act 1985 requires that:

> All income and charges relating to the financial year to which the accounts relate shall be taken into account, without regard to the date of receipt or payment.[25]

This is one of the basic accounting principles referred to in Chapter 1. It is similar to the 'accruals' concept contained in SSAP 2 *Disclosure of accounting policies*:

> ...revenue and costs are accrued (that is, recognised as they are earned or incurred, not as money is received or paid), matched with one another so far as their relationship can be established or justifiably assumed, and dealt with in the profit and loss account of the period to which they relate;[26]

It is therefore necessary to try to establish the relationship between the debits and the credits. Credits relating to the current period are included in the profit and loss account together with their matching debits. Current period debits expected to be matched with credits of a future period, are taken to the balance sheet. Debits incapable of being matched are written off in the profit and loss account. Their fate is sealed by the 'prudence' concept. SSAP 2 requires that 'where the accruals concept is inconsistent with the "prudence" concept, the latter prevails'.[27] The 'prudence' concept stipulates that:

> ...revenue and profits are not anticipated, but are recognised by inclusion in the profit and loss account only when realised in the form either of cash or of other assets the ultimate cash realisation of which can be assessed with reasonable certainty; provision is made for

all known liabilities (expenses and losses) whether the amount of these is known with certainty or is a best estimate in the light of the information available.[28]

The rules outlined so far suggest that the preparer's task is a difficult one. Its complexity is illustrated by the following examples.

Today's debits tomorrow?

Most transactions entered into by the reporting entity are expected to contribute towards an increase in revenue. Some of the revenue will, however, only materialise in future periods. In accordance with the 'accruals' concept, an attempt has to be made to match today's debits with tomorrow's credits. Where a 'relationship can be established or justifiably assumed' today's debits are deferred, pending recognition in tomorrow's profit and loss account:

Illustration 4.4: *Forte Plc (1992)*

Accounting policies

INTEREST, INTERNAL PROFESSIONAL FEES AND PRE-OPENING EXPENSES:

Interest on capital employed on land awaiting development and on the construction and major redevelopment of hotels and restaurants and internal professional costs incurred until these enterprises start to trade are capitalised as part of the costs of construction. In addition, pre-opening and development expenses incurred up to the commencement of full trading are deferred and written off over five to ten years. Expenses incurred on major information technology projects are capitalised and written off over five years.

The costs described above have all been incurred in expectation of future benefits. To present a meaningful profit and loss account in these circumstances, the preparer has to deal with the uncertainty attaching to the existence of the future benefits and the period over which they are expected to materialise.

In other instances, the uncertainties appear to be less problematic. Different preparers are, however, likely to adopt different approaches to essentially the same issue. For example, the directors of Tesco PLC seem to be more confident about the recoverability of their group's expenditure on freehold and long leasehold buildings, than rival J Sainsbury plc:

Illustration 4.5: Tesco PLC (1992)

Accounting Policies

Fixed Assets and Depreciation (extract)

No depreciation is provided on United Kingdom freehold buildings or leasehold buildings held on leases in excess of 125 years. The group follows a programme of regular refurbishment and maintenance of its properties, which includes the reinstatement of the fabric of the buildings, where necessary, in order to maintain them to a high standard. Accordingly, in the opinion of the directors, any element of depreciation would be immaterial and no provision has been made.

Illustration 4.6: J Sainsbury plc (1992)

ACCOUNTING POLICIES

Depreciation (extract)

Depreciation is provided on freehold and long leasehold properties if, in the opinion of the Directors, the estimated residual value of any property will be less than its book value after excluding the effects of inflation, so that the shortfall is written off in equal annual instalments over the remaining useful life of the property.

Allocating expenditure on buildings to different accounting periods is clearly not a straightforward process. It must, however, be easier than dealing with intangible assets like brand names. The accounting principle involved is similar: how to allocate today's expenditure to benefits expected tomorrow.

Illustration 4.7: Guinness PLC (1991)

Accounting Policies

BRANDS

The fair value of businesses acquired and of interests taken in associated undertakings includes brands, which are recognised where the brand has a value which is substantial and long term. Acquired brands are only recognised where title is clear, brand earnings are separately identifiable, the brand could be sold separately from the rest of the business and where the brand achieves earnings in excess of those achieved by unbranded products.

Amortisation is not provided except where the end of the useful economic life of the acquired brand can be foreseen. The useful economic lives of brands and their carrying value are subject to annual review and any amortisation or provision for permanent impairment would be charged against the profit for the period in which they arose.

Deciding whether a brand name has suffered a diminution in value is likely to be a difficult process. Identifying its existence in the first place sometimes requires considerable expertise:

Illustration 4.8: WPP Group plc (1991)

ACCOUNTING POLICIES

4 Intangible fixed assets

Intangible fixed assets comprise certain acquired separable corporate brand names. These are shown at a valuation of the incremental earnings expected to arise from the ownership of brands. The valuations have been based on the present value of notional royalty savings arising from ownership of those brands and on estimates of profits attributable to brand loyalty. The valuations are subject to annual review. No depreciation is provided since, in the opinion of the directors, the brands do not have a finite useful economic life.

There are essentially two aspects to the matching processes described in all of the examples above. The first is to decide whether today's debit will be covered by a surplus of tomorrow's credits, either by using the asset in the business or by the proceeds expected on its sale. Once recoverability has been established, the second issue is to decide how to allocate the debit to future periods in the most sensible manner. Opinions vary as to how this should be done.

Illustration 4.9: Tesco PLC (1992)

Accounting Policies

Fixed Assets and Depreciation (extract)

Leasehold properties with less than 125 years unexpired are amortised by equal annual instalments over the unexpired period of the lease.

Illustration 4.10: Granada Group PLC (1991)

Accounting policies

4 Depreciation (extract)

Motorway Service Areas held subject to short leaseholds are not depreciated whilst their value is maintained or increased. Depreciation thereafter is provided on a straight line basis over the residual period of the lease.

There is a fundamental difference in approach in the policies adopted by Tesco and Granada. The former regards depreciation as an allocation of past debits to future periods. All the periods receive a share of the debit. By contrast Granada treats depreciation as a measure of the decline in the value of the asset, to be recognised only in those periods where the decline occurs. Both policies are based on a desire to establish a sensible relationship between past debits and future credits. Some policies have even attempted to incorporate the effect of inflation into the matching process:

Illustration 4.11: *Charterhall PLC (1989)*

INTANGIBLE ASSETS (extract)

Goodwill
On the acquisition of subsidiaries and businesses, the purchase consideration is allocated over the underlying net tangible assets, significant intangible assets and goodwill. Goodwill arising on the acquisition of subsidiaries has been capitalised and is amortised (after taking account of the anticipated impact of inflation on future earnings) through the Profit and Loss Account over a period not exceeding 40 years, estimated by the Directors to be the useful economic life.

Given the complexity of the measurement issues and the many uncertainties involved, it is not surprising that different preparers have tackled the task of allocating today's debits to tomorrow's profit and loss accounts in different ways.

Tomorrow's debits today?

The SSAP 2 requirement that the 'prudence' concept should override the 'accruals' concept means that tomorrow's debits sometimes have to appear in today's profit and loss account. The 'prudence' concept stipulates that provision has to be made for all known liabilities. This is similar to another of the accounting principles contained in the Companies Act 1985, as noted in the first chapter:

all liabilities and losses which have arisen or are likely to arise in respect of the financial year to which the accounts relate or a previous financial year shall be taken into account, including those which only become apparent between the balance sheet date and the date on which it is signed on behalf of the board of directors in pursuance of section 233 of this Act.[29]

These requirements are relatively easy to understand in the context of product warranty claims and losses expected to result from litigation instituted against the reporting entity. It seems appropriate to charge an estimate of these future debits in the current year's profit and loss account. The losses originate from events in the current year or one prior to that.

The position is, however, less certain when management decides to reorganise the company's activities. Illustration 4.1 revealed that British Telecom made a provision of £390 million in its financial year ended 31 March 1990, to cover the costs of restructuring and refocusing the group's operations. Most of the money was to be spent in future accounting periods. A liability to third parties in the amount of £390 million did not exist at 31 March 1990. The decision to spend the money was presumably taken in the expectation that it would achieve a future benefit. The group reported a profit of £2,692 million before charging this provision. Despite the need to restructure and refocus its operations, it was expected to continue to report substantial profits in the years when the money was to be spent. How should the 'prudence' and 'accruals' concepts be applied in these circumstances? Is it appropriate to bring the debits of future years into the current year? Does this enable a meaningful profit to be calculated for any of the affected years?

FRS 3 contains some guidance on the issue of providing for future debits. It applies only in the context of decisions to sell or terminate an operation. It is a consequence of the new requirement to show discontinued operations separately in the revised profit and loss account referred to earlier in this chapter. The guidance is based on the principle that an obligation only arises when 'the reporting entity becomes demonstrably committed to the sale or termination.'[30] In the case of an intended sale a legally binding contract must exist. Failing this, 'no obligation has been entered into by the reporting entity; accordingly, provisions for the direct costs of the decision to sell and for future operating losses should not be made.'[31] In the case of an intended termination, it is sufficient for a public announcement to have been made which effectively obliges the entity to complete the termination. The provision allowed should cover only the direct costs of the sale or termination and any future operating losses. In determining these amounts, account has to be taken of any profits expected from the operation in the future or on disposal of its assets.

It is not clear whether the FRS 3 principle should also be applied to the reorganisation or refocusing of existing operations. As suggested by the British Telecom example, current practice is usually to make a provision for the expected costs of implementing decisions taken in the current year. In many instances, the reporting entity is not 'demonstrably committed' to incurring all of the costs involved.

Today's credits today?

The problems of allocation discussed in the previous two sections are not confined to debits. A similar difficulty exists with the allocation of credits to individual accounting periods.

Illustration 4.12: The Burton Group PLC (1991)

ACCOUNTING POLICIES

I Developers' contribution

Contributions from developers are, as appropriate, deducted from the capital cost of fitting out the store or treated as deferred income and released to profit over a five year period. The benefit of rent free periods is taken as it arises.

A common feature in a depressed property market has been the ability of tenants to negotiate rent-free periods, usually at the inception of their leases. This results in an obvious cash flow benefit but creates some uncertainty as to the appropriate accounting treatment. Should the profit and loss account show that there is no legal obligation to pay rent in the current accounting period? Or should the issue be viewed from a longer perspective, requiring the net rental cost to be accounted for in aggregate? The second approach would cause the benefit of the rent-free period to be spread over the lease term.

The first of these two approaches has been adopted by The Burton Group in the illustration shown above. It has some similarity with the practice of charging depreciation only in those periods when an asset suffers a decline in value (see Illustration 4.10). In both instances the preparer is attempting to relate the debits and credits to specific accounting periods.

The issue of allocating credits to individual accounting periods arises in another, more fundamental, context. It concerns the start of the revenue recognition process itself. The following example illustrates this point:

Example 4.1

There is consistently strong demand for a highly successful product. Production is stepped up accordingly. At the financial year end, the manufacturer's warehouse is full. Customers are approached with a view to finalising delivery schedules for the following year.

If an established customer agrees to take delivery of certain minimum quantities of product at specified dates in the following year, can the manufacturer treat these quantities as sales in the current financial year?

Most answers to this question will probably involve a discussion about whether a legally enforceable sale has taken place in the current year. It is not certain, however, whether this should be the decisive issue for accounting purposes. SSAP 9 *Stocks and long-term contracts* allows revenue to be recognised as contract activity progresses, without there having to be a legally enforceable debtor at the year end.

In this instance, there are a number of arguments in favour of recognising the credit in the current period. The product has a successful track record, its manufacture is complete and it is ready for delivery. It is clear that the established customer wants the goods, has evidenced this fact, will almost certainly take delivery on the specified dates and pay for the goods in full.

Example 4.1 illustrates that revenue recognition is essentially concerned with narrowing a range of uncertainty. A sale becomes a sale for accounting purposes when uncertainty is reduced to a comfortable level. The range of possibilities, in order of decreasing uncertainty, is as follows:

- when the customer has placed an order?
- when the goods have been manufactured?
- when the goods have been set aside for delivery?
- when the goods have been delivered?
- when the goods have been paid for?
- when the warranty period has expired?

As noted earlier in this chapter, SSAP 2 provides some guidance in these circumstances. The 'prudence' concept prevents revenue from being recognised until it is 'realised either in the form of cash or of other assets, the ultimate cash realisation of which can be assessed with reasonable certainty'.[32] The most prudent approach is clearly to wait until payment has been received and the warranty period has expired. If revenue is recognised at an earlier stage in the process, the quality of information provided to the user becomes a function of the preparer's ability to deal with the uncertain outcome of a future event.

ALL THE DEBITS?

The discussion of the 'accruals' concept in the previous section has proceeded on the basis that all debits eventually end up in the profit and loss account. It is simply a question of deciding when this should happen. This premise is, however, not completely true. The example of the new layout for the profit and loss account shows that it is essentially a component of another primary statement, the *Statement of total recognised gains and losses*. Certain debits, those arising on the revaluation of assets and on the retranslation of foreign currency net investments, appear in the latter statement. To prevent confusion, debits can be taken to one of the statements only. They are not allowed to appear in both. The reasons for the exclusion from the profit and loss account of the two debits mentioned above are discussed in the following sections.

Asset valuation debits

The Companies Act 1985 allows companies to choose whether to record certain assets at their acquisition cost or at a valuation. When the second option is chosen, the difference between the amount of the valuation and the cost of acquiring the asset gives rise to a debit or a credit. Valuation shortfalls result in debits. Provided that the asset is a fixed asset and that it has not suffered a permanent decline in its value, the resulting debit is not considered to represent a real loss. It could, after all, reverse itself in the future. It is therefore allowed to be excluded from the profit and loss account.

If the asset is a current asset, the debit is thought to be more significant. Current assets are, by definition, not intended for continuing use in the company's business. Valuation shortfalls usually mean that a loss on the sale of the asset is imminent. These debits therefore have to appear in the profit and loss account. What happens when an asset's classification is changed from current to fixed assets? Confusion surrounding the appropriate accounting treatment gave rise to the Trafalgar House investigation, discussed in Chapter 2.

Foreign currency translation debits

The reasoning behind the exclusion of certain foreign currency translation debits from the profit and loss account is best explained by way of an example.

Example 4.2

A UK holding company establishes a subsidiary in the USA when the exchange rate is £1.00 = $1.50. It invests £60 million which the US company converts into $90 million. This is invested in plant and working capital. In its first year, the US company makes a profit of $20 million. At the end of that year, the exchange rate is £1.00 = $2.00. The UK holding company does not trade during the year.

- How has the UK company's investment fared?
- Should the financial statements of the group headed by it reflect a profit or a loss?

The obvious answer to the first question is that the UK company is poorer to the extent of £5 million. Its sole asset is a US company with net assets of $110 million (share capital of $90 million increased by the profit of $20 million). This asset is worth £55 million at the end of the financial year ($110 million at £1.00 = $2.00). At the start of the year, the UK company had cash of £60 million. Therefore, it must be £5 million worse off.

The answer to the second question confirms that the group is £5 million worse off. However, this loss will be split into two components for financial reporting purposes. The profit and loss account will show a profit of £10 million, being the US company's profit of $20 million translated at the year-end exchange rate. (The UK company has the option of translating the profit at the average exchange rate for the year instead.)

Where does the loss come in? The statement of recognised gains and losses will reflect a loss of £15 million, being the decline in the sterling value of the opening investment when translated at the year end exchange rate ($90 million at $2.00 = £1.00 compared with $90 million at $1.50 = £1.00).

Read together, the two primary statements disclose the expected overall loss of £5 million. A profit of £10 million appears in the profit and loss account and a loss of £15 million is shown in the statement of total recognised gains and losses.

What should the user make of the exclusion of certain revaluation and foreign currency translation debits from the profit and loss account? Are they less significant than those charged in the profit and loss account? Are the two primary statements introduced by FRS 3 of equal importance? The philosophy behind the FRS suggests that both statements are important. They are intended to reveal different components of the reporting entity's financial performance. The user is nevertheless likely to wonder why the earnings per share calculation, for example, appears to attach greater emphasis to the debits in the profit and loss account.

Goodwill debits

Prior to December 1991, another category of debit was allowed to bypass the profit and loss account. These debits originate as follows. When one company acquires another, the purchase price of £20 million might exceed the net assets of the acquired entity. If the latter are worth £15 million, there is a difference of £5 million. This debit is deemed to represent the goodwill of the acquired company. The purchaser is prepared to pay the additional amount because it represents certain attributes which are not reflected in the acquired company's balance sheet. These could be its well established reputation or the special talents of its employees, for example.

In order to achieve consistency of treatment with the goodwill of the acquiror, SSAP 22 *Accounting for goodwill* allows purchased goodwill to be eliminated from the group balance sheet by a direct charge to reserves. The accounting standard explains that:

> ...if purchased goodwill is treated as an asset whilst non-purchased goodwill is not, a balance sheet does not present the total goodwill of a company (or group); it reflects only the purchased goodwill of the acquired business(es) at the date of acquisition, to the extent that it has not been written off.[33]

This approach allows purchased goodwill to be ignored on the disposal of the acquired company. The resulting profit or loss can be calculated without reference to the portion of the purchase price attributed to goodwill. Using the figures in the example, it would be possible for the acquirer to reflect a profit on sale even if the acquired company were sold for less than its £20 million purchase price. UK companies were therefore able to report the outcome of business disposals and closures in a more favourable light than their North American counterparts:

Illustration 4.13: Maxwell Communication Corporation PLC (1991)

CANADIAN SHAREHOLDER INFORMATION (extract)

	Year 31st March 1991 £m	Year 31st March 1990 £m
Profit after taxation and after deducting minority interests, in accordance with UK GAAP	99.2	126.8
Adjustments for Canadian GAAP:		
Deferred taxation	(1.3)	(2.2)
Goodwill amortisation	(11.7)	(11.8)
Pension contributions	1.8	2.2
Tax effect of the above adjustments	(0.6)	(0.8)
	87.4	114.2
Discontinued operations:		
Net losses arising from business disposals and discontinuance of printing-related activities (disclosed as extraordinary items under UK GAAP)	(49.5)	(25.7)
Related goodwill written off	(31.6)	(190.8)
Related deferred taxation	-	4.4
Net earnings adjusted to Canadian GAAP	6.3	(97.9)

The table shows that Maxwell Communication Corporation's earnings were significantly better off when prepared on a UK GAAP basis. The differences are huge – £224.7 million in 1990 and £92.9 million in 1991. They are due mainly to the 'related goodwill written off' line. At the time, UK GAAP did not require purchased goodwill arising on the acquisition of these businesses to be charged in the profit and loss account when calculating the loss on their disposal or discontinuance. Eliminated against reserves on acquisition, it ceased to exist for accounting purposes thereafter.

Accounting practice in this area has subsequently been amended by UITF Abstract 3 and FRS 2. Although purchased goodwill is still allowed to be eliminated against reserves, it must be brought back into the profit and loss account when the acquired business is sold or discontinued. A difficult measurement problem looms should an acquirer decide to sell portion of an acquired business. An allocation of the acquired goodwill would then have to be made. Furthermore, in the period from the acquisition of a business until its sale or closure, the goodwill is effectively in limbo. The existing rules mean that any loss caused by a decline in its value need only be revealed when the business is sold or discontinued. In recognition of the unsatisfactory nature of this situation, the chairman of the ASB recently commented that:

> The issue of the accounting treatment of goodwill has been the subject of major controversy in the United Kingdom for many years. As its starting point to the goodwill project the Board reviewed the responses received to the ASC's exposure draft ED 47. Thereafter, the Board commissioned a research project undertaken by a team headed by Professor John Arnold. The theoretical paper issued by the team advocated broadly that goodwill be retained on the balance sheet unless its value could not be substantiated.
>
> Following on from this the feasibility of the theoretical proposals is being investigated by the goodwill Project Director together with members of Professor Arnold's team. They are undertaking a number of interviews with major companies with a view to determining whether any reliable tests can be devised that would measure whether or not the carrying value of goodwill has diminished.[34]

Devising a reliable way of determining whether purchased goodwill has maintained its value will not be easy. It is difficult enough to ascertain what gave rise to it in the first place.

Reorganisation cost debits

The amount of goodwill arising on an acquisition will be increased if the acquirer intends to reorganise certain aspects of the acquired business. The costs of doing so are currently allowed to be incorporated into the goodwill figure. These debits are therefore excluded from the profit and loss account until the acquired business is sold or closed. The reasoning behind this treatment is explained in the following example.

Example 4.3

A retailer, company A, wishes to acquire a competitor, company B. The book value of the latter's net assets is £20 million. Included in these assets is a range of merchandise which company A wishes to discontinue. It proposes to sell these items by way of auction immediately after the acquisition. This is expected to result in their sales proceeds being £2 million less than their book value. Company A also intends to spend £1 million on the reorganisation of certain aspects of company B's business, to integrate the two companies into a single retail entity.

Working on the basis that company B's other assets and liabilities are considered to be worth their book values, but in anticipation of the £2 million loss and the outlay of £1 million, company A is able to negotiate a purchase price of £17 million.

In the first year after the acquisition, company A makes a net profit of £5 million from its own activities. Company B makes a profit of £2 million from its own activities, before accounting for the £2 million stock loss and the £1 million spent on the reorganisation of its business.

In the first year after the acquisition, is the profit of the combined group £7 million or £4 million?

The issue to be addressed is as follows. Has the purchaser effectively recovered the two debits amounting to £3 million from the seller? Does this allow them to be excluded from the group profit and loss account?

An argument in favour of excluding them could proceed along the following lines. Company B's net assets at the date of acquisition were £20 million. The subsequent year's profit of £2 million causes an increase to £22 million, which is then offset by the stock loss of £2 million and the reorganisation costs of £1 million. This leaves £19 million. The cost of company A's investment in company B is £17 million. As this investment is represented by net assets of £19 million, company A is better off by £2 million. In addition, it has also made a profit from its own activities of £5 million. The group profit and loss account should, therefore, reflect a profit of £7 million.

This seems to be the right answer. Although Company B's net assets had a book value of £20 million at the date of acquisition, Company A paid only £17 million to acquire them. The decline from £20 million to £19 million reflected in Company B's books is irrelevant. The starting point from Company A's perspective is £17 million, not £20 million. There has accordingly been an increase of £2 million, not a decline of £1 million. When this increase is added to Company A's own profit of £5 million, the group's profit is £7 million.

The conceptual appeal of this argument is presumably why the ASC allowed reorganisation costs to be excluded from the profit and loss account. ED 53 *Fair value in the context of acquisition accounting,* stipulated that two conditions had to met. There had to be a 'clearly defined programme of reorganisation' combined with 'evidence that in formulating its offer, the acquirer took account of plans or proposals for such reorganisation and associated costs.'[35]

The ASB seems set, however, to embark on a different approach. Noting that 'acquisition accounting continues to be the focus of much criticism in the financial community because of the opportunities that existing practices provide to obscure the true performance of combined businesses', the chairman of the ASB commented in November 1992 that:

> ...the Board is questioning the present practice of deeming as liabilities of the acquired company such items as provisions for future trading losses, reorganisations, and the disposal of duplicate facilities. Under the approach being considered the costs of post-acquisition restructuring would be disclosed as charges in the post-acquisition profit and loss account of the group, which would be consistent with accounting for the costs of restructuring that is unrelated to an acquisition. One effect of this proposal, if adopted, would be to reduce the amounts shown in the accounts as goodwill on acquisitions.[36]

The last sentence provides a clue as to why the ASB disapproves of the practice of excluding post-acquisition restructuring costs from the profit and loss account. To illustrate the point, it is necessary to make a slight alteration to the facts in Example 4.3. The accounting principle involved is identical, however.

Example 4.4
The facts are the same as in Example 4.3 except that company A paid £20 million to acquire company B, instead of £17 million. It believed that the extra £3 million was justified by the skills of company B's experienced management team.

Under this scenario, Company B's net assets are still £19 million one year later. However, the starting point from Company A's perspective is now £20 million, not £17 million. Company A is £2 million better off only when the goodwill of £3 million is added to Company B's net assets of £19 million. Without the addition for goodwill, there is a decline of £1 million from the £20 million starting point. If this is deducted from Company A's profit of £5 million, the group profit is only £4 million. It seems that the profit of £7 million in the previous answer can only be justified if the goodwill of £3 million is still intact.

Despite the current initiative of Professor John Arnold's team to establish a reliable way of measuring whether the value of goodwill has been maintained, it seems likely that the ASB will banish the establishment of reorganisation provisions in acquisition accounting. These debits seem set to return to the profit and loss account.

ALL THE CREDITS?

The practice of excluding items from the profit and loss account is not confined to debits. The revaluation and foreign currency differences referred to in the previous section could also be in the form of credits. They would accordingly also be excluded from the profit and loss account. This section is, however, concerned with two other categories of credits. Their inclusion in the profit and loss account is often a source of controversy.

Business disposal credits

FRS 3 was adopted by the assenting votes of eight of the ASB's nine members. Mr Robert Bradfield, Head of UK Equity Investment Research at Cazenove & Co, dissented. He did not like the way the FRS fails to separate business disposal profits from trading results. Under SSAP 6, business disposal profits were usually shown as extraordinary items. This excluded them from the reporting entity's profit before tax, profit after tax and minorities, and earnings per share figures. Mr Bradfield dissented because he feared that, by combining trading and business disposal profits on the face of the profit and loss account the FRS 'could frequently produce misleading measures of performance.'[37] The Appendix to FRS 3 notes that:

> Business disposal profits reflect internally generated goodwill often accrued over many years, together with an element of inflation; they are different in kind from the trading results of the year. Pending realisation, they constitute a hidden reserve. They may attract little tax and rarely contain a minority interest. By contrast, Mr Bradfield notes, it is the magnitude and quality of the earnings from trading, after tax and minority interests, that are the focus of attention for the shareholder as he uses the financial statements to assess the continuity of the source of dividends.[38]

FRS 3 does not require the effects of tax and minorities on the trading results to be shown on the face of the profit and loss account. In Mr Bradfield's opinion, users may therefore be unable to determine the underlying trend in the trading profits attributable to shareholders.

The appropriate accounting treatment of asset disposal profits has been a source of controversy for a long time. By requiring these profits to be shown as a separate component of profit before tax, the FRS will eliminate many of the variations seen in the past. Some companies have insisted that these profits are part of their operating income whereas others have shown them separately as non-operating items. A third category has always excluded them from earnings per share by deeming them to be extraordinary items. The FRS should also result in improved disclosure of these profits. It has not always been easy for users to identify their existence:

Illustration 4.14: Hanson PLC (1990 and 1991)

Consolidated Profit and Loss Account for the year ended September 30, 1990 (extract)	As reported in 1990 £ million	As reported in 1991 £ million
Sales turnover	7,153	7,153
Costs and overheads less other income [extracted from the supporting note]	5,868	5,868
Changes in stocks of finished goods and work in progress	1	1
Raw materials and consumables	3,572	3,572
Employment costs	1,107	1,107
Depreciation	172	172
Depreciation of finance leases	8	8
Other operating charges	1,248	1,349
Share of profit of related companies	(43)	(43)
Interest receivable	(824)	(824)
Interest payable	638	638
Profit on disposal of fixed assets	(11)	(11)
Profit on disposal of natural resources assets		(101)
Profit on ordinary activities	1,285	1,285

In the 1990 profit and loss account, Hanson showed the profit on disposal of natural resources assets as part of 'Other operating charges'. A different method of presentation was used when the 1990 results were reproduced in the comparative column of the 1991 profit and loss account.

Implementation of FRS 3 will result in standardised disclosure of the profits or losses on the sale or termination of a business operation and the disposal of fixed assets. It is, however, unlikely to settle the argument about the significance of these profits compared with those from trading activities.

Credits arising from sales to related parties

The debate about the inclusion of business disposal credits in the profit and loss account will be an ongoing one. There is more unanimity about the need to exclude another category of credit from the profit and loss account. FRS 2 requires that where goods are sold to a subsidiary of the seller the whole of the resulting profit should be eliminated from the group profit and loss account. This is uncontentious. A profit can only be made when the reporting entity trades with an outside party. Transactions between holding and subsidiary companies, being internal to the reporting entity, should not feature in its consolidated financial statements.

The position is less certain when the other party is an associated undertaking of the seller, one 'over whose operating and financial policy it exercises a significant influence.'[39] Is it possible for the group to report a profit under these circumstances? Because associated undertakings are not controlled by the reporting entity, they are not consolidated in the latter's financial statements. The existing rules allow a portion of the profit to be recognised. If the reporting entity owns 30 per cent of the buyer, it can recognise a profit to the extent of the 70 per cent outside interest in the buyer. It is deemed to be trading with itself only to the extent of 30 per cent. The principle is illustrated by the following extract:

Illustration 4.15: *Grand Metropolitan Public Limited Company (1991)*

16. Inntrepreneur Estates Ltd (extract)

On 28th March 1991 the group and Courage merged their tenanted pub estates into a joint venture company called Inntrepreneur Estates Ltd (IEL) which is incorporated in England. The group has a 50% shareholding in the IEL share capital and IEL has been treated as an associate within these financial statements.

25 Reserves (extract)	Profit and loss £m
At 30th September 1990	3,382
Exchange adjustments	(18)
Retained profit for year	214
Unrealised profit on sale of tenanted pub estate	23
Transfer of goodwill on disposal	(235)
Realisation of reserves on disposal	395
At 30th September 1991	3,761

INFORMATION FOR US SHAREHOLDERS

(f) Sale of assets to an associated company (extract)
Under UK GAAP, where an asset is sold to an associated company, the proportion of the gain or loss relating to the group's share of the equity in the associated company is generally accounted for as unrealised and is taken directly to retained surplus. Under US GAAP, the timing of and accounting treatment for, the sale of assets to an associated company may differ from UK GAAP as it depends on the amount of cash realised and the extent of guarantees given in respect of the associated company's indebtedness.

Under US GAAP no gain has been recognised on the sale of assets to Inntrepreneur Estates Ltd either in the statement of income or in retained surplus.

Note 25 reveals that the unrealised profit on the sale of the tenanted pub estate amounted to £23 million. Of the total profit of £46 million, £23 million must have been recognised in the profit and loss account for the year. It is worth noting that the group's net worth has, however, benefited to the extent of the full £46 million. Under US GAAP, no profit would be recognised on this transaction.

The UK accounting rule for associates is very different to that for subsidiaries. When the ownership interest is 50 per cent, as in the example above, half the profit on the sale of the asset can be recognised. Should the ownership interest be increased to 51 per cent, FRS 2 would prevent any profit from being recognised. It is, however, not necessary to increase the ownership interest to change the accounting treatment. Whether an undertaking is classified as a subsidiary or an associate depends on whether 'significant' or 'dominant' influence is exerted over it. The practical application of this difficult concept clearly has important accounting implications.

Transactions with associated undertakings are always going to be a source of controversy. This is to be expected when one party is, by definition, able to exert influence over the other. There is currently no requirement to disclose the value of sales made to associates. That this information might be of some significance to users, is implied by the following news report:

> ...The share shed 675c after publication of an article in the London *Sunday Telegraph* of July 19 reporting speculation by UK analysts that De Beers had manipulated the Central Selling Organisation (CSO) sales figures by selling diamonds to a CSO associate, Diamdel.
>
> The CSO wrote to the newspaper, rejecting the allegations and demanding a correction. The CSO says that while Diamdel is a sightholder and buys diamonds from the CSO, it is part of the regular diamond sales system. Diamdel breaks its purchases down into smaller parcels for sale to diamond dealers who are not large enough to have direct access to the sights. Sales to Diamdel have been proportionately lower this year than the overall drop in market sales.[40]

The possibility that the seller, the Central Selling Organisation, might have used its influence over a customer to improve its sales figures was clearly of concern to users of its financial statements. Whether transactions of this kind warrant separate disclosure is an issue plagued by difficulties of defining the related party and of establishing what constitutes an arm's length transaction.

MEASURING THE DEBITS AND THE CREDITS

Determining whether an article has been sold at a profit or a loss is normally a straightforward matter. The cost of acquiring it is simply deducted from its sale proceeds. An obvious difficulty arises, however, when the acquisition cost has to be determined by a process of allocation.

Debits arising on the acquisition of companies

When a company is acquired as a going concern, a process of allocation has to be used to determine the cost of the individual assets owned by it. The values assigned to the assets determine the profits reported by the enlarged group in the post-

73

acquisition period. The complexity of the accounting allocation process is illustrated by the following example, taken from the much publicised acquisition of Distillers by Guinness in April 1986.

Illustration 4.16: Guinness PLC (1986)

15 Effect of the acquisition of Distillers on the Consolidated Balance Sheet (extract)

	Unaudited Distillers consolidated accounts at 31 March 1986 £m	Fair value accounting adjustments £m	Total £m
Net assets/(liabilities) acquired			
Tangible assets	297	198	495
Investments	70	103	173
	367	301	668
Stocks of maturing whisky	661	-	661
Other stocks	229	(9)	220
Debtors	295	(1)	294
Cash and deposits	232	-	232
Bank loans and overdrafts	(29)	-	(29)
Other creditors falling due within one year	(220)	(62)	(282)
Net current assets	1,168	(72)	1,096
Loan stocks and bank loans	(256)	-	(256)
Other creditors falling due after one year	(1)	(8)	(9)
Provisions and other creditors	(5)	(276)	(281)
Deferred taxation	(64)	129	65
Increase in consolidated reserves from 31 March 1986 to 18 April 1986	-	7	7
Realised on disposals, after taxation	-	11	11
Total net assets acquired	1,209	92	1,301

Guinness paid £2,695 million to acquire Distillers. The book value of the latter company's net assets at the date of acquisition was £1,209 million. In order to determine the cost to Guinness of the individual assets owned by Distillers, it is necessary to assess what Guinness would have paid for each asset had it been acquired individually. This process concluded that the total cost would have amounted to £1,301 million, after making a £70 million adjustment to creditors and a provision of £276 million for certain reorganisation costs and trading losses. The difference between £1,301 million and the price paid to acquire the whole company is, by definition, what Guinness paid for Distillers' goodwill. At £1,394 million it represented 52 per cent of the total purchase price.

Although the accounting allocation process produced a relatively small net adjustment of £92 million, the individual adjustments are more significant. They were explained as follows:

Illustration 4.17: *Guinness PLC (1986)*

15 Effect of the acquisition of Distillers on the Consolidated Balance Sheet (extract)

(c) Fair value accounting adjustments
Adjustments have been made to the book values of the net assets acquired to reflect their fair value and to align the accounting policies of Distillers with those of the Group.

The principal adjustments are as follows:

(i) Fixed assets
Tangible assets have been included at fair value based principally on external professional valuations and after writing off surplus capacity. Listed investments have been included at market value.
(ii) Stocks
Stocks have been included at fair value which has been determined by taking account of costs of production, including financing costs, and after writing off surplus stocks and providing for costs of realisation.
(iii) Provisions
Provisions have been made for the cost of reorganising manufacturing, distribution, marketing and administration operations and for related trading losses pending reorganisation.
(iv) Deferred taxation
A deferred tax asset has been established to take account of the effect of the utilisation of reorganisation provisions on future tax liabilities.

The fair value accounting adjustments establish the cost of the assets for profit measurement purposes. It is important to note that it is not necessary to allocate the entire purchase price of £2,695 million over all of the assets and liabilities in the table. To the extent that it remains unallocated, it is deemed to be goodwill. As noted earlier in this chapter, the goodwill portion remains in limbo until the disposal or closure of the acquired entity, or any part thereof.

By contrast, the portion of the purchase price allocated to assets other than goodwill has a direct impact on profit. For example, if the stocks of maturing whisky are eventually sold for an amount in excess of the £661 million allocated to them in the table, a profit will be recorded on their disposal. The larger the portion of the purchase price allocated to the whisky stocks, the smaller the resulting profit on their sale. At first glance, the accounting treatment of the whisky stocks shown in Illustration 4.16 looks a little odd:

On the face of it, this note suggests that no adjustment has been made to the figure of £661m for stocks of maturing whisky shown in the Distillers' accounts. However, closer examination suggests that in fact two very large adjustments have been made, which happen to cancel each other out. This is explained as follows.

The note describing the basis of inclusion of the stock says that it includes finance charges and is after writing off surplus stocks and providing for costs of realisation. Elsewhere in the accounts, a note discloses that the valuation of £661m includes £344m of notional finance charges, leaving only £317m of stock exclusive of such charges. Now, according to their last published accounts, it was not the policy of Distillers to include finance charges in the valuation of stock, and presumably the figure of £661m in the first column of the note [Illustration 4.16] is drawn up using their own policy; it therefore appears that a writedown, also of £344m must have been made in respect of surplus stocks and realisation costs, and when set against the notional finance costs this produces a net adjustment of nil in the middle column.

Overall, Guinness' approach to the inclusion of the Distillers' stock could be regarded as rather surprising. The objective of the fair value exercise is to determine what the stock is worth to the acquiring company – what they would have hypothetically been prepared to pay in an arm's length transaction for what is, effectively, a second hand asset. Given that such transactions, albeit not of such colossal size, do occur between members of the whisky industry, I would have thought that it might have been possible to arrive more directly at a valuation for the stock, rather than to start with Distillers' historical cost, add a finance cost which Guinness has not in fact incurred in the transaction, and then deduct a provision which has the apparent effect of bringing it back to the number they first thought of.[41]

Another way of approaching the allocation of the purchase price to the individual assets and liabilities of an acquired business, is to be guided by the proceeds received on the sale of the acquired assets. If certain of the assets are sold shortly after the acquisition, their selling price must be a good indicator of their fair value. Recording the acquired assets at their selling price means, of course, that no profit can be recognised on their disposal. The following extract shows how Guinness dealt with a problem of this kind in 1986:

Illustration 4.18: *Guinness PLC (1986)*

15 Effect of the acquisition of Distillers on the Consolidated Balance Sheet (extract)

Disposals of assets and businesses	Distillers Book Value £m	Acquisition Adjustments £m	Fair Value £m
Tangible assets	11	22	33
Investments	19	81	100
Net current assets	14	-	14
	44	103	147
Proceeds on sale			175
Surplus on disposal			28

Of the surplus on disposal of assets acquired with Distillers, an amount of £8m has been taken to profit before taxation (Note 6), representing post-acquisition gains; the balance of £20m, less attributable taxation of £9m, has been treated as a net £11m adjustment to the fair value of the net assets acquired.

The extract shows that Guinness sold certain of Distillers' assets and businesses for £175 million shortly after the April 1986 acquisition of the entire company. In

Distillers' books they had been reflected at a value of £44 million. On their incorporation into Guinness's books, the accounting allocation process had assessed their fair value at £147 million. This represents their cost to Guinness. Selling them for £175 million suggests that a profit of £28 million had been made. Guinness decided, however, that the profit reflected in the profit and loss account should be £8 million, being the appreciation in the value of these assets and businesses in the post-acquisition period. In other words, it felt that the fair value previously assigned to these assets had been understated by £20 million. This figure, net of tax of £9 million, was therefore adjusted against the goodwill residual of £1,394 million. Further adjustments to the goodwill residual were deemed necessary in the years after the Distillers acquisition. The following extract is taken from the 1989 financial statements, three years after the acquisition. It illustrates again just how difficult the accounting allocation process is. It also reveals that its impact on the profit and loss account can be very significant:

Illustration 4.19: Guinness PLC (1989)

11. REVIEW OF THE FAIR VALUE ACCOUNTING FOR THE ACQUISITION OF DISTILLERS (extract)

In view of the size and complexity of the reorganisation required following the acquisition of Distillers in 1986 and of the resulting fair value accounting for its assets and liabilities, the Group adopted the policy that if, after a reasonable period, the estimates on which fair values, provisions and similar adjustments were based proved to be in excess of amounts required, the fair values would be restated as a recalculation of goodwill.

After a review of the fair values adopted on the basis of experience since the acquisition, the following adjustments increasing the net assets at acquisition have been made:

	£m
Adjustment of stock to revised fair value	157
Reorganisation provisions released	27
Release of fixed asset adjustments	51
	235
Deferred tax asset written off	(38)
Increase in net assets	197

The increase in net assets has been accounted for by reducing the goodwill arising on the acquisition of Distillers and has not been included in the results for the year. The effect of these adjustments on the results for the period from acquisition to 31 December 1989 is immaterial and no prior year adjustment has been made.

It is worth noting that the value originally assigned to the whisky and other stocks in 1986 was increased by £157 million in 1989. Had this and the other adjustments shown above not been made, Guinness's 1989 profit and loss account would have been better off by £197 million. Is it appropriate to use 'experience since the acquisition' to adjust the original allocation of the total purchase price? Does it produce a more meaningful profit figure in the post-acquisition period?

One extreme view would say that any information which only comes to light after the acquisition should not be taken into account in the allocation of fair values because it cannot have been known to the acquirer, cannot therefore have influenced the acquisition price, and should accordingly result in a post-acquisition gain or loss rather than an adjustment to fair values. However, such an approach would clearly be impracticable, because acquisitions are seldom based on a detailed evaluation of the assets of the target, particularly in the circumstances of a public bid; rather they are based on expectations of earnings, cash flows or similar factors. Accordingly it is necessary to allow some time after the acquisition for the acquirer to investigate what he has got for his money so that he can account for it on the basis of a sensible allocation.

The other extreme view would then let the acquirer go on indefinitely making adjustments to the fair values in the light of subsequent information as it gradually emerged. However this would be equally absurd because it would effectively mean that no kind of good or bad news which subsequently came to light would ever be reported in the group profit or loss account.

Accordingly it is sensible to impose some limit to the period during which fair values can continue to be refined.[42]

The difficulty, of course, lies in determining the time period during which the fair values have to be finalised. Profits reported in the post-acquisition period are a function of whatever decision is made in this regard.

Hidden debits

A common feature of many acquisitions made during the 1980s was that the purchase price was not finalised on conclusion of the agreement. Instead it was made contingent upon the acquired company's profits in the post-acquisition period. The following simplified example illustrates the existence of the hidden debit which usually arises in these circumstances:

Example 4.5

A company negotiates the acquisition of a competitor for a price of £100 million. The acquired company operates in a service industry and has negligible tangible assets. It made a profit of £10 million in its latest financial year. Two options are proposed for the payment of the purchase consideration:

- £100 million in cash on signature of the agreement; or
- £50 million on signature of the agreement and £55 million in one year's time, provided that the acquired company's profit amounts to at least £10 million in that year. If the profit is less than £10 million, the second instalment will be reduced using a profit-linked formula.

Will the accounting treatment adopted for each of these options produce the same result, assuming that the purchaser has £100 million in cash, currently earning interest at 10 per cent per annum?

It is important to note that the present value of the purchase consideration under both options is £100 million. The higher consideration payable under the second option is offset by interest of £5 million earned on the cash left over after paying the first instalment. To achieve the same accounting result, however, it is necessary to record a notional interest charge on the second instalment of £55 million. This amount should be split into its interest and capital components, of £5 million and £50 million respectively.

The position is more complicated when the financial year end of the acquirer occurs before the second instalment falls due. The calculation of a meaningful profit figure becomes dependent upon a reliable estimate of the second instalment and the selection of an appropriate discount rate. In many instances, however, the existence of an unquantifiable second instalment is simply disclosed in a note to the financial statements. When the amount is settled, the interest portion of £5 million is written off to reserves as additional goodwill, bypassing the profit and loss account altogether. Use of the second payment option therefore usually results in the profit and loss account showing a higher profit.

Accounting practice in the UK has not developed to a point where the time value of money is recognised as a matter of course. In some instances, this significantly impairs the usefulness of the information contained in the profit and loss account.

Profit and revaluation credits

FRS 3 has amended the way in which profit is calculated on the sale of a revalued asset. It is possible that the new requirement is the start of a fundamental change in approach to the measurement and reporting of financial performance in the UK. The FRS stipulates that the profit or loss on the sale of an asset should be based on the difference between the sale proceeds and the asset's carrying value. This ruling prevents the surplus arising on the revaluation of an asset from appearing in the profit and loss account. For example, an asset originally acquired for £10 million might have been revalued to £15 million some years later. Under FRS 3, its sale for £14 million will result in a loss of £1 million having to appear in the profit and loss account. Prior to the FRS, it would have been possible to record a profit of £4 million, being the difference between the cost of acquiring the asset from one third party and the proceeds received on its sale to another. The reasoning behind the new requirement is explained in the standard as follows:

> ...a gain on the revaluation of a fixed asset should be reflected directly in the statement of total recognised gains and losses of the period in which the revaluation takes place. The realisation, or part realisation, of such a gain on the sale of the asset in a subsequent period is not itself a gain of that later period but, rather, confirmation of a gain that had already occurred by the time of the revaluation.[43]

By moving away from the concept of profit based on the outcome of transactions with third parties, the FRS appears to have introduced a fundamental change in approach. The extract stresses the importance of the change in the value of the entity's net assets during the reporting period. Whether these changes are the outcome of transactions with third parties or the product of internal revaluations is irrelevant. The origin of the change simply determines which of the two primary statements is used to report the resulting gain.

Taken to its logical conclusion, the new approach would require an annual valuation of all the assets and liabilities. Only by doing this, would it be possible to identify the gains which have occurred during the reporting period. Whether these valuations could ever be done in a sufficiently objective manner to convince users of the reliability of the outcome, looms as a major obstacle should this path be chosen by the ASB.

CONCLUSION

Profit has long been considered a primary indicator of the health of the reporting entity. It is unlikely to lose its status in the eyes of preparers and users of financial statements. This chapter has, however, illustrated that it is a somewhat elusive concept. Different people have different ideas as to how it should be calculated. Some methods are considered to produce more meaningful answers than others. To this end, the format of the profit and loss account has recently been revised. The latest approach seeks to widen the focus by highlighting various components of financial performance. This has resulted in the introduction of yet another primary financial statement, the *Statement of total recognised gains and losses*. The changes would also appear to represent a fundamental shift in approach, requiring more emphasis to be placed on measuring changes in net asset values and less on the outcome of transactions with third parties.

This chapter has highlighted the difficulty in formulating a set of rules designed to measure financial performance. Changing the approach does nothing to simplify the complexity of many of the underlying issues. It is often difficult to decide which entities to include in the financial statements in the first place. The allocation of debits to individual reporting periods is affected by uncertainties attaching to the recoverability of assets, some of which are of an intangible nature. The treatment of future expenditure in a prudent manner sometimes appears to destroy the significance of the annual profit and loss account. The allocation of credits to reporting periods is a function of the need to minimise uncertainty about the collectability of future revenue. The appropriate treatment of debits representing goodwill and the costs of reorganising an acquired business, currently excluded from the profit and loss account, remains difficult to determine. A better understanding of the nature and origin of goodwill is required. How to deal with sales to related parties is an issue plagued by difficulties of definition. Finally, there are problems of measurement. These affect the assignment of fair values to the individual assets and liabilities in an acquired business. They also complicate the discounting and estimation of contingent purchase consideration. The allocation of changes in the values of assets to different reporting periods in an objective manner seems to be an insurmountable problem.

The sensible way to deal with these difficulties is to acknowledge their existence and to view the primary statements of financial performance in their proper context. They are essentially crude attempts to deal with a complex present and an uncertain future.

1   Sylvie and Bruno (1889), 'The Mad Gardener's Song'.
2   Accounting Standards Board (1991), 'The objective of financial statements', Exposure Draft of Chapter 1, *Statement of Principles* (London: ASB), July, para. 12.
3   Companies Act 1985, Sch. 4, para. 8.
4   SSAP 6, Revised August 1986, para. 30.
5   *Ibid.*, para. 29.
6   *Ibid.*, para. 28.
7   Accounting Standards Board (1991), UITF Abstract 2, *Restructuring costs* (London: ASB), October, para. 3.
8   Financial Reporting Council (1992), *The State of Financial Reporting – Second Annual Review*, November, para. 2.12.
9   Accounting Standards Board (1992), FRS 3, *Reporting Financial Performance* (London: ASB), October, para. 35.
10 *Ibid.*, para. 56.
11 *Ibid.*, Appendix, Profit and loss account example 2.
12 *Ibid.*, para. 48.
13 *Ibid.*, para. 59.
14 *Ibid.*, para. 52.
15 Ernst & Young (1992), *Reporting Financial Performance A Guide to FRS 3* (London: Ernst & Young), p.35.
16 FRS 3, The Development of the Standard, para. iii.
17 *Ibid.*
18 *Accountancy Age* (1992), 'The search for a reliable single earnings measure', 26 November.
19 Accounting Standards Board (1992), FRS 2, *Accounting for subsidiary undertakings* (London: ASB), July, para. 59.
20 *The Globe and Mail* (1992), Saturday, 7 November, p.B8.
21 Companies Act 1985, s 258(4)(a).
22 FRS 2, para. 7b.
23 *Ibid.*, para. 73.
24 Waller, David (1991), 'Taking account of the prize', *Financial Times*, 16 May, p.31.
25 Companies Act 1985, sch. 4, para. 13.
26 SSAP 2, *Disclosure of accounting policies* (1971), November, para. 14.
27 *Ibid.*
28 *Ibid.*
29 Companies Act 1985, sch. 4, para. 12.
30 FRS 3, para. 45.
31 *Ibid.*
32 SSAP 2, para. 14.
33 SSAP 22, *Accounting for goodwill*, Revised July 1989, para. 6.
34 *The State of Financial Reporting – Second Annual Review*, paras. 3.19–3.20.
35 Accounting Standards Committee (1990), ED 53, *Fair value in the context of acquisition accounting* (London: ASC), July, para. 75.
36 *The State of Financial Reporting – Second Annual Review*, para. 3.17.
37 Appendix to FRS 3, *Dissenting View*.
38 *Ibid.*
39 Companies Act 1985, schedule 4A, para. 20.

40   *Financial Mail* (1992), 7 August, p.83.
41   Paterson, R. M. (1988) 'Fair value accounting following an acquisition', in L. C. L. Skerrat and D. J. Tonkin (eds) *Financial Reporting 1987–88 – A Survey of UK Published Accounts* (London: ICAEW), p. 58.
42   *Ibid.*, p. 61.
43   FRS 3, para. 37.

5: Gearing and the Balance Sheet

He thought he saw a Garden-Door
That opened with a key:
He looked again, and found it was
A Double Rule of Three:
'And all its mystery,' he said,
'Is clear as day to me!'

Lewis Carroll[1]

INTRODUCTION

The Chairman's Statement in the 1990 Annual Report of Cadbury Schweppes Public Limited Company contained the following paragraph:

> Following implementation of our 1990 funding strategy, the Balance Sheet shows strength, with net borrowings at £364 million, down £60 million from [the] 1989 year end, interest cover at 5.8 times and gearing at 49.7%.

There is nothing remarkable about this statement. An equivalent is to be found in the annual report of virtually every UK company. Its significance derives from the importance it attaches to the balance sheet as an indicator of financial strength. As noted in Chapter 3, existing and potential investors are likely to take a keen interest in the financial position of the reporting entity. The extract suggests that preparers of financial statements are well aware of the user's desire for this information. Its tone is reassuring – a strategy is in place to manage the company's finances in a prudent manner and the balance sheet provides evidence of its successful implementation. The purpose of this chapter is to examine whether the balance sheet is capable of providing valuable information about the reporting entity's financial position.

THE GEARING RATIO

The fact that Cadbury Schweppes' net borrowings amounted to £364 million at the group's 1990 year end does not, of itself, mean a great deal. Of more significance is the relative amount of the borrowings. For this reason the extract goes on to refer to the group's gearing as being 49.7 per cent. Users unfamiliar with the concept would find an explanation on page 32 of the Annual Report. This page contains particulars of a number of financial ratios covering the 1986 to 1990 period. One of these is the gearing ratio:

Illustration 5.1: *Cadbury Schweppes Public Limited Company (1990)*

FINANCIAL RATIOS (extract)

			1990	1989	1988	1987	1986
Gearing Ratio	$\dfrac{\text{Net borrowings}}{\text{Ordinary shareholders' funds} + \text{minority interests}}$	%	49.7	62.4	(0.5)	21.6	14.7

Because it compares net borrowings to the total of ordinary shareholders' funds and minority interests, the gearing ratio is regarded by many users as a sound indicator of financial risk. It reveals the significance of the net borrowings figure. If the percentage is high, the ratio indicates that extensive use has been made of finance provided by bankers and other lenders. A low percentage suggests that the group's assets have largely been financed by shareholders and trade creditors.

The gearing ratio does have another, more positive, connotation. Its name implies that borrowings can be used to enhance, or gear up, the returns earned for shareholders. If the borrowed funds are invested to earn a return that exceeds their cost, the surplus accrues to shareholders. Companies capable of earning a high return on funds employed are sometimes encouraged to increase their gearing in order to maximise their shareholders' wealth. The formula used to calculate the ratio is relatively simple. It involves extracting a numerator and a denominator from the balance sheet. What these numbers mean and whether the ratio is a useful indicator, needs to be examined in more detail.

CALCULATING THE NUMERATOR

The gearing ratio used by Cadbury Schweppes is fairly typical of those used by other major UK companies. Its numerator is the net borrowings of the group at the balance sheet date. The term 'net borrowings' is not defined on the page containing the summary of the group's financial ratios. It is, however, relatively easy to extract from the published balance sheet.

Finding borrowings on the balance sheet

In addition to specifying the format of the profit and loss account, the Companies Act 1985 contains rules governing the layout of the balance sheet. Of the two options allowed by paragraph 8 of schedule 4, Format 1 is most commonly used in practice. It stipulates that the following items should appear on the face of the balance sheet:

> Called up share capital not paid
> Fixed assets
>   Intangible assets
>   Tangible assets
>   Investments
> Current assets
>   Stocks
>   Debtors
>   Investments
>   Cash at bank and in hand
> Prepayments and accrued income
> Creditors: amounts falling due within one year
> Net current assets
> Total assets less current liabilities
> Creditors: amounts falling due after more than one year
> Provisions for liabilities and charges
> Accruals and deferred income
> Capital and reserves
>   Called up share capital
>   Share premium account
>   Revaluation reserve
>   Other reserves
>   Profit and loss account

The first difficulty facing the calculator of a gearing ratio is that the list does not contain an item called 'borrowings'. Reference to the details contained in the Creditors notes would not be particularly helpful either. The legislature requires the total of the amounts shown for Creditors to be analysed into the following components: debenture loans, bank loans and overdrafts, payments received on account, trade creditors, bills of exchange payable, amounts owed to group undertakings, amounts owed to undertakings in which the company has a participating interest, other creditors including taxation and social security, and accruals and deferred income. An exhaustive list, but one that does not contain an item called 'borrowings'.

The 1990 Cadbury Schweppes balance sheet is more helpful in this regard. On the face of the balance sheet, the amounts shown under the Creditors headings are split into two sections: Borrowings and Other. A supporting note to the balance sheet explains that the former category is made up as follows:

Illustration 5.2: Cadbury Schweppes Public Limited Company (1990)	
18 Borrowings (extract)	1990
	£m
Secured	
Bank overdrafts	0.6
Other loans	14.2
Unsecured	
13[$\frac{1}{4}$]% Guaranteed Notes 1993 (A$75m)	30.1
8% Convertible bonds 2000 (US$0.8m)	0.4
Commercial paper (US$34.8m)	18.1
Bank loans in foreign currencies	164.7
Bank overdrafts	2.4
Other loans	95.7
Obligations under finance leases	84.1
Acceptance credits	10.9
	421.2
Obligations under perpetual subordinated loan (FFr 1,206m)	123.0
	544.2

For ease of reference, the amounts due within and after one year have been added together in the table. The comparative figures for 1989 have not been reproduced.

It is significant that the numerator in the gearing ratio includes only some of the items under the Creditors heading. Notable exclusions are amounts owed to trade creditors and accruals and deferred income. In the Cadbury Schweppes 1990 group balance sheet these amounted to £515.4 million. Their exclusion is probably related to the second purpose of the gearing ratio noted earlier in this chapter. To indicate the ability of the group to gear up the returns earned for shareholders, the ratio focuses on so-called 'interest-bearing' debt only. 'Interest-free' debt owed to trade and other creditors is therefore ignored.

The distinction between 'interest-bearing' and other debt appears to be artificial. As noted in Chapter 4, all liabilities are made up of interest and capital components. Most creditors are well aware of the time value of money. The longer a debt is outstanding, the less it is worth. Creditors will seek to protect themselves against this loss by increasing the amount of the debt whenever interest is not formally provided for.

Accounting practice has not reached the point where the distinction between capital and interest is made as a matter of course. The gearing ratio's emphasis on 'interest-bearing' debt and its usefulness as an indicator of financial risk should be seen in this context. Companies cease to exist when they are unable to pay their debts. Whether the interest element of these debts was separately recognised is irrelevant.

Finding net borrowings on the balance sheet

The previous section revealed that the total borrowings of the Cadbury Schweppes group at its 1990 year end amounted to £544.2 million. This is £180 million more than the chairman's net borrowings figure of £364 million. The origin of the difference is, however, easily found on closer scrutiny of the balance sheet. The following items are included under the Current Assets heading:

	£m
Investments – short term loans and deposits	118.0
Cash at bank and in hand	62.6

It seems appropriate to deduct these items from the total of the borrowings. They represent surplus funds, invested to earn interest pending their deployment elsewhere in the business. The practice of deducting interest-bearing assets from interest-bearing liabilities to arrive at the numerator in the gearing ratio is well established. Some users might wonder, however, why the surplus cash has not been used to reduce the liabilities. After all, the rate of interest charged on the liabilities is usually higher than that earned on the assets.

An obvious answer is that it is not always possible to coordinate the raising of finance on advantageous terms with its investment in capital projects. Another explanation is that some businesses are able to earn a superior after-tax return by borrowing money in one currency and investing it in another. A third answer has more significant implications for the usefulness of the gearing ratio as an indicator of financial risk.

It should be remembered that the figures in the group balance sheet are an aggregation of those in the balance sheets of all the entities in the group. These entities are, by definition, controlled by the parent company. Its ability to access the surplus cash resources held in certain subsidiaries may, however, not be a simple matter of being able to control these entities. If they are not wholly owned by the parent company, their directors may be unable to respond to the latter's wishes simply by advancing the funds required. The directors are obliged by law to take the interests of all the company's shareholders into account. In these circumstances, the argument in favour of deducting interest-bearing assets for gearing ratio purposes is less compelling. It suggests that users need to know more about the circumstances surrounding the surplus funds. This might also reveal the existence of legal or governmental restrictions. Alternatively, it could be that the funds are committed to future capital projects. The case for deducting them in order to measure financial risk, is often no more convincing than that which could be applied to other assets.

Which balance sheet?

Users seeking to calculate the net borrowings figure for Grand Metropolitan Public Limited Company at its 1991 year end, might wonder what to make of Note 16 to its financial statements:

Illustration 5.3: Grand Metropolitan Public Limited Company (1991)

16. Inntrepreneur Estates Ltd (extract)

On 28th March 1991 the group and Courage merged their tenanted pub estates into a joint venture company called Inntrepreneur Estates (IEL) which is incorporated in England. The group has a 50% shareholding in the IEL share capital and IEL has been treated as an associate within these financial statements. Summarised accounts based on the audited interim management accounts of IEL and its subsidiaries for the period 29th March 1991 to 30th September 1991 are as follows:

Balance sheet	30th September 1991 £m
Investment properties	2,227
Other properties	108
Net current assets	14
	2,349
Loans from the Grand Metropolitan group	(311)
Bank loans – four to five years	(1,325)
– one to two years	(113)
Net assets	600
Group share of net assets	300
Loans	311
Group investment in IEL (note 15)	611

Note 16 reveals the existence of bank loans totalling £1,438 million. Because IEL has been treated as an associate, these borrowings do not appear on Grand Metropolitan's balance sheet. The latter document includes only one item relating to IEL, the group's investment of £611 million. Are the borrowings which appear on IEL's balance sheet relevant to Grand Metropolitan's gearing ratio? Given that the ratio is meant to be an indicator of financial risk, one way of answering this question might be to ask whether Grand Metropolitan could be obliged to repay any of these loans. This information is also contained in note 16:

Illustration 5.4: Grand Metropolitan Public Limited Company (1991)

16. Inntrepreneur Estates Ltd (extract)

Notes

(ii) The group and Foster's Brewing Group, the ultimate parent of Courage, have a limited joint and several obligation to ensure that IEL does not breach a specified interest coverage ratio, and also have several and equal obligations to ensure that the effective rate of interest borne on the secured loans does not exceed certain levels. IEL is obliged under its financing arrangements to maintain certain specified loan to asset ratios.
(iii) The group and Foster's Brewing Group have severally guaranteed the £113 million bank loan. This loan is secured on properties held for disposal.

It is difficult for an outsider to understand the full implications of the obligations described in note (ii). Note (iii) is easier to follow. Both suggest that IEL's financial position is not irrelevant to a proper understanding of Grand Metropolitan's.

Further consideration of this issue also suggests that the existence of guarantees or other commitments should not necessarily be regarded as the decisive factor in determining the relevance of the borrowings. These criteria are not used in deciding whether to include a subsidiary company's borrowings, for example. They are included regardless of whether they have been guaranteed by the parent company.

Another way of trying to determine the relevance of the IEL borrowings is to ask whether the interest payable on them affects Grand Metropolitan's profits. The answer to this question can be found in note 16. The note contains the following summarised version of IEL's profit and loss account:

Illustration 5.5: Grand Metropolitan Public Limited Company (1991)

16. Inntrepreneur Estates Ltd (extract)

Profit and loss account	6 months 1991 £m
Rental and other operating income	104
Costs and sundry income	(20)
Trading profit	84
Profit on sale of property	3
Interest	(109)
Loss on ordinary activities before taxation	(22)
Attributable to the group	(11)

The extract reveals that the interest payable on IEL's borrowings exceeded the rentals receivable from its tenanted pub estates. By virtue of its 50 per cent ownership interest, Grand Metropolitan is required to account for half the overall loss of £22 million. The interest payable on IEL's borrowings clearly has an impact on Grand Metropolitan's profits. Where all of this leaves a calculator of the gearing ratio is not entirely clear. Because they do not appear on the group balance sheet, the borrowings of associates would normally be excluded from the numerator. Yet the impression remains that they are somehow relevant to a proper understanding of the reporting entity's financial position. Their interest costs have a direct impact on its profit and loss account and it might be obliged to repay some of these debts should the associate default on its commitments.

Confusion about the significance of the borrowings of associates probably arises from the impact of transactions like the one described in the following example. These were not uncommon in the period prior to the 1989 amendment of the Companies Act 1985.

Example 5.1

Company A sells its properties at their book value of £100 million to a newly incorporated entity, company B. The latter uses finance borrowed from company A's bankers to settle the purchase consideration. It receives an annual rental from company A, which continues to occupy the properties. The rental income is used to pay the interest on the bank loans, which are guaranteed by company A.

Company B's share capital consists of two ordinary shares of £1 each, both owned by company A, and two 5 per cent preference shares of £1 each, both owned by company A's bankers. The preference shares, which participate equally with the ordinary shares in company B's profits when they exceed £500 million in any one year, have no voting rights unless the preference dividend is in arrear. Company A and its bankers each appoint 2 directors to company B's board. Company A's directors have two votes each whereas the bankers' directors have one vote each.

The sale of the properties for £100 million enables company A to repay £100 million of its borrowings.

Should company A's gearing ratio reflect an improvement under these circumstances?

Although company A owns all of company B's ordinary shares, it owns only half of its equity share capital. The preference shares' right to participate in profits under certain circumstances means that they qualify as 'equity' under the Companies Act 1985. Company A is also not entitled to appoint the majority of company B's directors in number. Prior to the amendment of the Companies Act 1985 by the 1989 Act, company B would not have been a subsidiary of company A. Being an associated company, its borrowings would have been excluded from company A's group balance sheet. As a consequence they would be excluded from its gearing ratio.

For the gearing ratio to reflect an improvement under these circumstances would seem to be inappropriate. Company A's bankers have changed the form of their lending without altering its substance. Their money has been advanced to company B but its repayment has been guaranteed by company A. They are effectively still owed £100 million by company A. If the gearing ratio is to be a meaningful indicator of financial risk, it would need to include the borrowings reflected in company B's balance sheet.

Transactions of the kind described above have ceased since the 1989 revision of the Companies Act 1985. The new *subsidiary undertaking* definition would require company B to be included in company A's group balance sheet. The legislature's attempt to counteract the innovative proposals put forward by various bankers is, however, not the major issue facing the calculator of the gearing ratio. The real difficulty lies in determining the relevance of the borrowings to a ratio intended to be an indicator of financial risk. Whether they are shown in the balance sheet or in a note to the group financial statements does not resolve this issue.

Sale and leaseback transactions

Transactions of the type described in Example 5.1 involve the sale of an asset without giving up the right to use it or to benefit from an appreciation in its value. In that example, the asset was sold to a newly incorporated company beneficially owned by the seller. A similar outcome is achieved when the seller is granted the right to re-purchase the asset at a price unrelated to its market value. Particulars of these transactions are not required to be disclosed in company financial statements. Examples are therefore hard to find. The Extel Financial News Card for Bromsgrove Industries PLC does, however, provide an interesting example:

Illustration 5.6: Bromsgrove Industries PLC

COMPANY ANNOUNCEMENTS (extract)

ASSETS – *Sale & Leaseback*

[Oct 15 1990] Co announces disposal of freehold premises at Forge Lane, Minworth to Endless Enterprises IV Ltd, a Sub of Norfina PLC, for £2.25m in cash. Endless has granted Co a 25 year operational lease on these premises at an initial rent of £225,000 pa.

Co has also disposed of freehold premises at Hillbottom Road, High Wycombe, to Endless for £2.75m which has been fully satisfied in cash. Co has again been granted an operational lease on similar terms at an initial rent of £275,000 pa.

At end of fifth year of each lease, Co has right to re-purchase freehold reversions for £5m in aggregate subject to payment of its financial obligations thereunder and a transaction fee of 4.15% pa of consideration.

The transactions described above raise another difficult issue for the calculator of a gearing ratio. Bromsgrove has received an amount of £5 million on the disposal of its properties to Endless. It is, however, also obliged to return this sum to Endless at the rate of £500,000 per annum by way of rental for the properties. Furthermore, repayment of the £5 million will probably be accelerated if the properties appreciate in value. In these circumstances, it is likely that Bromsgrove would want to exercise its right to re-purchase them after five years. Should the £5 million received on the sale of the properties be regarded as being more in the nature of a repayable loan? Treating it as such would cause the gearing ratio to remain unchanged. Deducting it from the carrying value of the properties, the normal accounting treatment when an asset is sold, would result in a £5 million reduction in the gearing ratio numerator.

SSAP 21 *Accounting for leases and hire purchase contracts* provides some guidance on accounting for sale and leaseback transactions. It requires the seller to determine whether the leaseback agreement is a finance lease or an operating lease. The former is a lease 'that transfers substantially all the risks and rewards of ownership of an asset to the lessee.'[2] If the leaseback is deemed to be a finance lease, the standard requires the asset to remain on the seller's balance sheet. It is difficult to disagree with the reasoning behind this requirement. After all, if the risks and rewards of ownership have not been transferred to the lessor, that party can hardly be said to have bought the asset from the lessee. The 'sale' proceeds, being in the nature of a repayable advance, would not be deducted from the asset's carrying value. They would instead be shown as a creditor in the lessee's balance sheet.

There is an obvious difficulty in applying the SSAP 21 requirement in practice. Determining whether a lease 'transfers substantially all the risks and rewards of ownership' can be problematic. The agreements are rarely straightforward and they usually provide for a sharing of the risks and rewards of ownership. One prominent company has decided to revise its accounting treatment in expectation of 'likely developments in accounting practice':

Illustration 5.7: The Burton Group PLC (1991)

ACCOUNTING POLICIES

B Changes in accounting bases and the presentation of financial information (extract)

In the light of the introduction of the Companies Act 1989 and likely developments in accounting practice, a comprehensive review of accounting policies and the presentation of financial information has been undertaken. As a result, certain changes have been made to the bases of accounting for fixed assets and the presentation of financial information adopted in previous years as follows:

(i)   The results, assets and liabilities of High Street Property Investments Limited (HSPI) have been consolidated. HSPI was formerly treated as an associated undertaking;

(ii) Certain properties disposed of in 1988 under the terms of sale and leaseback transactions with a capital value of £75 million have been reflected in the Group's fixed assets and the related lease obligation included in creditors. These transactions were previously treated as operating leases in accordance with the provisions of Statement of Standard Accounting Practice No. 21;

(iii) The redeemable preference shares owned by banks in Debenhams (Aruba) NV, one of the Group's subsidiary undertakings, have been treated as a component of borrowings rather than as a minority interest;

These items all affect the calculation of the group's gearing ratio by increasing the numerator. The first item was discussed in the previous section. It shows the impact of the new subsidiary undertaking definition which requires HSPI, previously classified as an associate, to be consolidated in the group balance sheet. The third item will be discussed later in this chapter.

The second item has been addressed in this section. By amending the classification of the leaseback agreements, the amount received on the 'sale' of these properties has been treated as being in the nature of a repayable loan. Note 24 to the 1991 accounts contained additional information about the group's obligations under the leaseback agreements:

Illustration 5.8: The Burton Group PLC (1991)

NOTES TO THE ACCOUNTS

24 LEASE OBLIGATIONS

In 1988, the Group sold properties at market value for £75.5 million to certain banks on 125 year leases at peppercorn rents and entered into full tenant repairing sub-leases for 125 years. The rentals payable are structured so as to give the lessors a return linked to LIBOR in the first 25 years and, in the following 10 years, a LIBOR linked return together with the repayment of capital. Thereafter, market rentals are payable subject to revision every 5 years. The Group has certain rights up to the 25th year of the lease to re-acquire the properties concerned at prices based on their original sales proceeds. In view of likely developments in accounting practice, these leases have been reflected in the Group's fixed assets.

Other lease obligations

In the previous section, the importance of the distinction between finance and operating leases was highlighted. It determined whether the proceeds received under a sale and leaseback agreement would be treated as a creditor or deducted from the cost of the asset concerned. The favourable impact of the second option on the gearing ratio was noted.

The purpose of this section is to consider why this distinction should have an effect on the gearing ratio. Are the commitments assumed under operating leases any different from those under finance leases? If the gearing ratio is meant to be an indicator of financial risk, why should it include only those obligations arising out of finance lease agreements?

Example 5.2

A company decides to expand its business by moving into new premises and acquiring additional plant and machinery. It signs a 5-year lease for the premises at an annual rental of £1 million, payable in advance.

The supplier of the plant and machinery offers the following choice:
- a cash price of £4.17 million payable immediately; or
- five annual lease rentals of £1 million each, payable in advance. The useful economic life of the plant and machinery is five years. It will be scrapped at the end of the lease, which does not have an early termination option.

If the cash price option is selected, the company will need to borrow the money at an interest rate of 10 per cent per annum.

How would these transactions affect the company's gearing ratio?

The two options offered by the supplier of the plant and machinery would have the same impact on the company's balance sheet. The lease clearly transfers all the risks and rewards of ownership of the plant and machinery to the lessee. The company in the example would be its sole user and it is obliged to reimburse the lessor for the latter's cost of acquiring it. The lease would accordingly be classified as a finance lease. It would have to be capitalised at the present value of the lessee's obligation, £4.17 million. This results in the inclusion in the lessee's balance sheet of a fixed asset and a creditor. The cash price option produces the same outcome. The acquisition of the plant brings in an asset costing £4.17 million, matched by a loan for the same amount, included under creditors.

The lease of the premises is, by contrast, an operating lease. The company in the example can vacate the premises after five years, leaving the landlord with the problem of having to find another tenant. Substantially all the risks and rewards of owning the property have clearly not been transferred to the lessee. The lessee's obligations under this agreement would therefore not appear on its balance sheet.

If the lease option is chosen for the plant and machinery, the company's expansion plans would both involve an obligation to pay £1 million per annum for five years. A gearing ratio based on its balance sheet would, however, ignore the commitment arising under the lease of the premises.

The example illustrates an important point about the purpose of the balance sheet. It is clearly not a summary of outstanding future obligations. Instead, it seems designed to show the assets acquired by the reporting entity and the manner in which they have been financed. Because an operating lease agreement is not regarded as being equivalent to the purchase of an asset, the resulting obligation does not appear on the balance sheet.

Other obligations

Operating lease agreements are but one example of future obligations not currently required to be included in the balance sheet. Take-or-pay contracts present another potential problem for the calculator of a gearing ratio. The authors of *UK GAAP – Generally Accepted Accounting Practice in the United Kingdom* have summarised the issue as follows:

Under these contracts, the purchaser is obliged to pay a certain minimum amount even if, in the event, he does not take delivery of the goods or use the services he has contracted for. The accounting question which therefore arises is whether the purchaser has to account for a liability (his commitment under the contract) together with a corresponding asset (his right to use the facilities he has contracted for).[3]

The authors note that the recognition principles contained in ED 49 *Reflecting the substance of transactions in assets and liabilities* appear to require the inclusion of these items on the balance sheet. Because 'this would be a radical departure from present practice', they question whether the recognition principles provide an appropriate basis for resolving the issue.[4] The potential significance of these contracts is illustrated by their example taken from ICI's 1991 commitments note.

Illustration 5.9: Imperial Chemical Industries PLC (1991)

34 COMMITMENTS AND CONTINGENT LIABILITIES (extract)

A subsidiary company has entered into a take-or-pay contract to purchase electric power commencing 1 April 1993 for fifteen years. The subsidiary is obligated to make monthly payments including a fixed capacity charge and a variable energy charge. The present value of the commitment to purchase electric power over the period of the agreement is estimated at £560m.

Obligations of the kind described in the extract would appear to be as relevant to the gearing ratio numerator as commitments arising under finance lease agreements.

A meaningful numerator?

This section has outlined some of the uncertainties and limitations attaching to the numerator used in the calculation of most gearing ratios. It is often difficult to decide which entities to include in the group balance sheet in the first place. Where borrowings are excluded, they sometimes appear to be as relevant to a proper understanding of the entity's financial position as those that are included. The numerator includes only those creditors that are 'interest-bearing', yet this distinction appears to be arbitrary. 'Interest-bearing' assets are deducted, apparently without further consideration of their availability to reduce the 'interest-bearing' liabilities. Determining the appropriate classification of the disposal proceeds under sale and leaseback agreements is often difficult. Of more fundamental concern is the apparent inability of the balance sheet to capture the existence of many other obligations entered into by the reporting entity. Operating lease agreements and take-or-pay contracts are but two examples.

CALCULATING THE DENOMINATOR

Cadbury Schweppes' definition of the gearing ratio suggests that the denominator should be relatively easy to calculate. It is simply the total of ordinary shareholders' funds and minority interests. The rules in the Companies Act 1985 governing the layout of the balance sheet should help to locate these figures. The relevant section of Cadbury Schweppes' 1990 balance sheet has been reproduced in Illustration 5.10.

Illustration 5.10: Cadbury Schweppes Public Limited Company (1990)	
GROUP BALANCE SHEET (extract)	**1990**
	£m
Capital and Reserves	
Called up share capital	174.7
Share premium account	381.6
Revaluation reserve	95.8
Profit and loss account	115.8
	767.9
Minority Interests	116.0
	883.9

Although it seems that the denominator in the gearing ratio is the figure of £883.9 million shown at the foot of the extract, the issue is a little more complicated. The Companies Act 1985 does not draw a distinction between ordinary and preference share capital. Both appear under the 'Called up share capital' and 'Share premium account' headings. It should be remembered that the denominator in the Cadbury Schweppes gearing ratio is the total of *ordinary* shareholders' funds and minority interests. The table of financial ratios on page 32 of the company's 1990 Annual Report reminds readers that the gearing ratio excludes preference shares at their redemption value (£152.1 million at the 1990 year end). This is the first of four important issues affecting the calculation of the denominator.

Preference shares

The background to the exclusion of the preference shares from the denominator in Cadbury Schweppes' gearing ratio is explained in the following extract. It describes the first of four arrangements forming part of the group's funding strategy:

Illustration 5.11: Cadbury Schweppes Public Limited Company (1990)

FINANCIAL REVIEW (extract)

FUNDING

The Group began the year with net borrowings of £424 million which mainly resulted from the acquisitions in 1989. Over half was repayable within two years. A strategy was agreed to put longer term funding in place, including standby facilities, with the following three objectives:

- match overseas borrowings with overseas assets and currency flows;
- avoid covenants and constraints which might prejudice the Group's flexibility in future;
- minimise after-tax interest rates.

The key arrangements in place are:

- US$227.5 million (£118 million) and Can$75 million (£34 million) of issued preference shares (including premiums). The Series 1 (US$52.5 million) and Series 2 (Can$75 million) shares were privately placed into Canada and the dividend in each case is fixed at 75% of the US and Canadian dollar short-term market interest rates for a 5 year period. Dividends on the Series 3 to 6 shares (US$175 million in all) are set every 28 days at auction in New York and these shares were privately placed into the USA, Canada and the UK. These two structures give significant benefits to the Company over the more normal placement into the US 28-day auction market alone. These preference shares provide additional share capital at marginally more than the cost of equivalent debt and do not participate in future earnings growth;

Although the preference shares described in the extract are classified as share capital for company law purposes, Cadbury Schweppes clearly regards them as an alternative form of borrowing. They are redeemable at the company's option and their holders 'do not participate in future earnings growth'. They also bear a cost related to the interest rates payable on other forms of borrowing. The company's decision to exclude them from the gearing ratio denominator is consistent with the ASB's recent initiative to amend the balance sheet presentation of these instruments.

In December 1992, the ASB issued a Financial Reporting Exposure Draft (FRED) titled *Accounting for Capital Instruments*. One of its proposals requires 'an analysis to be presented of shareholders' funds between the amounts attributable to equity and non-equity shares. In consolidated financial statements a similar analysis is to be presented of the amounts of minority interest attributable to equity and non-equity shares issued by subsidiaries.'[5] Because their dividend entitlement is linked to market interest rates, the preference shares issued by Cadbury Schweppes would be non-equity shares as defined by the FRED. The shareholders' funds' total of £767.9 million would therefore have to be analysed between the amounts attributable to ordinary and preference shares.

The information needed to present the required analysis was clearly disclosed in Cadbury Schweppes' 1990 Annual Report. The impact of the new disclosures proposed by the FRED is, however, likely to be more significant where non-equity shares have been issued by subsidiary companies. At present, there is no requirement to present any information about the Minority Interests' figure (shown as £116.0 million in Illustration 5.10) in the group balance sheet. That is why the information provided by The Burton Group PLC in 1991 was of such significance. The relevant portion of Illustration 5.7 has been reproduced in the next extract.

Illustration 5.12: *The Burton Group PLC (1991)*

ACCOUNTING POLICIES

B Changes in accounting bases and the presentation of financial information (extract)

(iii) The redeemable preference shares owned by banks in Debenhams (Aruba) NV, one of the Group's subsidiary undertakings, have been treated as a component of borrowings rather than as a minority interest;

Without disclosure of this kind, the calculator of the gearing ratio would not have known what was included in the minority interests' figure. Conversion of the FRED into a financial reporting standard will ensure that the missing information is disclosed.

Convertible capital instruments

A further complication affecting the calculation of the gearing ratio denominator is contained in the following extract, taken from the 1990 group balance sheet of Saatchi & Saatchi Company PLC.

Illustration 5.13: *Saatchi & Saatchi Company PLC (1990)*

GROUP BALANCE SHEETS (extract)	**1990** **£million**	**1989** **£million**
CAPITAL AND RESERVES		
Called up share capital	115.4	115.3
Share premium account	9.0	7.6
Special reserves	-	-
Goodwill reserves	(305.7)	(434.6)
Profit and loss account	(197.0)	47.5
	(378.3)	(264.2)
Called up preference share		
capital issued by a subsidiary	176.5	176.5
Minority interests	11.7	9.0
	(190.1)	(78.7)

The positioning of the 'Called up preference share capital issued by a subsidiary' caption is interesting. At first glance, it appears to be similar to the proposed new requirement to attribute the minority interests' figure to its equity and non-equity share components. That would, however, require the amount of £176.5 million to be shown underneath the Minority interests' heading. Why present it above? The answer is revealed by closer examination of the relevant note to the balance sheet:

Illustration 5.14: Saatchi & Saatchi Company PLC (1990)

15. SHARE CAPITAL (extract)	1990	1989
	£million	£million
Authorised:		
279,000,000 Ordinary shares of 10p each (1989 - 279,000,000)	27.9	27.9
125,000,000 6.3% Convertible Cumulative		
Redeemable Preference shares of £1 each (1989 - 125,000,000)	125.0	125.0
Authorised share capital of the Company	152.9	152.9
Allotted, called up and fully paid:		
159,914,982 Ordinary shares of 10p each (1989 - 158,494,618)	16.0	15.8
99,443,442 6.3% Convertible Cumulative		
Redeemable Preference shares of £1 each (1989 - 99,445,078)	99.4	99.5
Called up share capital of the Company	115.4	115.3
176,470,416 6.75% Redeemable Convertible Preference shares		
2003 of £1 each issued by a subsidiary (1989 - 176,478,516)	176.5	176.5
Called up share capital of the Group	291.9	291.8

The item of most significance in note 15 is that the share capital of a subsidiary company, £176.5 million, has been added to the holding company's share capital, £115.4 million. A new concept, the Called up share capital of the Group, is thereby introduced. This form of presentation is not allowed on the face of the balance sheet because the subsidiary's preference shares are owned by shareholders other than Saatchi & Saatchi Company PLC. As such they would ordinarily have to be shown as part of the 'Minority interests' total. To understand why Saatchi & Saatchi has treated them as a component of the group's share capital, it is necessary to consider the terms of their issue:

Illustration 5.15: Saatchi & Saatchi Company PLC (1990)

15. SHARE CAPITAL (extract)

The 6.75% Redeemable Convertible Preference shares 2003 of £1 each issued by a subsidiary (Saatchi & Saatchi Finance NV incorporated in the Netherlands Antilles) are guaranteed on a subordinated basis by the Company. These shares are convertible into Ordinary shares of the Company at any time after 1st October 1989, at the option of the shareholder, at a price of 441p per Ordinary share. The shares have a final redemption date of 15th July 2003 and can be redeemed at the option of the holder on 15th July of each year from 1993 to 1998 inclusive at a price to yield a compound annual rate of return to the holder of 9.98%. A provision has been made for the additional interest accrued to 30th September 1990 that would be payable if the shares are redeemed in 1993.

Unlike the preference shares in the Cadbury Schweppes example, those issued by the Saatchi & Saatchi subsidiary are convertible into ordinary shares of the holding company. An expectation that they might one day become ordinary shares of Saatchi & Saatchi Company PLC appears to be the reason for showing them above the 'Minority interests' caption in the balance sheet. It would also explain why they were considered to be part of the 'Called up share capital of the Group' in note 15.

The conversion option presents the calculator of a gearing ratio with a dilemma. If converted, the preference shares become part of the denominator. If redeemed, they are no different to the other borrowings used as the numerator in that ratio. One way of dealing with this problem is to try to predict which option the preference shareholder is likely to choose. This clearly hinges on the performance of the company's ordinary share price.

In the Saatchi & Saatchi example, conversion would be an attractive option whenever the ordinary share price exceeded the conversion price of 441p. The ordinary share prices for Saatchi & Saatchi Company PLC at its respective financial year ends are shown below:

Last trading day in:	Share price	Conversion price
September 1988	354p	441p
September 1989	291p	441p
September 1990	32p	441p

Although it might have been possible to anticipate conversion of the preference shares at the 1988 and 1989 balance sheet dates, the 1990 collapse in the ordinary share price made it certain that the preference shareholders would prefer to have them redeemed instead. Ironically the share price collapse was precipitated by an expectation that the company might be unable to find the cash necessary to redeem these shares in 1993. As this became increasingly likely, a recapitalisation of the company took place in March 1991. The holders of the Saatchi & Saatchi Finance NV preference shares received 617,646,300 ordinary shares, then worth approximately £100 million, on redemption of their 176.5 million preference shares.

Although the preference shares did eventually become part of the ordinary share capital of Saatchi & Saatchi Company PLC, the terms of exchange were rather different to those anticipated when the earlier balance sheets were drawn up. The original 441p conversion price would have resulted in the issue of 40 million new ordinary shares. The 1991 recapitalisation meant that 617.6 million had to be issued instead. The ordinary shares were then trading at approximately 16p each. Saatchi & Saatchi's balance sheet presentation of these preference shares would not be permitted if the proposals contained in *Accounting for Capital Instruments* are converted into an accounting standard:

> Shares issued by subsidiaries other than those held by companies within the group should be accounted for in consolidated financial statements as liabilities if any member of the group has an obligation to transfer economic benefits in connection with the shares, for example under a guarantee of payments to be made in respect of the shares. In all other cases they should be reported as minority interests.[6]

The Saatchi & Saatchi Finance NV preference shares were guaranteed by the holding company, Saatchi & Saatchi Company PLC. The new proposals therefore require them to be shown as liabilities in the consolidated balance sheet.

Whether this resolves the treatment of convertible debt instruments for gearing ratio purposes is less certain. Some companies will be able to mount convincing arguments that their convertible debt will eventually become part of their shareholders' funds. Like the Saatchi & Saatchi subsidiary's preference shares, the Convertible Capital Bonds 2005 issued by British Airways Plc in October 1989 would have to be shown as liabilities under the new proposals:

> Conversion of debt should not be anticipated. Convertible debt should be reported within liabilities and the finance cost should be calculated on the assumption that the debt will never be converted. The amount attributable to convertible debt should be stated on the face of the balance sheet separately from that of other liabilities.[7]

The proposed treatment outlined above contrasts sharply with British Airways' presentation of the bonds in the first balance sheet after their issue:

Illustration 5.16: *British Airways Plc (1990)*

Group Balance Sheet (extract)

£million	Note	1990	1989
CAPITAL AND RESERVES			
Called up share capital	17	180	180
Reserves	18		
Revaluation		121	167
Other		(18)	(9)
Profit and loss account		629	411
		912	749
Convertible Capital Bonds 2005	19	320	
Minority interests			1
		1,232	750

19 CONVERTIBLE CAPITAL BONDS 2005 (extract)

In October 1989 British Airways Plc raised £320 million through the issue of $9\frac{3}{4}$ per cent Convertible Bonds 2005 by a subsidiary, British Airways Capital Limited. The Bonds were offered by way of rights to existing ordinary shareholders of the Company on the basis of four Bonds of £1 each for every nine British Airways Plc shares then held. The terms of the Bonds allow the holders to convert into British Airways Plc ordinary shares during the period 1993 to 2005 on the basis of one ordinary share for each £2.43 of Bonds held. The terms also provide that on maturity in 2005 the Company may require remaining bondholders to convert their Bonds into ordinary shares of the Company which would be sold on their behalf. If the proceeds of such sale are less than the issue price of the Bonds the Company has to fund any deficit from its own resources.

In these circumstances the Directors consider that it is highly probable that the proceeds of the issue of the Convertible Capital Bonds will become part of the Company's called up share capital in due course and therefore will be available to the Group on a permanent basis. Accordingly the Convertible Capital Bonds have been included in the Group balance sheet under Capital and Reserves.

Whether convertible debt should be treated as part of the numerator or the denominator in a gearing ratio, is an issue which will not be resolved by rules governing its balance sheet presentation. Companies will continue to try to convince the users of their financial statements that their directors are well placed to judge the outcome of uncertain future events.

Goodwill and other intangible assets

The extract taken from Saatchi & Saatchi's 1990 balance sheet (Illustration 5.13) reveals the existence of another problem affecting the calculation of a gearing ratio. In both the 1989 and 1990 columns, the total of shareholders' funds and minority interests is a negative number. Determining the appropriate classification of the 6.3 per cent Convertible Cumulative Redeemable Preference shares and the 6.75 per cent Redeemable Convertible Preference shares (discussed in the previous section) is clearly not the only issue which needs to be addressed.

A gearing ratio based on a negative denominator is not going to produce a sensible answer. Although Saatchi & Saatchi's profit and loss account reflected an accumulated loss of £197 million at its 1990 year end, this is not the major reason for the overall deficit on shareholders' funds. At that date, the gross goodwill written off against shareholders' funds amounted to £787.6 million. This explains why the holding company's balance sheet reflected positive shareholders' funds of £493.2 million when the group balance sheet showed a deficit of £378.3 million.

As noted in Chapter 4, SSAP 22 prefers goodwill to be eliminated against reserves immediately after the acquisition of the business concerned. This does not mean that the purchased goodwill has suddenly become worthless. The SSAP explains that the deduction is made simply to achieve consistency of treatment with non-purchased goodwill, which is not reflected in the balance sheet of the group.

To calculate a gearing ratio when significant amounts of goodwill have been eliminated against reserves, it is necessary to decide whether the purchased goodwill has actually lost any of its value. If its value has been maintained, the SSAP 22 elimination against reserves can be ignored. A clue as to its fate is sometimes provided by the holding company's balance sheet. This should reveal whether the directors consider its value to be intact. When the goodwill loses its value, it is usually necessary to reflect this by writing down the holding company's investment in, or loans to, the subsidiary which gave rise to the goodwill. A loss in the value of purchased goodwill tends to be accompanied by a loss in the holding company's books. Whether Saatchi & Saatchi's holding company balance sheet, which showed a surplus of £493.2 million at the 1990 year end, was of much help in this regard is doubtful. It does, however, serve to illustrate the difficulty of calculating a sensible gearing ratio under these circumstances.

Reflecting purchased goodwill as an asset in the group balance sheet is unlikely to solve the problem either. Attempts to determine whether it has suffered a decline in value will always be fraught with difficulty. It is often not clear what gave rise to the goodwill in the first place. One company which has attempted to analyse the origin of the large amounts of goodwill eliminated against its reserves, is the WPP Group plc. In 1987 it acquired the JWT Group, Inc. and with it the J Walter Thompson and Hill and Knowlton corporate brand names. Goodwill arising on this acquisition amounted to £277.5 million. Eliminating it against reserves in the group balance sheet caused WPP's shareholders' funds to become a negative £65.5 million. In 1988, WPP decided to reconsider the appropriateness of the goodwill elimination arising on the JWT Group acquisition.

Illustration 5.17: WPP Group plc (1988)

CHAIRMAN'S STATEMENT (extract)

Brand Valuation

The Company has seriously considered and decided to incorporate the values of its brand names in its Balance Sheet. These revaluations total £175 million, are confined to J Walter Thompson Company and Hill and Knowlton, and are on a conservative basis. The Board feels that in the absence of such a revaluation the Balance Sheet would significantly understate the value of the Group's total and net assets and that traditional accounting concepts fail adequately to value intangible assets such as brand names and the values of which our clients are well aware. The Henley Centre, a Group company which has done similar work for our clients, prepared a report which was reviewed by our Investment Bankers, Samuel Montagu & Company, which values the Group's brands conservatively.

In effect, WPP decided that £175 million of the total goodwill of £277.5 million arising on the JWT Group acquisition was attributable to the brand names owned by JWT. Recording these brand names as an asset in its consolidated balance sheet had the following impact on the shareholders' funds' figure:

Illustration 5.18: WPP Group plc (1988)

CONSOLIDATED BALANCE SHEET (extract)	1988 £000	1987 £000
Capital and Reserves		
Called up share capital	3,973	3,670
Merger reserve	(150,603)	(89,423)
Other reserves	185,259	13,233
Profit and loss account	21,052	6,963
Shareholders' Funds	59,681	(65,557)
Minority interests	1,180	1,065
Total Capital Employed	60,861	(64,492)

Recording the brand names at a valuation of £175 million is the major reason for the increase in 'Other reserves' from £13.233 million to £185.259 million. WPP's change in accounting policy removes the anomaly of a deficit on shareholders' funds at a time when management regards the group as being in a sound financial condition. Whether it results in a meaningful denominator for gearing ratio purposes is less certain. Confining the valuation to the J Walter Thompson and Hill and Knowlton brand names and valuing these on a conservative basis suggests that the balance sheet has not overcome the chairman's concern that it understates the true value of the group's total and net assets.

Asset valuations and the revaluation reserve

The extract taken from the British Airways Plc balance sheet (Illustration 5.16) highlights another important factor in the calculation of the gearing ratio denominator. At 31 March 1990, the group balance sheet included a 'Revaluation reserve' amounting to £121 million. The existence of this reserve is optional. As noted in an earlier chapter, the Companies Act 1985 allows companies to record their assets either at their original acquisition cost or at a valuation. When the latter option is selected the excess of the valuation over the cost of the asset is credited to the revaluation reserve.

There is, however, currently no requirement for the valuations to be updated nor need they be applied to all the assets in the same category. UK company balance sheets tend, as a result, to be comprised of some assets recorded at acquisition cost, others at outdated valuations and a third category at current valuations. The shareholders' funds' section of the balance sheet will obviously be affected by the method used to record the assets.

A meaningful denominator?

The uncertainties and limitations attaching to the numerator used in the gearing ratio were outlined in the previous section. This section has revealed that the calculation of the denominator is also affected by many difficult issues. The appropriate classification of convertible capital instruments hinges on the outcome of an uncertain future event. Their presentation in the balance sheet may not always be the best guide to their treatment for gearing ratio purposes. Items which appear to resemble the numerator occasionally appear in the section used to calculate the denominator. The ASB's new proposals may cause items which are very likely to become part of the denominator to be shown in the section used for the numerator. More importantly, the denominator is often depleted by a substantial goodwill elimination, the relevance of which is difficult to judge. Further consideration of the goodwill issue reveals that the balance sheet probably fails to capture the true value of many other assets.

CALCULATING THE GEARING RATIO

The start of this chapter contained the following extract from Cadbury Schweppes' 1990 Annual Report:

Illustration 5.19: Cadbury Schweppes Public Limited Company (1990)								
FINANCIAL RATIOS (extract)								
			1990	1989	1988	1987	1986	
Gearing Ratio	$\dfrac{\text{Net borrowings}}{\text{Ordinary shareholders' funds} + \text{minority interests}}$	%	49.7	62.4	(0.5)	21.6	14.7	

It reveals that the 1990 gearing ratio is lower than the 1989 figure. The section in this chapter dealing with the calculation of the numerator has noted that the group's net borrowings amounted to £363.6 million at its 1990 year end. The total of its shareholders' funds and minority interests at the same date was £883.9 million. Expressing the former as a percentage of the latter produces a gearing ratio of 41.1 per cent. The reason for the difference between this figure and that shown in Illustration 5.19 was explained in the section covering the treatment of preference shares. Cadbury Schweppes decided that it was appropriate to exclude them from the denominator at their redemption value of £152.1 million. Reducing the denominator by this amount produces a figure of £731.8 million and the gearing ratio of 49.7 per cent shown in the table.

It is, however, tempting to wonder why the preference shares were not included as part of the numerator. The group's 1990 funding strategy, outlined in Illustration 5.11, involved the issue of preference shares to redeem other borrowings. If those preference shares are not considered to be part of the group's permanent capital, are they any different to the borrowings they have replaced? Treating the preference shares as part of the numerator produces a gearing ratio of 70.5 per cent (£515.7 million expressed as a percentage of £731.8 million).

An increase in the gearing ratio from 62.4 per cent in 1989 to 70.5 per cent in 1990 would be consistent with the trend revealed by two other ratios. The group's table of Financial Ratios shows that interest cover declined from 8.8 to 5.8 times and fixed charge cover from 6.9 to 4.7 times over the same period.

CONCLUSION

This chapter has outlined some of the uncertainties and limitations attaching to the numerators and denominators used in the calculation of most gearing ratios. They would appear to compromise the ability of the ratio to be a meaningful indicator of financial risk, or of anything else. The gearing ratio nevertheless continues to feature prominently in loan covenants, takeover documents and fund raising proposals. The importance attached to it by bankers, investment analysts, financial journalists and fund managers is hard to explain. It is equally difficult to understand why preparers of financial statements should spend so much time and effort trying to improve users' perceptions of it.

The financial community's fascination with the gearing ratio is, however, an issue of relatively minor importance. The uncertainties and limitations identified in this chapter apply equally to the balance sheet's ability to be a meaningful statement of financial position. It does not represent the value of the reporting entity's assets, nor does it contain particulars of all of its obligations. It is a limited document, badly misunderstood by many preparers and users of financial statements.

1   Sylvie and Bruno (1889), 'The Mad Gardener's Song'.
2   SSAP 21, *Accounting for leases and hire purchase contracts* (1984), August, para. 15.
3   Davies, Mike, Paterson, Ron and Wilson, Allister of Ernst & Young (1992), *UK GAAP – Generally Accepted Accounting Practice in the United Kingdom* (London: Macmillan Publishers Ltd), p. 792.
4   *Ibid.*, p. 793.
5   Accounting Standards Board (1992), FRED 3, *Accounting for capital instruments* (London: ASB), December, para b.
6   *Ibid.*, para. 43.
7   *Ibid.*, para. 22.

6: All of the People, All of the Time?

If one tells the truth, one is sure, sooner or later, to be found out.

Oscar Wilde[1]

BACKGROUND

In September 1990, Carr, Kitcat & Aitken published an investment analyst's report on Polly Peck International PLC. The company's shares were then trading at approximately 260p each. Impressed by the strength of trading in Polly Peck's food and electronics divisions, the Carr, Kitcat & Aitken analyst predicted a substantial improvement in pre-tax profit in 1990 and 1991. He recommended that Polly Peck's shares be bought at their current price of 260p.

A mere six days after publication of the report, on 20 September 1990, trading in the shares of Polly Peck International was suspended on the London Stock Exchange. The suspension prompted The Lex Column in the *Financial Times* of the following day to comment that:

> The market has reached the end of its tether with Polly Peck. Whatever one's views of fresh fruit, Cypriot hotels or the prospects for Turkish electronics, they fade into the background compared to the sheer chaos of yesterday's events. The shares plunged so fast, and in circumstances so bizarre, that Polly Peck's market price has lost all contact with fundamentals. At 108p, the prospective p/e is 2.3 and the gross yield 19.8 per cent, a death-bed rating that companies reach only when nearly bust. Yet that is surely not Polly Peck's position. At £864m-odd, its debt is high but manageable, unless the group's fruit and electronics suffer an apocalyptic collapse, which seems very unlikely.[2]

Carr, Kitcat & Aitken's analyst and The Lex Column were both wrong about the future prospects for Polly Peck International. Trading in the shares never resumed. They are today considered to be worthless.

The purpose of this chapter is to examine the ability of users to draw meaningful conclusions from financial statements. What do investment analysts look for when writing reports about companies' future prospects? Why did experienced analysts think that a company like Polly Peck International was capable of increasing an already substantial level of pre-tax profit by over 50 per cent in its current financial year with a further gain to follow in the year thereafter? What prompted the *Financial Times* to regard debt of nearly £1 billion as 'manageable'? Were these users misled by the financial statements? Is 'creative accounting' capable of presenting a false picture of the underlying reality? Does the stockmarket see 'creative accounting' for what it is?

There are no completely satisfactory answers to any of these questions. To claim to provide any would be presumptuous. Instead, the approach adopted in this chapter is based on an examination of some of the proposals put forward by other commentators. If this helps to develop a better understanding of the behaviour of the investor user group, it may shed some light on whether financial statements actually serve a useful purpose.

THE ROLE OF INVESTMENT ANALYSTS

Interpreters of financial statements?

Following the collapse of Polly Peck International, an article titled 'Polly Peck: Where Were The Analysts?' appeared in the January 1991 issue of *Accountancy* magazine. Written by David Gwilliam and Tim Russell of the University of Cambridge, it explored why analysts took a positive view of the company's prospects despite the existence of various 'danger signs' in the financial statements. The article began by noting the role analysts are expected to play in the processing of financial information:

> Most textbooks on accounting and finance agree that a key aspect of stockmarket efficiency is the markets' ability to absorb new information rapidly and to adjust the price of securities accordingly. Information will be evaluated whether it is highlighted in the p&l account or buried in the notes. But since the great majority of investors pay almost no attention to the details contained in financial statements, the focus is on the role of professional financial analysts in researching the minutiae of financial statements. It was the collapse of Polly Peck that brought this role into the public spotlight.

The article then focused on the ability of analysts to question the favourable impact of the group's accounting treatment of interest receivable and exchange losses. It also explored whether the analysts should have been able to detect signs of the liquidity crisis that precipitated the company's downfall. Not surprisingly, the authors noted that 'there were significant differences between analysts in the quality and depth of their analysis.' The authors were concerned about the lack of adequate explanation for the group's large interest receivable figure and the superficial treatment of the large exchange variances in many brokers' reports. They concluded that:

A significant proportion of analysts, perhaps the majority, either did not dig sufficiently deep into the disclosed information or failed to understand its importance. What does emerge is a pattern of judgments which appear to have been based on a relatively uncritical assessment of information formally or informally released by the company rather than on the financial statements.

The suggestion that the analysts paid more attention to information released by the company than to the financial statements themselves is particularly interesting. It is worth examining the Trafalgar House controversy in this light. As discussed in Chapter 2, an investigation by the Financial Reporting Review Panel resulted in the restatement of the company's consolidated profit and loss account for the year to 30 September 1991. The matter in dispute concerned the presentation of losses on property developments. The losses were not included in the consolidated profit and loss account but their existence was disclosed in notes 12, 14 and 24 to the 1991 accounts. An analyst wishing to look beyond the figures in the profit and loss account would have been able to make the necessary adjustment without difficulty.

How much attention did the analysts pay to the Trafalgar House financial statements for 1991? Were they guided instead by information released by the company? Did they detect the existence of the property losses? Were the losses considered to be relevant to an assessment of Trafalgar House's financial performance? If they were neither relevant nor significant, what did the Review Panel achieve by requiring a restatement of the profit and loss account? One way of attempting to answer these questions is to compare the analysts' forecasts of Trafalgar House's 1992 profits in the periods before and after the announcement that the 1991 profit and loss account would be restated.

Trafalgar House's results for the year to 30 September 1991 were released in December 1991. The company's 1991 annual report contained the following profit and loss account:

Illustration 6.1: *Trafalgar House Public Limited Company (1991)*

CONSOLIDATED PROFIT AND LOSS ACCOUNT (extract)

	Year ended 30th September 1991 £m	Year ended 30th September 1990 (restated) £m
Operating profit	148.9	206.3
Interest and finance charges	32.5	62.4
Operating profit after interest and finance charges	116.4	143.9
Profits less losses of associated companies	6.0	7.6
Profit on ordinary activities before taxation	122.4	151.5

Also included in the 1991 annual report was information revealing the existence of losses amounting to £102.7 million arising on the valuation of certain property developments. These losses were excluded from the profit and loss account shown above. Following an investigation by the Review Panel into the treatment of these losses, the company issued a press release on 15 October 1992. It announced that it would:

> ...restate the 1991 comparative figures in its 1992 accounts to comply with the requirements of Urgent Issue Task Force Abstract No. 5 issued on 22nd July 1992. As a result the 1991 comparative figures will show deficits on revaluation of properties of £102.7 million as a charge to the profit and loss account rather than to reserves.[3]

The restatement would reduce the previously reported pre-tax profit of £122.4 million to £19.7 million.

By February 1992, most analysts covering the company had released their forecasts of the 1992 consolidated profit before tax (PBT) figure. The summary of their early expectations shown in the following table has been extracted from the March 1992 issue of *The Estimate Directory*. It is reasonable to assume that the 1992 forecasts would be influenced by the analysts' assessments of the company's 1991 financial performance. They would have to decide whether the group was capable of improving on the 1991 result, or whether it was unlikely to be repeated.

One option would be to base their assessment of the company's 1991 performance on the profit of £122.4 million shown in the profit and loss account. Strauss Turnbull's analyst, for example, appears to have used this figure when initially predicting an unchanged performance in 1992. Alternatively, the analysts could have used a reduced figure of £19.7 million, had they considered the losses of £102.7 million disclosed in the notes to be relevant.

Figures in £m	Date of forecast	9/92F PBT	Date of forecast	9/92F PBT
BZW	6/1/92	150.0	30/10/92	60.0
Carr Kitcat	18/2/92	145.0	28/10/92	52.5
Charles Stanley	22/1/92	150.0	2/10/92	60.0
Charterhouse Tilney	28/12/91	130.0	3/8/92	100.0
County NatWest	24/1/92	185.0	30/10/92	60.0
Credit Lyonnais Laing	30/1/92	145.0	29/10/92	60.0
Fleming Securities	25/2/92	142.0	19/10/92	65.0
Greig Middleton	n/a		15/10/92	75.0
Hoare Govett	7/2/92	155.0	2/11/92	75.0
James Capel	27/1/92	138.0	2/11/92	41.0
Kleinwort Benson	27/1/92	140.0	26/10/92	60.0
Lehman Brothers	n/a		7/10/92	75.0
Nikko	3/12/91	125.0	30/9/92	55.0
Nomura	7/2/92	140.0	29/10/92	60.0

Panmure Gordon	10/2/92	126.0	19/10/92	50.0
Smith New Court	27/2/92	130.0	8/10/92	100.0
Strauss Turnbull/S.G.S.T. Securities	10/2/92	122.4	1/11/92	65.0
UBS Phillips & Drew	5/2/92	140.0	28/10/92	98.0
Warburg	6/2/92	145.0	2/11/92	45.0
Williams de Broe	3/2/92	142.0	27/10/92	70.0
Consensus		141.7		66.3
% Change on Previous Year (122.4)		+16		−46

By November 1992, a great deal had happened to cause the analysts to amend their consensus forecast of a 16 per cent increase in 1992 pre-tax profit to £141.7 million. Interim results were released in May. The company had become the subject of a partial tender offer by Hong Kong Land. In October it announced that its 1991 results would be restated in the 1992 annual report. The 1992 forecasts extracted from the mid-November 1992 issue of *The Estimate Directory* therefore reflect a vastly different picture. As shown in the last column above, the earlier consensus forecast of £141.7 million had been reduced by 53 per cent to £66.3 million.

In formulating their revised forecasts, the analysts would have considered many factors in addition to those listed in the previous paragraph. It is not possible to determine the degree of importance attached to any factor. It is, however, significant that the two highest revised forecasts for 1992, of £100 million, were both made prior to the press release of 15 October which announced the restatement of the 1991 profit and loss account.

In formulating their original forecasts for 1992, it would appear that none of the analysts paid any attention to the property losses disclosed in the notes to the 1991 accounts. There are two possible explanations for this. Either the losses were considered to be irrelevant to the group's prospects for 1992 or the analysts failed to spot their existence. The first explanation could imply that the Urgent Issues Task Force and the Review Panel pursued a matter considered by an important user group to be of little relevance to their decision-making. The second explanation suggests that analysts are not particularly good at looking beyond the figures disclosed in the profit and loss account.

The chairman of the Accounting Standards Board (ASB) might be expected to side with the second explanation. In the July 1992 edition of *Accountancy* magazine he is reported to have said of analysts in another context:

> I find it frightening – some people are just lifting the numbers and using them as sacrosanct. You shouldn't be an analyst if you do that. That's why we exploded the p&l account into its components – they have to look behind the figures. But there are good analysts and bad ones. I remember once, a rumour went around that we were thinking of abolishing equity accounting, and share prices fell. What are they *doing*? It wouldn't affect cash flow, so why did share prices fall? Some of them would be better off driving buses – it would be safer for a lot of us.

Pursuing another objective?

The need to see the role of the analyst in its proper context has been stressed by other commentators. The March 1991 edition of *Accountancy* magazine contained an article written by Geoffrey Holmes and Alan Sugden in response to the criticism by David Gwilliam and Tim Russell noted earlier in this chapter. Titled 'Corporate Failure – Analysing the Analysts', it stressed the importance of understanding the 'real situation in which brokers' analysts operate.' Holmes and Sugden identified two reasons why analysts might be unwilling to be overly critical of the companies they report on:

> First, if their firm is the company's broker, it is liable to be sacked if the analyst is too frank, although we are glad to say that from time to time the roles are reversed, and the broker decides to ditch the company.
>
> Second, even if the analyst is not from the company's brokers, the company may refuse to speak to him or her ever again, or may complain vehemently to the broker's chairman or to the top management of the broker's parent company.

Their article also contains an unusual proposition that brokers' reports should not be read too literally:

> But it can be pretty misleading to judge an analyst's ability on the basis of his or her published recommendations, unless you feed in a 'reality factor'. We always check whether the note is from the company's own broker; if it is, we interpret 'Long term buy' as meaning 'Don't buy now – consider selling', and 'Weak hold' as a straight sell. Most analysts have built up a store of euphemisms for use when giving what is, in effect, a 'Sell' recommendation, to reduce the risk of offending the company concerned: 'High enough', 'Take profits', 'Remain underweight' to mention but three.

The continued use of the terms in this extract is presumably dependent on the companies concerned not reading the Holmes and Sugden article.

The authors were also critical of 'the scope our present accounting rules give companies for pulling the wool over the analysts' eyes' and they expected the ASB to effect an improvement in this regard. Of more interest in the context of this chapter, is their assertion that:

> Another factor that can influence analysts is the pressure in some firms to generate business. It is not uncommon for an analyst's note to be returned for 'improvement' because it wouldn't generate enough business as it stood. If anything, this has got worse since Big Bang, as financial houses that paid over the odds for broking firms try desperately to screw a reasonable return out of their investment.

The above extract raises an important point, one which is critical to understanding the investment analysts' role. It suggests that analysts are probably hired for another purpose. To criticise them for failing to research the finer details of company reports might be inappropriate. Their task is to respond to the perceived needs of their employers' clients. Is it possible that stockbrokers' clients want analysts to provide another service, one that is considered to be more relevant to the investment decision-making process? Do they want brokers' reports to be written by accounting experts?

One view is that making successful investment decisions is about understanding the dynamics of the market place in which companies sell their goods and services. It is about recognising opportunities and threats well ahead of time. It is about developing a feel for the capabilities of the people who manage the companies that operate in this challenging environment. It requires knowledge of the strengths and weaknesses of these individuals and their ability to adapt their companies to change. These are the priorities of the investment manager.

The possibility that accounting expertise might not be particularly relevant to the investment manager's role is also suggested by the following job advertisement, taken from the *Financial Times* of 2 September, 1992. It provides a clue as to the qualifications and abilities investment managers would like to see in their analysts. There is little in the advertisement to suggest that the individual concerned needs to have a strong accounting background.

The advertisement does not distinguish between experience gained in a stockbroking firm or an investment management firm. Both positions tend to be filled by individuals possessing similar qualifications and abilities.

The services which investment analysts are expected to provide are wide-ranging. Is it appropriate to criticise people who are not accounting specialists for failing to provide expertise of that kind? Do stockbrokers' clients attach a particularly high degree of importance to accounting expertise? Stockbrokers' reports are hardly going to be characterised by rigorous analyses of accounting practices if accounting expertise is not considered to be of paramount importance by the readers of the reports. If these observations are to be believed, there are a number of important implications for the system of financial reporting. The most radical is the possibility that company financial statements might not be particularly relevant to the investor's decision-making process.

Are company financial statements relevant?

The observation by David Gwilliam and Tim Russell that the analysts in the Polly Peck International case seemed to pay more attention to information released by the company than to the financial statements themselves, is supported by other research. A survey conducted by David Bence, Roger Hussey and Catherine Wilkie[4] produced the following ranking of analysts' sources of information:

Source of information	Rank
Preliminary statements	1
Personal interviews with company	Equal 2
Interim statements	Equal 2
Company presentations	4
Annual reports	5
Telephone calls to company	6
Company PR Department	7
Visits to company	8
Trade journals	9
Company literature other than financial statements	10
Data stream or similar	11
Industry and government statistics	12
Other analysts	13

The researchers noted that the analysts surveyed were largely concerned with the timeliness of information. This could explain the relatively low ranking accorded the annual report. They also stressed that 'these findings are specific to one company where the success of one of its individual products and the process of research and development are seen as critical factors in investment decisions.' Although their research is still continuing, their findings shed important light on analysts' priorities.

Of the 21 analysts surveyed, only one 'was conducting a rigorous fundamental analysis of the accounts.' Others commented that 'I will possibly never read the annual report – there shouldn't be anything new in it'; and 'the annual report is advertising, using coded language. I discount it.'

If analysts do not attach a particularly high priority to the financial statements contained in the annual report, how do they go about writing their reports? The link between share prices and earnings, noted in Chapter 3, could be taken as a useful starting point. The need to form an opinion about future growth prospects was identified as the key to successful investing. Investment analysts' reports are therefore likely to be concerned primarily with future earnings. The cornerstone of these reports would then be an evaluation of the company's growth prospects. This could be done as follows. The first stage is to develop an understanding of the company's business. Then its management's plans for the future need to be investigated. The annual report could be used for these purposes. It usually contains a fair amount of detail about the nature of the company's activities and it might include an outline of management's strategy and objectives. It is probably not an ideal source for the analyst, though. They are, after all, looking to generate business for their employers. They need to differentiate their reports from their competitors'. The information contained in the annual report is available to all analysts. A better source of information about a company's business and its management's plans for the future is direct contact with senior executives of the company. This usually enables the analyst to offer a different insight into the company's prospects. Direct contact with management also helps with the detailed forecasting of the profit before tax, earnings and dividends per share figures.

Are financial statements ignored in the report writing process? The analyst's report will probably need to explain why the company has performed significantly better or worse than previously expected. The financial statements are a useful source of information in this respect. Their role is, however, essentially confirmatory. They are a way of establishing whether management's plans are being achieved. This can be done by examining a few key numbers and ratios. Turnover growth, operating margin, interest cover, earnings per share, and the gearing ratio are most commonly used. All of this information is contained in the preliminary announcement. The problem with financial statements is that they usually appear at least three months after the company's financial year end. They merely confirm the results contained in the preliminary announcement, made some weeks before. Are hours spent poring over detailed notes in support of a profit and loss account and balance sheet released to the public in an earlier preliminary announcement, going to generate much additional business for the analysts' employers?

THE STOCKMARKET AND COMPANY FINANCIAL STATEMENTS

The previous section has suggested that company financial statements might not be particularly relevant to the investment decision-making process. Should this proposal be taken seriously? Is there another explanation why investment managers and analysts do not appear to have the accounting expertise needed to perform an exhaustive analysis of the financial statements?

One way of attempting to answer these questions is to examine the relationship between share prices and the information contained in the financial statements. For purposes of this book, a small sample of four companies which featured prominently in the financial press in the early 1990s will probably suffice.

Brent Walker PLC

After a period of dramatic growth in earnings and dividends per share, Brent Walker suffered a sharp reversal of fortune in 1990:

Example 6.1: *Brent Walker PLC*

Financial years to 31 December:	1987	1988	1989	1990	1991
Basic earnings/(loss) per share – pence	30.6	54.0	116.8	(299.8)	(763.1)
Net dividend per share – pence	8.0	11.0	15.0	5.0	-

Source: Extel Financial UK Quoted Companies Service

The following graph shows the company's share price at the end of each quarter during the period from December 1987 to June 1992:

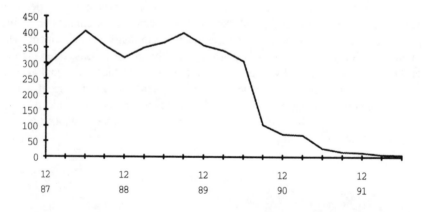

Figure 6.1. Brent Walker PLC – quarterly share price in pence per share

The graph shows a clear correlation between the company's share price and the earnings and dividend per share statistics in the previous table. The 1987–9 period is characterised by dramatic growth in earnings and a buoyant share price. The losses in 1990 and 1991 would appear to have provoked the 1990 collapse in the share price.

Harder to explain is the relationship between the company's share price and the steady increase in the level and cost of its borrowings. Example 6.2 shows that borrowings increased from £57.7 million at December 1987 to £1,230.3 million at December 1989. The cost of servicing these borrowings represented 44 per cent of the 1989 profit before interest payable. This information was contained in the 1989 financial statements, released to the stockmarket in the early part of 1990. At end-June 1990, six months after the company's 1989 year end, the company's share price still exceeded 300p. Two years later, it had fallen to 6p.

The share price eventually collapsed under the weight of the group's borrowings. The stockmarket appears, however, not to have been particularly interested in the borrowings. As long as the group was able to report sharply higher earnings per share figures, it appears to have received the benefit of any doubt regarding its ability to service its borrowing commitments.

Example 6.2: *Brent Walker PLC*

All figures in £000

Year to 31 December:	1987	1988	1989	1990	1991
Profit/(loss) before interest	20,449	47,096	116,748	(6,605)	(151,455)
Interest receivable	1,527	5,745	12,910	9,148	6,070
Interest payable	(1,172)	(11,150)	(56,968)	(125,327)	(241,882)
At 31 December:					
Cash	19,568	78,672	47,304	10,922	9,004
Borrowings	57,714	407,598	1,230,292	1,453,514	1,570,335

Borrowings comprise bank loans and overdrafts, commercial paper, convertible bonds, hire purchase and finance lease creditors and loan stock.

Source: Extel Financial UK Quoted Companies Service

There is some similarity between the stockmarket's treatment of Brent Walker and that accorded the WPP Group plc.

WPP Group plc

Example 6.3: WPP Group plc

Financial years to 31 December:	1987	1988	1989	1990	1991
Earnings per share – pence	32.1	55.0	73.0	78.1	27.9
Net dividend per share – pence	6.4	17.8	24.2	–	–

Source: Extel Financial UK Quoted Companies Service

Between 1987 and 1989, WPP's earnings per share increased by 127 per cent. There was a near quadrupling in the dividend during this period. Not surprisingly, the stockmarket reacted favourably to these statistics. The company's share price at the end of 1989 was 64 per cent higher than that ruling at the end of 1987. The subsequent downturn in the company's profitability provoked a severe reaction from the stockmarket:

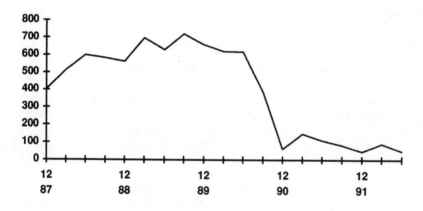

Figure 6.2. WPP Group plc – quarterly share price in pence per share

As in the Brent Walker example, the relationship between the company's share price and the change in the level of its borrowings is harder to explain. Financing the growth in earnings during the 1987–9 period caused gross borrowings to increase from £179 million to £559 million. In the 1989 year, servicing the cost of these borrowings and paying the dividends due on the group's preference shares accounted for 44 per cent of the profit before these charges. As in the Brent Walker example, this information was available to the stockmarket in early 1990. At the end of June of that year the company's share price was still comfortably above 600p, more than 50 per cent higher than the December 1987 level. Two years later it was trading at 50p.

Example 6.4: *WPP Group plc*

All figures in £000

Year to 31 December:	1987	1988	1989	1990	1991
Profit before interest	21,454	51,436	102,482	132,971	101,912
Interest receivable	3,739	7,926	16,072	14,275	9,429
Interest payable	(11,076)	(19,044)	(43,515)	(57,206)	(55,236)
Preference dividends			(8,413)	(17,648)	(17,640)
At 31 December:					
Cash	72,616	92,591	233,617	229,455	205,478
Borrowings	179,281	133,242	558,975	526,956	539,293

Borrowings comprise amounts owed to bankers, loan notes, bank loans and hire purchase and finance lease creditors.

Source: Extel Financial UK Quoted Companies Service

In both the Brent Walker and WPP Group examples, there is a long-term correlation between the fall in the companies' share prices and their decreased ability to service their borrowing commitments. What is of interest, however, is that the stockmarket seemed unconcerned about changes in borrowing levels for as long as the companies were able to report healthy increases in earnings and dividends per share. Both companies' 1989 annual reports showed a sharp increase in borrowing commitments. Their share prices held up for some months thereafter, presumably because both reports also contained significantly higher earnings per share figures.

Polly Peck International PLC

Another example of the stockmarket's willingness to be guided by earnings and dividends is provided by the Polly Peck International disaster. The performance of the company's shares during the period from end-December 1987 to end-June 1990 contains no hint of their suspension on 20 September 1990, referred to at the start of this chapter. During the period covered by the graph, the stockmarket appears to have been influenced by the company's record of steady increases in earnings and dividends per share, shown in Example 6.5.

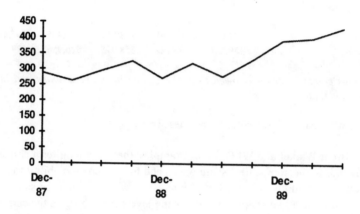

Figure 6.3. Polly Peck International PLC – quarterly share price in pence per share

Example 6.5*: Polly Peck International PLC*

Years to 31 August/*31 Dec:	1985	1986	1987	*1988	*1989
Basic earnings per share – pence	31.0	33.2	36.1	40.6	44.6
Net dividend per share – pence	3.1	4.0	5.6	9.5	13.0

Source: Polly Peck International Annual Reports

The impressive earnings record appears to have outweighed any concern the stockmarket might have had about the sharp increase in the group's borrowings during this period.

Example 6.6: *Polly Peck International PLC*

All figures in £million

Year to 31 Aug/*31 Dec:	1985	1986	1987	*1988	*1989
Trading profit	63.7	76.0	93.4	118.6	139.0
Interest and other income	0.7	8.1	12.6	32.3	77.4
Interest payable	(5.7)	(14.1)	(21.3)	(38.7)	(55.6)
At 31 Aug/*31 Dec:					
Cash	3.0	18.1	20.6	124.2	249.3
Borrowings	65.9	103.5	171.8	377.9	1,106.2

Borrowings comprise bank loans, overdrafts, mortgage loans, loan stock, guaranteed bonds and finance lease and hire purchase creditors.

Source: Polly Peck International Annual Reports

The near seventeen-fold increase in borrowings from £65.9 million in 1985 to £1,106.2 million in 1989 contrasts sharply with the modest doubling in trading profit from £63.7 million to £139.0 million during this period. Even if the dramatic increase in trading profit forecast for 1990 had been achieved, it is clear that the group's risk profile had altered beyond recognition. The stockmarket seemed prepared to tolerate this, presumably in expectation of further increases in earnings and dividends per share.

Saatchi & Saatchi Company PLC

The three previous examples have revealed instances of the stockmarket's faith in the ability of companies to cope with significant increases in their borrowings. In all three instances, the market's optimism appeared to be sustained by a healthy trend in historic earnings and dividends. The Saatchi & Saatchi example suggests that this optimism might, on occasion, be based on expectations of a turnaround in earnings.

In the year to September 1989, Saatchi & Saatchi reported a loss after many years of impressive growth in earnings per share. The 1988 result had also been disappointing, with earnings per share only marginally higher than the previous year.

Example 6.7: *Saatchi & Saatchi Company PLC*

Period to 30 Sept/*31 Dec:	1987	1988	1989	1990	*1991
Earnings/(loss) per share – pence	37.9	39.7	(19.1)	(12.6)	(9.1)
Net dividend per share – pence	12.0	13.2	7.4	–	–

Earnings and dividend per share statistics are prior to the share consolidation in May 1992

Source: Extel Financial UK Quoted Companies Service

The company's share price had weakened from 421p at end-December 1987 to 249p at end-December 1989. Although the decline of 41 per cent was significant, it is doubtful whether it reflected the full extent of the increase in the group's borrowing commitments.

Example 6.8 reveals that, if a subsidiary company's preference shares are counted as borrowings in view of the redemption option granted to their holders, the group's gross borrowings had increased by £379.7 million during the 1987–9 period. Adding a £132.2 million decline in cash balances brings the increase in the group's net borrowings to over £500 million during this period.

Example 6.8: *Saatchi & Saatchi Company PLC*

All figures in £million

Period to 30 Sept/*31 Dec:	1987	1988	1989	1990	*1991
Profit/(loss) before interest	100.3	133.3	44.1	63.9	(33.7)
Interest receivable	37.3	19.7	6.0	17.6	10.1
Interest payable	(13.5)	(15.0)	(28.3)	(45.9)	(40.0)
Preference dividends	(6.3)	(8.8)	(18.2)	(15.1)	
– additional provision				(13.4)	
At 30 Sept/*31 Dec:					
Cash	200.3	182.3	68.1	99.5	103.3
Borrowings	36.3	127.1	239.5	318.6	292.5
Company preference shares	99.5	99.5	99.5	99.4	–
Subsidiary preference shares		176.5	176.5	176.5	–

Borrowings comprise amounts owed to bankers, debentures, unsecured loan stock and finance lease creditors.

Source: Extel Financial UK Quoted Companies Service

Seen in the context of the £500 million increase in net borrowings during the 1987–9 period, the share price of 249p at end-December 1989 says a great deal about the stockmarket's optimism.

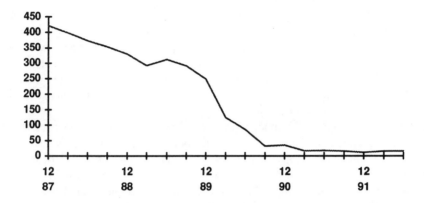

Figure 6.4. Saatchi & Saatchi Company PLC – quarterly share price in pence per share

The group was, in the event, unable to service the higher level of borrowings. Within a year, the share price had lost 86 per cent of its value. Chapter 5 highlighted the unusual balance sheet presentation of the preference share capital issued by a Saatchi & Saatchi subsidiary company. It is interesting to speculate whether this influenced the stockmarket's perceptions of the group's recovery prospects. Were these preference shares considered to be borrowings or as part of shareholders' funds?

CONCLUSION

This chapter has explored the relevance of company financial statements to the economic decisions made by the investor user group. It has attempted to answer questions such as the following. Do investment analysts have the ability to draw sensible conclusions from financial statements? If they appear to lack the accounting expertise necessary, is this a function of the relatively low priority that investment decision-makers seem to attach to it?

The suggestion that company financial statements might not be a particularly important part of the investor's decision-making process can probably be rejected. The evidence examined in this chapter suggests that the statements provide valuable information about the reporting entity. An inability to service borrowing commitments eventually results in a collapse in the share price.

There is a better explanation for the relatively low priority which investors seem to attach to accounting expertise. It is probably due to a belief that they should be able to take the integrity of financial statements for granted. They regard this as being the responsibility of the ASB and the auditor. It is the task of the ASB and the auditor to ensure that the statements are 'true and fair' and clear and unambiguous.

These conclusions are significant when viewed against those reached in previous chapters. Chapters 4 and 5 have questioned the ability of financial statements to provide unequivocal measures of financial performance and financial condition. Chapter 2 has highlighted the danger of relying on any system of financial reporting to safeguard the quality of the financial statements produced by it. Investors' faith in the reliability of financial statements should be seen in this context. It is extremely doubtful whether their integrity can ever be guaranteed.

What are the implications of all of this for the system of financial reporting in the UK? It seems clear that if the reliability of financial statements cannot be taken for granted their limitations should at least be clearly understood. It is significant that investors appear to attach more importance to reported earnings than to changes in the cost and level of borrowings. This approach fails to recognise that the latter is a more objective indicator of financial health than the former. Users need a better understanding of the limitations inherent in the financial statements if they are to draw the right conclusions from the mass of information presented to them.

1   Chameleon (1894), *Phrases and Philosophies for the Use of the Young*, December.
2   *Financial Times* (1990), 21 September.
3   Trafalgar House Press Release (1992), 15 October.
4   Bence, David, Hussey, Roger and Wilkie, Catherine (1992), 'Producers, Investment Analysts and the Annual Report', paper presented at the British Accounting Association Annual Conference, Warwick University, April.

7: Unravelling the Profit and Loss Account and the Balance Sheet

The numerical exactitude of business accounts and calculations must not prevent us from realizing the uncertainty and speculative character of their items and of all computations based on them. The essential elements of economic calculation are speculative anticipations of future conditions. There is accuracy in the keeping of books. But they are accurate only with regard to these rules. The book values do not reflect precisely the real state of affairs.

Ludwig von Mises

INTRODUCTION

The ASB's statement of the objective of financial statements requires them 'to provide information about the financial position, performance and financial adaptability'[1] of the reporting entity. To use more common terminology, financial statements have to include a balance sheet, a profit and loss account, a statement of total recognised gains and losses and a statement of cash flows, in addition to various note disclosures.

At the start of this book, doubt was expressed as to whether this was the best way of providing useful information about the reporting entity. Chapters 4 and 5 have suggested that today's profit and loss accounts and balance sheets might not be reliable indicators of financial performance and financial position. The purpose of this chapter is to explore whether there is another alternative open to users of financial statements. Do they have to rely on the profit and loss account and the balance sheet as the major sources of useful information about the reporting entity?

PROFIT AND LOSS ACCOUNTS AND BALANCE SHEETS

It is tempting to think of the profit and loss account and the balance sheet as two entirely separate documents. Chapter 1 of the ASB's draft *Statement of Principles* is a useful reminder that this is not the case. It notes that 'the component parts of the financial statements interrelate because they reflect different aspects of the same transactions or other events.'[2]

Although the profit and loss account and the balance sheet interrelate with one another, the precise nature of their relationship has not been easy to establish. Deciding which statement should be accorded primary status is an issue that has plagued the development of accounting standards in nearly every country. A brief look at the nature of the problem sheds important light on the limitations of both statements. It also provides a clue as to how the user might unravel them in an attempt to improve their usefulness.

The balance sheet approach to measuring profit

By according primary status to the balance sheet, this approach measures profit by reference to the opening and closing positions reflected in that statement. The procedure involves setting criteria for the recognition of assets and liabilities, so as to make the balance sheet a meaningful statement of financial position.

The balance sheet approach was adopted by David Solomons in formulating his *Guidelines for Financial Reporting Standards*. The Institute of Chartered Accountants in England and Wales (ICAEW) sponsored this project in the hope that it would produce greater consistency in the approach to setting accounting standards. Solomons' *Guidelines* define assets as 'resources or rights incontestably controlled by an entity at the accounting date that are expected to yield it future economic benefits.'[3] Liabilities are 'obligations of an entity at the accounting date to make future transfers of assets or services (sometimes uncertain as to timing and amount) to other entities.'[4] Deducting the total of the liabilities from the total of the assets produces a figure for net assets. Profit is derived from the change in net assets during the period. The balance sheet approach has been criticised on the basis that it:

> ...abandons the matching concept in many instances. I think this is inappropriate both because it flies in the face of much of generally accepted practice and, more importantly, because it would often give rise to meaningless figures in the profit and loss account.
>
> In addition, I doubt whether the recognition criteria for assets and liabilities which underlie this approach are workable, because I think that financial accounting as we know it has its roots in transactions, and that this is where recognition criteria must start.[5]

The profit and loss account approach to measuring profit

This method is based on the allocation of revenue and expenses to individual reporting periods. The unallocated portion of these items is taken to the balance sheet, to await recognition in future profit and loss accounts. Solomons dislikes this approach because it:

...threatens the integrity of the balance sheet and its value as a useful financial statement. Its value is maximized if it can be seen as a statement of financial position; but it can only be that if all the items in it are truly assets, liabilities, and equity, and not other bits left over from the profit and loss account, and if all such items that are capable of being recognised are included in it.[6]

APPLYING THE DIFFERENT APPROACHES IN PRACTICE

The argument as to which approach should underlie the development of detailed accounting standards is unlikely to be settled. Of greater interest to users of financial statements is whether either approach provides useful information about the reporting entity. The problems affecting both approaches are best illustrated by way of an example.

On 6 March 1992, THORN EMI plc entered into a conditional agreement to acquire the Virgin Music Group. The financial position of the latter as reflected in its latest available audited balance sheet at 31 July 1991, was as follows:[7]

	£m
Fixed assets:	
Intangible assets	6.6
Tangible assets	25.9
Investments	0.8
Current assets:	
Cash at bank and in hand	22.1
Other	119.4
Liabilities:	
Borrowings	(74.3)
Other	(97.3)
Net assets	3.2

The purchase consideration payable by THORN EMI was set at £510 million. The newspaper extracts which follow help to explain the discrepancy between the purchase price and the net assets of the acquired business. They also provide a clue as to the factors that could be taken into account in determining the appropriate accounting treatment for the transaction. The *Evening Standard* of the same day commented that:

> The £510 million price and the assumption of £50 million of Virgin's debt may appear generous. However, higher offers were around so Thorn shareholders have no need to be overly concerned.
>
> Although the business made operating profits of £21 million last year these were depressed by US Investments, the benefits of which will accrue to Thorn.
>
> Thorn chairman Colin Southgate is not only securing a quality business he is also paving the way for considerable synergies.

The financial benefits will be generated from those arising in manufacture, marketing and distribution. As a consequence he is able to estimate that earnings per share should be enhanced after the first year.

The Tempus column in *The Times* of the following day observed that:

In any other industry, the deal which Thorn EMI struck with Virgin yesterday would be considered crazy. Thorn is paying £510 million for a business with net assets of £3.2 million and post-tax profits of £483,000. Even assuming a nominal tax rate of 35 per cent for Virgin, Thorn is paying around 60 times earnings. Virgin Music's actual tax rate was 96 per cent of pre-tax profits last year.

The advertising agency deals of the mid-Eighties spring to mind. While Saatchi and WPP were paying in instalments for goodwill, intangible assets were walking out the door.

In the world of recorded music, however, yesterday's deal was hailed as a triumph for Thorn, whose shares rose 25p to 810p, despite news of a £516 million rights issue. On closer inspection the market is probably right. Virgin is the last independent record producer to come up for sale. It has a catalogue of artists the envy of its rivals and, while it may still be classed as intangible, Virgin Music's back catalogue is a secure revenue producing asset that accounted for 35 per cent of its £330 million turnover last year.

...While the assets may be intangible, the synergies for Thorn are very real. Derek Brock at Nomura calculates that Thorn can lift Virgin Music's £21 million operating profits to £61 million in the year ending March 1993. Virgin Music's distribution and manufacturing, now farmed out to third parties, will be taken in-house.

In one swoop Thorn takes market share from 14 per cent to 18 per cent and gains the benefits of negotiating power from being the joint number one player.

Determining the appropriate accounting treatment for the £510 million purchase price is clearly going to have a significant impact on the measurement of Thorn's financial performance in the post-acquisition period. Would the balance sheet approach provide the most useful information in this regard? Or should the profit and loss account approach be adopted?

The balance sheet approach to measuring profit

There is little doubt that THORN's acquisition of the Virgin Music Group means that it owns 'resources or rights ... that are expected to yield it future economic benefits.' Solomons' *Guidelines* would require these to be included in the balance sheet at their value to the business. By this is meant the loss THORN would suffer if deprived of the assets concerned. The annual profit figure would be derived from changes in the value of these assets.

The balance sheet approach is relatively easy to adopt in the context of an investment company with a portfolio of shares quoted on the stock exchange. Applying it to Virgin Music's catalogue of artists and music copyrights is going to be difficult. Whether it could be done in a sufficiently reliable manner for users to feel confident about the profit figure produced as a by-product of the process is not certain. The problem would be exacerbated by THORN's intention to merge the business of the Virgin Music Group with its own EMI Music division.

The profit and loss account approach to measuring profit

This approach requires the cost of acquiring the Virgin Music business to be matched with the revenues expected to be generated by it. The obvious difficulty with this approach lies in determining the period over which to allocate the cost of £510 million. The unallocated portion at the end of each reporting period would be reflected in the balance sheet. Its recoverability would have to be assessed to ensure that it was covered by revenue expected in the future.

Implications for the user of financial statements

Although existing accounting practice has more in common with the profit and loss account approach, there are indications that the ASB prefers the balance sheet approach. As noted in Chapter 4, FRS 3 *Reporting Financial Performance* has loosened the link between the profit and loss account and the outcome of certain transactions with third parties. A surplus arising on the sale of a revalued asset has to be excluded from the profit and loss account if it 'is not itself a gain of that later period, but, rather, confirmation of a gain that had already occurred by the time of the revaluation.'[8] Whether FRS 3 heralds the start of a new approach which places greater emphasis on changes in the balance sheet values of assets and liabilities in measuring financial performance, is not entirely clear.

What is clear, though, is that both approaches are heavily dependent on the exercise of judgement. The reliability of the information contained in profit and loss accounts and balance sheets is a function of their preparers' ability to anticipate the outcome of uncertain future events. The two statements are intertwined in the sense that one is derived from the other. They are both affected by the same uncertainties, estimates and predictions about the future.

AN ALTERNATIVE APPROACH TO MEASURING FINANCIAL PERFORMANCE

Prior to the establishment of the ASB in August 1990, financial accounts intended to give a 'true and fair' view were required to contain three primary statements. In addition to the profit and loss account and the balance sheet, a source and application of funds statement had to be prepared. SSAP 10 *Statements of source and application of funds* was issued in July 1975. However, the perception that the funds statement was a document of limited usefulness eventually led to its replacement by the ASB's FRS 1 *Cash flow statements* in September 1991.

SSAP 10's failure to capture the imagination of users of financial statements reveals something about their approach to analysing financial information. The funds statement provides a summary of the transactions entered into by the reporting entity during the period covered by the financial statements. It is the allocation of these transactions that gives rise to the profit and loss account and the balance sheet. The funds statement is, by contrast, untainted by the exercise of judgement. It provides a useful backdrop against which to assess the information contained in the profit and loss account and the balance sheet. This is best illustrated by a simple example.

Example 7.1

Company A commences business as a retailer by acquiring freehold premises for £15 million, financed by a bank loan repayable in 10 years' time. In its first year of trading, the company purchases 2 million items for £10 each and sells 1 million for £20 each. The sales are made evenly throughout the year. Suppliers are paid in cash but customers are granted six months' credit.

The preparation of a profit and loss account and a balance sheet for company A under the existing accounting framework requires decisions to be made about:

- the allocation of the cost of the premises to individual reporting periods. Should the buildings be depreciated or will they be maintained in a sufficiently good condition for the amount of any depreciation to be insignificant?
- the collectability of the £10 million owed by customers at the end of the period;
- the saleability of the unsold stock costing £10 million.

The usefulness of the information contained in the profit and loss account and the balance sheet depends on their preparer's ability to predict the outcome of the three uncertain future events described above.

The funds statement is, by contrast, a more objective document. It will reveal that:

- merchandise costing £20 million was paid for in cash;
- sales totalling £20 million resulted in an increase in debtors of £10 million and an inflow of cash of £10 million;
- premises were acquired at a cost of £15 million, financed by a bank loan.

The SSAP 10 funds statement was rejected because it was felt to contain information of little value to users. At first glance this seems to be true of the information shown in Example 7.1 above. Could it be of any use to readers of company A's financial statements?

The ASB has identified the following primary characteristics that make accounting information useful:

To be useful, information must be relevant to the decision-making needs of users. Information has the quality of relevance when it influences the economic decisions of users by helping them evaluate past, present or future events or by confirming, or correcting, their past evaluations.[9]

To be useful, information must also be reliable. Information has the quality of reliability when it is free from material error and bias and can be depended upon by users to represent faithfully in terms of valid description that which it either purports to represent or could reasonably be expected to represent.[10]

The information contained in the funds statement in Example 7.1 meets the second of the two criteria above. It is certainly reliable. Its relevance to the decision-making needs of users depends on how it is interpreted. Revising the layout of the funds statement could be of significant assistance in this regard.

Revising the layout of the funds statement

If the funds statement is to provide useful information, it should focus on the issues that matter most to the owners of the reporting entity. Their objective in investing in the business is, ultimately, a relatively simple one. They want to get more cash out of it than they have put into it. They would probably like to know the answers to the following questions:

- Has the business generated a cash surplus during the period?
- How much of the surplus has been reinvested in expanding the business?
- Has it been necessary to use funds provided by bankers and other financiers to operate and expand the business?

The answers to these questions might be more relevant to the owners of the business and others wishing to transact with it, than the information contained in the profit and loss account and the balance sheet. The financial health of the reporting entity is, after all, a function of its ability to generate cash surpluses and to finance the expansion of its operations in a prudent manner.

Amending the layout of the funds statement allows the user to focus on these issues. The transactions listed in Example 7.1 could, for example, be summarised as follows:

	£m
Net increase in borrowings	25
Cash shortfall from business operations	(10)
Finance available for capital expenditure	15
Capital expenditure during the period	15

The information shown above should be relevant to users' decision-making needs. It suggests that although the company may have been profitable during its first year of trading its financial health might be cause for concern. Unless it is able to generate a cash surplus from its business operations in the future, it is unlikely to be able to make distributions to its owners or repay the loan taken out to finance the purchase of its premises. Information of this kind is not evident from the profit and loss account or the balance sheet.

If the unsold stock and the uncollected debtors are both considered to be recoverable, the profit and loss account would show a gross profit of £10 million. Non-depreciation of the premises would cause the surplus of £10 million to contribute towards a healthy excess of assets over liabilities in the balance sheet. The gross profit of £10 million would cover the interest payable on the borrowings of £25 million. Given the potential usefulness of the information contained in the funds statement, it is surprising that users tended to ignore it. Example 7.1 is rather simplistic. The value of the funds statement is best demonstrated by a live example.

Interpreting the funds statement in practice

The calculation of Cadbury Schweppes' 1990 gearing ratio was discussed in Chapter 5. The company's consolidated financial statements for that year are a good example of the value of the information contained in the funds statement. To place the information in its proper context, it is necessary to take a brief look at the profit and loss account for that year and the balance sheet at the end of it. This enables the funds statement to be used as a backdrop against which to assess the allocation process used to create the profit and loss account and the balance sheet. The key features of the group's profit and loss accounts for 1990 and 1989 have been summarised in the following extract:

Illustration 7.1: *Cadbury Schweppes Public Limited Company (1990)*

GROUP PROFIT AND LOSS ACCOUNT
For the 52 weeks ended 29 December 1990 (extract)

	1990 £m	1989 £m
Sales	3,146.1	2,776.7
Trading Profit	333.9	272.6
Share of profits of associated undertakings	2.9	2.8
Net interest	(57.2)	(31.1)
Profit on Ordinary Activities Before Taxation	279.6	244.3
Tax on profit on ordinary activities	(78.0)	(69.5)
Profit attributable to minority interests	(22.2)	(17.0)
Profit before Extraordinary Items	179.4	157.8
Earnings Per Ordinary Share of 25p:		
Net basis	25.29p	24.22p

As noted at the start of this chapter, the profit and loss account is a product of an accounting allocation process. It consists of most, but not all, of the current year's transactions plus an allocation of others from previous years. Viewing the profit and loss account in isolation ignores the unallocated portion of the transactions entered into in the current and previous years. To gain a proper understanding of the reporting entity's activities, it is necessary to consider the balance sheet as well. Under the existing accounting framework, the balance sheet is a by-product of the allocation process that creates the profit and loss account. In addition to other items, it contains the 'bits left over from the profit and loss account', as explained by David Solomons in an earlier section of this chapter.

Illustration 7.2: Cadbury Schweppes Public Limited Company (1990)

SUMMARISED GROUP BALANCE SHEETS (extract)

	1990	1989	1988
	£m	£m	£m
Assets Employed			
Stock	328.2	334.8	253.4
Debtors	554.1	548.2	434.5
Cash, loans and deposits	180.6	90.7	242.0
	1,062.9	973.7	929.9
Short term borrowings	(136.3)	(133.7)	(114.1)
Other creditors and provisions	(934.3)	(933.2)	(736.8)
	(7.7)	(93.2)	79.0
Fixed assets	1,299.5	1,155.1	727.2
	1,291.8	1,061.9	806.2
	1990	1989	1988
	£m	£m	£m
Financed by:			
Capital of Cadbury Schweppes plc	174.7	173.6	153.7
Reserves	593.2	421.7	436.6
Perpetual subordinated loan	118.9	–	–
Long term loans	289.0	381.4	124.7
Minority interests	116.0	85.2	91.2
	1,291.8	1,061.9	806.2

The extract shown above has been taken from the table of summarised group balance sheets on page 33 of the 1990 Annual Report. Its format is accordingly very different to that specified by the Companies Act 1985.

The summarised balance sheets reveal that the unallocated portion of past transactions can be substantial. The amounts shown for fixed assets are a good example. At the 1990 balance sheet date, the largest items in this category were brand names (£304.0 million), land and buildings (£355.4 million) and plant and equipment (£554.6 million). The usefulness of the profit and loss account as a measure of financial performance depends to a significant extent on the treatment of these debits. Allocating them to individual reporting periods requires the preparer to predict the outcome of uncertain future events. How much revenue will be generated by these assets in the future? When will the revenue be earned?

The value of the information contained in the profit and loss account is clearly dependent on the reliability of the predictions made by its preparer. The funds statement is, by contrast, not based on predictions about the outcome of uncertain future events. It is simply a record of the transactions that have taken place during the year. It does not attempt to allocate capital expenditure debits to individual reporting periods. It is not concerned with the saleability of unsold stock. It ignores the collectability of unpaid debtors. It is true that it also ignores unpaid liabilities, yet this does not destroy its usefulness if it is interpreted correctly.

To draw the right conclusions from the funds statement, it is helpful to simplify its presentation. The problem with the traditional layout is that it contains too much

Illustration 7.3: Cadbury Schweppes Public Limited Company (1990)

STATEMENT OF GROUP SOURCE AND APPLICATION OF FUNDS (extract)

	1990 £m	1989 £m
Funds generated from operations		
Trading profit	333.9	272.6
Depreciation	99.3	79.6
Dividends from associates	0.4	0.4
	433.6	352.6
Changes in working capital		
Stock	21.0	(34.4)
Debtors	13.4	14.2
Creditors	(3.0)	14.2
Exchange restatement of working capital	(20.9)	2.6
	10.5	(3.4)
Changes in fixed assets		
Purchases of tangible assets	(212.8)	(200.2)
Disposals of tangible assets	27.8	17.1
Net change in investments	7.3	(2.8)
	(177.7)	(185.9)
Cash flow from operations	266.4	163.3
Net interest	(57.2)	(31.1)
Tax paid	(83.0)	(59.8)
Dividends paid to shareholders and minorities	(82.0)	(64.4)
	(222.2)	(155.3)
Net movement of funds after financing costs and tax	44.2	8.0
Shares issued	165.3	26.8
Acquisition of subsidiary undertakings [net of cash and borrowings acquired]	(147.2)	(428.6)
Non-operating items	(41.9)	(23.9)
Net inflow/(outflow) of funds	20.4	(417.7)
Net borrowings		
Net borrowings/(cash) at beginning of year	424.4	(3.2)
Exchange restatement	(40.4)	9.9
Net (inflow)/outflow of funds	(20.4)	417.7
Net borrowings at end of year	363.6	424.4

information, thereby complicating the task of analysing it. Much of the information is designed to reconcile the statement to the profit and loss account and the balance sheet. This could be relegated to a supporting note, to enable the user to focus on the more important features of the statement.

Before revising the layout of the funds statement, the matter raised at the end of Chapter 5 needs to be addressed. Cadbury Schweppes made an issue of redeemable preference shares during 1990 as part of its strategy to place greater emphasis on longer term funding. The group decided to exclude the preference shares from the denominator in the gearing ratio, at their redemption value of £152.1 million. How should the preference share issue be reflected in the funds statement?

The 1990 source and application of funds statement (see Illustration 7.3) shows that net borrowings declined from £424.4 million at the beginning of that year to £363.6 million at its end. The company's 1990 Annual Report sheds some light on one of the reasons for the reduction. It points out that:

> The interest cover ratio would have been marginally lower if we had not re-financed part of our borrowings by the issue of preference shares. This factor, in particular, has led us to give more attention to the fixed charge ratio. In concept, this is similar to interest cover but modified to incorporate other commitments, namely preference dividends (grossed up for tax) and the financing element of operating lease rentals.

The extract suggests that the finance sourced from the issue of the preference shares could be regarded as being more in the nature of borrowings than permanent equity. In revising the layout of the funds statement to achieve the objectives described earlier in this chapter, it seems appropriate to include the preference shares in the same section as the change in net borrowings. This enables the statement to highlight the use of funds provided by bankers and other financiers in the operation and expansion of the business.

What conclusions can be drawn from the information contained in the revised funds statement below? The first, and most important, is that the group's capital expenditure has been soundly financed. There is a healthy mix of finance from internal and external sources. The group's business operations have generated large cash surpluses in both years. Portion of this surplus has been returned to shareholders in the form of dividends. The balance has been reinvested in further expansion of the business.

Whether the capital expenditure represents money well spent is another matter entirely. It is beyond the scope of financial statements to predict the outcome of investments made by the reporting entity. The funds statement does, nevertheless, provide a reliable basis for believing that the business is in good financial shape. It confirms the favourable impression gained from the profit and loss account and the balance sheet. Existing operations have generated a cash surplus that could be returned to shareholders or reinvested in the business. The volatility of these surpluses is such that undue emphasis should not be placed on one year's results. Because it is not being managed on a one year time perspective, the need to judge management's performance over a longer period should, however be obvious to shareholders.

Example 7.2: *Cadbury Schweppes Public Limited Company*

REVISED FUNDS STATEMENT

	1990 £m	1989 £m
Net borrowings/(cash) and preference shares		
at beginning of the year	424.4	(3.2)
exchange restatement	(40.4)	9.9
at end of the year	515.7	424.4
Net increase during the year	131.7	417.7
Other sources of finance		
Share issues (excluding preference shares)	13.2	26.8
Business operations†	180.0	170.0
Total finance available for capital expenditure	324.9	614.5
Capital expenditure during the year		
Acquisition of subsidiary undertakings*	147.2	428.6
Purchases of tangible assets	212.8	200.2
Disposals of tangible assets	(27.8)	(17.1)
Net change in investments	(7.3)	2.8
	324.9	614.5

* After adjusting for cash and borrowings in the acquired entities.

† This figure would be reconciled to the profit and loss account in a supporting note. It comprises the following items extracted from Illustration 7.3 above: funds generated from operations, changes in working capital, net interest, tax paid, dividends paid to shareholders and minorities and non-operating items.

DIFFICULTIES WITH THE FUNDS STATEMENT

The source and application of funds statement is not an ideal document from which to prepare the revised funds statement outlined in this chapter. There are three major difficulties:

- The revised funds statement is heavily dependent on the distinction between cash flows resulting from capital expenditure decisions and those which are part of the other activities of the business. It is not possible to derive these figures with complete accuracy from the source and application of funds statement. For example, the 1990 changes in Cadbury Schweppes' debtors and creditors of £13.4 million and minus £3.0 million respectively (see Illustration 7.3 above), do not distinguish between fixed asset and other items. It is therefore necessary to scrutinise the 'Other debtors' and 'Other creditors' notes to see whether an adjustment should be made to the amounts shown under the 'Capital expenditure during the year' heading in the revised funds statement.

- When the reporting entity enters into a finance lease, the revised funds statement shows capital expenditure financed by an increase in borrowings (finance lease creditors are included under this heading). When this happens, the statement loses its objectivity because the finance lease entry is dependent on the preparer's interpretation of the lease agreement. There has not been an actual outflow of cash. It would be preferable to show the lease payments actually made during the year. Whether they are included under capital expenditure or as part of business operations is unlikely to make a significant difference to the user's ability to draw meaningful conclusions from the revised funds statement.
- The revised funds statement is only as good as the definition of the reporting entity. The problems associated with the inclusion or exclusion of certain subsidiaries and associates were outlined in Chapter 4. Because the funds statement is based on the consolidated financial statements, it will also be affected by the same problems.

The first and second of the difficulties noted above were resolved by the introduction of FRS 1 *Cash flow statements* in September 1991.

SOLVED BY THE CASH FLOW STATEMENT?

The introduction of FRS 1 will undoubtedly make it easier to produce a revised funds statement of the kind described in this chapter. Because the new standard focuses entirely on cash flows, it is a more useful document than its SSAP 10 predecessor. It also allows the user to locate the cash flows relating to the purchase and sale of fixed assets without difficulty. Presenting a revised cash flow statement along the lines of the revised funds statement is a relatively straightforward matter.

It might be argued that the new FRS 1 statement is a good approximation of the revised funds statement proposed in this chapter. It is true that the FRS 1 statement contains all the relevant information. Its emphasis on cash and so-called 'cash equivalents' means, however, that its layout is far from satisfactory. Its usefulness would be significantly enhanced by making a few alterations to its prescribed format. The nature of the problem is evident from the following extracts:

Illustration 7.4: Dunhill Holdings PLC (1992)

Note:
For the purposes of this consolidated statement of cash flows, which has been prepared in accordance with Financial Reporting Standard No. 1, cash and cash equivalents represent liquid funds having original maturities of up to three months. As will be seen from note f on page 28, the Group also has substantial bank deposits which at 31st March 1992 amounted to £162,514,000 (1991: £110,561,000). These are held with major banks and are generally placed on 12-month deposit but FRS 1 does not permit them to be treated as cash and cash equivalents.
The directors consider that this statement of cash flow is therefore of limited use in assessing the true liquidity of the Group.

Illustration 7.5: *Pearson plc (1991)*

Cash flow statements will be mandatory for 1992 under the new Financial Reporting Standard. The audited source and application of funds is shown on page 42, but the above unaudited summary shows the new format.

The Pearson source and application of funds contains two key measures: the movement in net debt (down £287 million) and the net movement of funds from operations (an inflow of £18 million). The new standard will make them both much less visible:

- there is a very narrow definition of 'cash and cash equivalents'. All other movements in liquid funds are treated as an investing activity thus reducing the apparent net cash inflow before financing in 1991 by £141 million; and
- the net cash inflow before financing is also calculated after acquisitions and disposals, making it harder to show whether the business is generating or consuming cash.

FRS 1's emphasis on the movement in cash and 'cash equivalents' makes it difficult to identify the change in the reporting entity's net borrowings. This figure is an essential part of the revised funds statement shown in Example 7.2. It is also needed in order to reconcile the cash flow information to the interest payable and receivable figures in the profit and loss account. The usefulness of this reconciliation is illustrated by the following example.

Example 7.3

Company B sells the same number of items in every month of the year. The cost of its first year's sales amounts to £60 million. Goods are marked up by 100 per cent on cost. Customers, who always pay on due date, are allowed a month's credit except in January when all the goods are sold for cash at their cost price. Annual sales total £115 million. The stock figure represents 3 months' purchases (or £15 million), except at the end of the January sales when it is allowed to fall to 2 month's purchases (or £10 million). Suppliers are paid on delivery of the goods in order to take advantage of trade discounts.

The company started trading on 1 February 19x1. Its first balance sheet is prepared at 31 January 19x2. If interest and all other transactions are ignored, would a cash flow statement covering the year to 31 January 19x2 provide comprehensive information about the company's sources and uses of cash?

The FRS 1 statement would reflect the following cash flows:

	£m
Cash inflow from operating activities*	45
Increase in cash and cash equivalents	45

*Profit of £55 million reduced by an increase in stock of £10 million.

What the statement does not reveal is that the company used a bank overdraft to finance its investment in stock and debtors for the first four months of the financial year. A breakdown of the FRS 1 statement showing the cumulative cash flows at the end of each month would be as follows:

End of Month: £ million	1	2	3	4	5	6	7	8	9	10	11	12
Cash (outflow)/inflow from operating activities	(20)	(15)	(10)	(5)	0	5	10	15	20	25	30	45
(Decrease)/Increase in cash and cash equivalents	(20)	(15)	(10)	(5)	0	5	10	15	20	25	30	45

At the end of the first month, the profit of £5 million shown in the profit and loss account is offset by an increase in stock of £15 million and an increase in debtors of £10 million. A payment of £20 million was made to suppliers for the goods sold in that month and to build up the stock on hand to three months' sales. Credit granted to customers meant that there were no cash inflows in the first month.

An interest rate of 12 per cent per annum would enable the company to earn net interest of approximately £1 million in the year. This is significantly less than that implied by the cash inflow of £45 million from operating activities. Although the company eventually accumulated a large cash surplus, the FRS 1 statement does not reveal the timing or direction of the cash flows during the year.

It would clearly be helpful if the information contained in the cash flow statement could be reconciled to the interest payable and receivable amounts shown in the profit and loss account. Pearson plc's view that its source and application of funds statement made the change in the group's net debt more visible than the new FRS 1 statement is significant. It is the opening and closing net debt figures that have to be reconciled to the net interest charge in the profit and loss account. The FRS 1 statement is clearly an improvement on the funds statement. Its value to the user would be enhanced by a simple revision of its layout along the lines suggested for the revised funds statement in Example 7.2.

CONCLUSION

Users of financial statements are in a fortunate position. They are provided with a profit and loss account, a balance sheet and a record of the transactions from which the first two statements are derived. This chapter has explained how the profit and loss account and the balance sheet interrelate, how one is derived from the other and how they reflect 'different aspects of the same transactions or other events.' The chapter has also stressed that the two statements are only as good as the accounting allocation process which creates them.

Users wishing to unravel the profit and loss account and the balance sheet have been able to do so without difficulty since SSAP 10 was introduced. The funds statement does not reveal whether the reporting entity has made a profit or a loss. It does not purport to show the value of its assets nor the extent of its obligations to third parties. It does not allow users to calculate a gearing ratio. It does not attempt to allocate the acquisition of subsidiaries or fixed assets to individual reporting periods. It does not attempt to amortise goodwill and other intangible fixed assets. It is not concerned with the establishment of reorganisation provisions. Despite all these limitations it is a document of great value to users of financial statements. Their good fortune has recently been increased by the introduction of the FRS 1 cash flow statement.

Users have, however, shown little inclination to give the funds statement the attention it deserves. Whether the cash flow statement will be more successful in diverting their attention from the profit and loss account and the balance sheet remains to be seen. The newspaper articles covering THORN EMI's acquisition of the Virgin Music Group seem preoccupied with the intangible nature of the latter's assets and the impact of the transaction on THORN's earnings per share. Relying on the profit and loss account and the balance sheet to provide useful information for decision-making purposes may not be sufficient. Investors in Polly Peck International will be aware of the pitfalls of adopting this approach. Users of financial statements need a backdrop against which to assess the accounting allocations that give rise to the profit and loss account and the balance sheet.

1   Accounting Standards Board (1991), 'The objective of financial statements', Exposure Draft of Chapter 1, *Statement of Principles* (London: ASB), July, para. 12.
2   *Ibid.*, para. 20.
3   Solomons, David (1989), 'Guidelines for Financial Reporting Standards', paper prepared for the Research Board of the Institute of Chartered Accountants in England and Wales, addressed to the Accounting Standards Committee (London: ICAEW), p. 20.
4   *Ibid.*, p. 21.
5   Paterson, Ron (1990), 'Primacy For The P&L Account', *Accountancy,* August, p. 82.
6   Solomons, David, 'Guidelines for Financial Reporting Standards', p. 18.
7   THORN EMI plc, Note 30 to the 1992 Accounts.
8   Accounting Standards Board (1992), FRS 3, *Reporting Financial Performance* (London: ASB), October, para. 37.
9   Accounting Standards Board (1991), 'The qualitative characteristics of financial information', Exposure Draft of Chapter 2, *Statement of Principles* (London: ASB), July, para. 23.
10 *Ibid.*, para. 26.

8: The Collapse of Polly Peck International

The art of prophecy is very difficult –
especially with respect to the future

Mark Twain

INTRODUCTION

Chapter 7 outlined the advantage of having a backdrop against which to assess the accounting allocation process which creates the profit and loss account and the balance sheet. The disadvantages of relying on these two statements as the primary sources of financial information about the reporting entity have been stressed throughout this book. The purpose of this chapter is to examine whether closer analysis of the funds statement might have assisted users of the last financial statements produced by Polly Peck International PLC. It also questions whether the traditional ratio based approach to financial analysis is capable of dealing with the uncertainties, estimates and predictions which underlie the preparation of the profit and loss account and the balance sheet.

BACKGROUND

On 17 April 1990, the directors of Polly Peck International PLC approved the company's financial statements for the year ended 31 December 1989. In his annual statement, the company's chairman commented that:

> 1989 was a remarkable year for Polly Peck International. It was a fitting conclusion to a decade in which we were one of the UK's fastest growing industrial and commercial companies, an achievement that was crowned by the purchase of two of the world's leading brand names. From modest beginnings as a small trading company, PPI has become a major force in the complex markets of food and electronics, and is well placed to benefit from the anticipated growth in world leisure in the 1990s. Our coming of age was aptly reflected in our admission during 1989 to the Financial Times Stock Exchange 100 share index. These are achievements to be proud of — as are our financial results for 1989.[1]

Illustration 8.1: *Polly Peck International PLC (1989)*

FINANCIAL HIGHLIGHTS (extract)

	12 months ended 31st December 1989 £ million	12 months ended 31st December 1988 £ million
TURNOVER	1,162.3	761.0
PROFIT ON ORDINARY ACTIVITIES BEFORE TAXATION	161.4	112.2
SHAREHOLDERS FUNDS	843.7	386.2
EARNINGS PER SHARE		
Basic	44.6p	40.6p
Fully diluted	43.2p	37.1p
NET DIVIDENDS PER ORDINARY SHARE	13.0p	9.5p

Note: Figures for 1988 are pro-forma, based on the audited results for the 16 months to 31st December 1988.

With annual turnover of £1.162 billion and shareholders' funds of £843.7 million, Polly Peck International PLC (PPI) was a large company. At 31 December 1989, its 378.7 million ordinary shares were quoted at 393p each on the London Stock Exchange. This price valued the whole company at £1,488 million. Its admission to the FTSE-100 share index confirmed its status as one of the larger companies in the UK.

The chairman's satisfaction with the group's financial results for 1989 appeared to be well founded. As shown in Illustration 8.1, turnover had increased by 53 per cent on the 1988 figure, profit before tax by 44 per cent and fully diluted earnings per share by 16.4 per cent. The chairman concluded his annual statement with the following comments about the group's future prospects:

> PPI intends to continue its unbroken record of growth and profitability into the 1990s and beyond. We will continually seek new sources for our existing product ranges, new products to expand those ranges and new markets into which to sell these products.
>
> ...Our financial objective remains to increase shareholder value through strong growth in earnings per share. We are also determined to ensure that PPI's share price reflects the true value of its underlying businesses. We are therefore continuing to examine a number of possibilities for restructuring our operating businesses, with this aim in mind.
>
> In conclusion, I am confident that 1990 will be an exciting start to a second decade of growth for the Group, and that the strategy we develop in the 1990s will be as successful as that implemented during the 1980s.[2]

The strategy implemented during the 1980s had indeed been very successful, especially when measured in terms of the return earned for shareholders. On 16 December 1989 *The Times* reported that PPI's shares had outperformed all other companies in the FTA All-share index during the period from end-December 1979 to end-November 1989. The newspaper article contained a table showing the top 10 performers during this period. To put Polly Peck's performance into perspective, that of several other well-known companies has been shown alongside the top 10 performers:

Top 10	%	Others	%
Polly Peck	120,545	Sainsbury	1,361
Albert Fisher	8,218	BTR	1,300
Mountleigh	4,109	BAT Inds	1,260
Williams Hdgs	4,065	Sun Alliance	878
Hazlewood Foods	4,005	Tesco	749
Priest Marians	3,861	Unilever	662
Southend Prop	3,325	Legal & General	651
Securicor Group	3,117	Lucas Inds	179
Wilson Connolly	2,698	BP	176
Glaxo	2,677	Midland Bank	107

Source: County NatWest Wood Mackenzie. Performance from end-December 1979 to end-November 1989.

The chairman's belief that 1990 would be a good year for PPI was reinforced five months after the publication of the 1989 Annual Report. On 3 September 1990, interim results covering the six months to 30 June 1990 were released. The announcement contained the following statement on Current Trading and Prospects:

> I am aware that unease has been expressed in some parts of the investment community and in the financial press as to the likely effects of the current situation in the Gulf. PPI's trading exposure to Iraq and Kuwait is minimal.
>
> Your Directors are confident that, based on current trading, the remainder of the financial year will continue to be highly successful. Furthermore, the Company is well-placed to grasp the opportunities that the 1990s will provide, enabling continued strong growth in earnings per share.[3]

The profit and loss account for the six months to 30 June 1990 provided ample support for the chairman's claim that:

> These record results are a comprehensive endorsement of the Group's strategy, and a tribute to the skills and efforts of its management and staff in carrying it out. Sales, operating profits, pre-tax profits and earnings per share have, once again, all advanced strongly to record levels. In particular, the results are clear evidence of the Board's commitment to increasing the rate of growth in earnings per share.[4]

Illustration 8.2: *Polly Peck International PLC (Interim Financial Statement 1990)*

UNAUDITED CONSOLIDATED PROFIT AND LOSS ACCOUNT for the half-year to 30th June 1990 (extract)	Half-year to 30th June 1990 £ million	Half-year to 30th June 1989 £ million
SALES	880.7	512.3
Operating costs	(752.7)	(452.8)
Share of profits of related companies	0.8	0.2
OPERATING PROFIT	128.8	59.7
Net interest and investment income	(18.3)	4.7
PROFIT BEFORE TAXATION	110.5	64.4
Taxation on ordinary activities	(16.4)	(9.6)
PROFIT ON ORDINARY ACTIVITIES AFTER TAXATION	94.1	54.8
Minority interests	2.8	(0.5)
Extraordinary item (profit on flotation of minority shareholding)	40.5	–
PROFIT ATTRIBUTABLE TO SHAREHOLDERS	137.4	54.3
Dividends	(26.1)	(12.9)
RETAINED PROFIT FOR THE PERIOD	111.3	41.4
EARNINGS PER SHARE		
Basic	22.4p	17.8p
Fully diluted	21.5p	16.6p
DIVIDEND PER ORDINARY SHARE	5.5p	4.5p

Eleven days after publication of the half-yearly results, Carr, Kitcat & Aitken released the analyst's research report referred to in Chapter 6. It estimated that profit before tax for the year to 31 December 1990 would increase substantially on the corresponding 1989 figure of £161.4 million. The rate of growth predicted by the analyst was probably influenced by the actual improvement of 72 per cent achieved in the half-year and the chairman's expectation that 'based on current trading, the remainder of the financial year will continue to be highly successful.'

Six days later, a mere seventeen after the release of the Interim Results, trading in Polly Peck International's shares was suspended on the London Stock Exchange. The following extract is taken from the *Financial Times* of 21 September 1990, the day after the suspension of the shares:

Polly Peck chief seen by fraud office as shares suspended

Polly Peck International, the fruit trading and consumer electronics group, was last night facing the worst crisis in its turbulent history as Mr Asil Nadir, chairman and largest shareholder, was interviewed by the Serious Fraud Office.

Mr Nadir left the SFO's headquarters in Elm Street, central London, at 6.30 pm after several hours of questioning. He sat smoking a cigarette in the back of a car which followed his own maroon Jaguar.

News of his visit coincided with a collapse in Polly Peck's share price. It lost more than half its market value, falling from £1.05bn to less than £468m before trading was suspended at 2.21pm yesterday.

PPI never recovered from this crisis. Trading in the shares did not resume. The company was placed in administration on 25 October 1990 and its shares are today considered to be worthless. Within six months of the publication of the 1989 Annual Report, shareholders' investments worth in excess of £1,000 million had been lost. The unaudited Interim Financial Statement, released within one month of the share suspension, gave no hint of the impending disaster. The balance sheet at 30 June 1990 showed shareholders' funds of £932.7 million.

ANALYSING THE FINANCIAL STATEMENTS

The purpose of this section is to outline how the average user might have tackled the task of analysing Polly Peck International's 1989 Annual Report. Were users guided by the information contained in the profit and loss account and the balance sheet? Is the traditional approach, of using financial ratios to analyse and interpret the financial statements, capable of dealing with the estimates, uncertainties and predictions which underlie the preparation of the profit and loss account and the balance sheet?

The user's first step would probably be to turn to the profit and loss account and the balance sheet. The consolidated profit and loss account for the year to 31 December 1989 has been reproduced in the following extract:

Illustration 8.3: Polly Peck International PLC (1989)		
CONSOLIDATED PROFIT AND LOSS ACCOUNT (extract)		
	12 months ended 31 December 1989	16 months ended 31 December 1988
	£ million	£ million
TURNOVER	1,162.3	967.1
Cost of sales	866.1	707.5
Gross Profit	296.2	259.6
Distribution costs	47.1	27.9
Administration expenses	110.1	85.0
TRADING PROFIT	139.0	146.7
Other income	77.4	38.0
	216.4	184.7
Interest payable	55.6	40.6
	160.8	144.1
Share of results of related companies	0.6	–
PROFIT ON ORDINARY ACTIVITIES BEFORE TAXATION	161.4	144.1
Taxation on ordinary activities	22.8	24.5
Profit on ordinary activities after taxation	138.6	119.6
Minority interest	0.9	1.7
Profit before extraordinary items	137.7	117.9
Extraordinary items	–	0.9
Profit for the financial period	137.7	118.8
Dividends	49.3	26.1
RETAINED PROFIT FOR THE FINANCIAL PERIOD	88.4	92.7
EARNINGS PER ORDINARY SHARE		
Basic	44.6	53.0
Fully diluted	43.2	48.4

The profit and loss accounts shown above present the user with an immediate problem. The comparative column for 1988 shows the group's results for a sixteen-month period. In that year, the company's financial year-end was changed from August to December. The 1988 financial statements prepared for statutory purposes were therefore required to cover the sixteen months from the beginning of September 1987 to the end of December 1988.

The statutory reporting requirement is not particularly helpful because most users want to make a line-by-line comparison of the current year's figures with those of the previous year. This is generally regarded as a useful starting point for an evaluation of the company's financial performance. Has the current year been better than the previous one? What is the rate of growth in earnings per share? A sixteen-month period in the comparative column makes it impossible to answer these questions.

PPI's solution was to calculate pro-forma figures for the 12 months to 31 December 1988, 'based on the audited results for the 16 months to 31 December 1988.'[5] The pro-forma figures are reproduced in Illustration 8.1 at the start of this chapter. Users will probably insert growth percentages next to the key figures:

Example 8.1: *Polly Peck International PLC*

CALCULATING GROWTH RATES

	12 months ended 31 December 1989 £ million	12 months ended 31 December 1988 £ million	Growth
TURNOVER	1,162.3	761.0	+53%
PROFIT ON ORDINARY ACTIVITIES			
BEFORE TAXATION	161.4	112.2	+44%
SHAREHOLDERS FUNDS	843.7	386.2	
EARNINGS PER SHARE			
Basic	44.6p	40.6p	+10%
Fully diluted	43.2p	37.1p	+16%

Source: 1989 Annual Report.

The trends shown above suggest that 1989 was a good year for the group. A substantial portion of the increase in turnover and pre-tax profit appears to be due to additional finance raised in the 3-for-7 rights issue during the year. In these circumstances, the earnings per share calculation is normally regarded as a better guide to the underlying growth rate. It adjusts for the impact of the new shares issued during the year. Users will probably use analytical review techniques to aid their analysis and interpretation of the profit and loss account.

Example 8.2: *Polly Peck International PLC*

RATIO ANALYSIS

Financial year ended:	Note	Dec 89	*Dec 88	Aug 87	Aug 86	Aug 85
Profit and loss account						
Gross profit margin (%)	(i)	25.5	26.8	35.7	36.0	38.1
Trading profit margin (%)	(ii)	12.0	15.2	24.6	27.8	31.0
Pre-tax profit margin (%)	(iii)	13.9	14.9	22.6	25.7	29.7
Interest cover (times)	(iv)	3.9	4.5	5.0	6.0	11.7
Dividend cover (times)	(v)	3.4	4.9	6.5	8.3	10.0

*16 month period.
Source: Company Annual Reports.

In order to place the 1989 figures in context, the ratios are usually calculated for a five year period. They are designed to provide a better understanding of the key features of the group's financial performance. The ratios are normally evaluated in absolute terms and relative to those calculated for previous years.

A technique similar to this is sometimes used by the auditor to determine whether there are any anomalies in the financial statements. Unusual percentages and trends would be investigated with the company's management.

The significance of each ratio shown in Example 8.2 could be explained as follows:

(i) The gross profit margin represents gross profit expressed as a percentage of turnover. A high percentage is usually indicative of a manufacturing or primary industry. The declining trend shown in Example 8.2 suggests a change in the mix of the group's activities.

(ii) The trading profit margin represents trading profit expressed as a percentage of turnover. The comments under (i) above also apply here. The ratio is similar except that it takes distribution costs and administrative expenses into account.

(iii) The pre-tax profit margin represents pre-tax profit expressed as a percentage of turnover. Comparing this ratio with the trading profit margin reveals the impact of non-trading income and the cost of servicing the group's borrowings.

(iv) Interest cover represents trading profit plus other income, divided by interest payable. It reveals whether the group's profit is large enough for it to be able to pay the interest due on its borrowings. Although a declining trend is usually cause for concern, the 1989 figure suggests that the risk of default is relatively low.

(v) Dividend cover represents earnings per share divided by dividends per share. It reveals the proportion of profit distributed to shareholders by way of dividend. The figures shown in Example 8.2 are indicative of a prudent distribution policy. A high proportion of profit is being retained in the business to finance its growth.

The analysis done so far would probably enable the user to draw the following conclusions:

- There has been a significant expansion in the scale of the group's activities in 1989, as evidenced by the large increase in turnover.
- Because the expansion was financed by a further issue of shares in 1989, the earnings per share figure has not increased at the same rate as the growth in turnover and pre-tax profit.
- Profit margins are healthy but the declining trend requires further investigation. It could be indicative of a change in the mix of the group's activities.
- The group is able to service its commitments to lenders and shareholders without difficulty. The declining trend in interest cover could be indicative of financing strain caused by rapid growth. It should also be investigated further.

The search for answers to the two issues raised above would usually involve closer examination of the annual report. This would reveal that profit margins had been affected by two main factors. The first was the increasing importance of the lower-margin Electronics division. In 1989, it accounted for 42 per cent of the group's turnover, compared with 14 per cent in 1985. The second was the declining margin in the Food division. A satisfactory explanation was provided on page 11 of the 1989 Annual Report:

> Net margins fell during 1989, reflecting the acquisition of our newly acquired downstream activities. This does not imply a deterioration of the business, as vertical integration allows us to guarantee outlets for our products, and so improve the quality of those margins.

The fall in interest cover would probably prompt the user to turn to the balance sheet, to see whether the group's borrowings were at a manageable level. The 1989 Financial Review contained the following commentary on the group's finances:

> In a year that has seen such important corporate developments for PPI, the Group's financial strategy remained unaltered, namely:
>
> - to maintain an adequate equity base, so enabling the Group to take advantage of opportunities as they arise;
> - to extend the maturity profile of the Group's borrowings;
> - to reduce the cost of servicing Group debt.
>
> We are particularly pleased with the progress that has been made in all these areas and with the resultant strength of the Group's financial structure. This will enable us to continue our growth in the 1990s.[6]

The Finance Director's satisfaction with the state of the group's finances would appear to be borne out by an examination of the 1989 balance sheet. In the extract which follows, two changes have been made to the layout actually used by PPI. Borrowings have been shown separately from other creditors on the face of the balance sheet. The necessary information was extracted from the creditors' notes. The second change was to condense the four columns actually used into two.

Illustration 8.4: Polly Peck International PLC (1989)

CONSOLIDATED BALANCE SHEET (extract)	1989 £m	1988 £m
FIXED ASSETS		
Acquired brands at cost	284.5	–
Tangible assets	1,015.8	514.8
Bank deposits	51.1	–
Investments	18.3	4.8
	1,369.7	519.6
CURRENT ASSETS		
Stocks and work in progress	246.5	128.1
Debtors	459.6	203.1
Cash and bank balances	249.3	124.2
	955.4	455.4
CREDITORS		
Borrowings	387.5	84.5
Other amounts falling due within one year	336.2	191.9
	723.7	276.4
NET CURRENT ASSETS	231.7	179.0
TOTAL ASSETS LESS CURRENT LIABILITIES	1,601.4	698.6
CREDITORS		
Borrowings	716.7	291.6
Other amounts falling due after more than one year	36.8	4.1
	753.5	295.7
PROVISION FOR LIABILITIES AND CHARGES		
Deferred tax	2.6	1.4
	845.3	401.5
CAPITAL AND RESERVES		
Called up share capital	38.5	25.1
Share premium account	478.3	186.5
Revaluation reserve	254.8	148.1
Other reserves	0.4	0.4
Retained profit	71.7	26.1
	843.7	386.2
Minority interest	1.6	15.3
	845.3	401.5

The significant expansion of the group's activities evident from the profit and loss account is confirmed by the balance sheet. The extract from the Chairman's Statement at the start of this chapter referred to the purchase of 'two of the world's leading brand names.' The acquisition of the tropical fruit division of the Del Monte Corporation for £557 million was completed in December 1989. It established the group 'as one of the world's largest suppliers of fresh fruit and vegetables', making it 'the largest distributor of pineapples and the third largest distributor of bananas in the world.'[7] The other acquisition was the purchase of a controlling interest in Sansui Electric Company for £68.7 million. This transaction was completed in January 1990 and, accordingly, had no effect on the 1989 balance sheet.

The Del Monte acquisition, by contrast, had a dramatic impact on the balance sheet. Additions to fixed assets in 1989 totalled £790.2 million. Of this figure, £547 million is attributable to the Del Monte transaction. Together with other smaller acquisitions, it also accounted for 45 per cent of the increase in stocks, 37 per cent of the increase in debtors and virtually the entire increase in creditors other than borrowings.

Despite the need to finance approximately £300 million of the Del Monte purchase price by term loans, the balance sheet at 31 December 1989 looks healthy. The £843.7 million excess of assets over liabilities is a substantial figure by any standards. It was presumably the major reason for the Finance Director's satisfaction 'with the progress that has been made in all these areas and with the resultant strength of the group's financial structure.'

As with the profit and loss account, users will probably use analytical review techniques to aid their understanding of the consolidated balance sheet. The first two categories shown in the following table deal exclusively with the balance sheet. The profitability and activity ratios are, by contrast, designed to relate information in the profit and loss account to that contained in the balance sheet.

Example 8.3: *Polly Peck International PLC*

RATIO ANALYSIS	Note	Dec 89	*Dec 88	Aug 87	Aug 86	Aug 85
Liquidity						
Current ratio (times)	(i)	1.3	1.6	1.8	1.7	1.9
Quick ratio (times)	(ii)	1.0	1.2	1.3	1.3	1.4
Risk						
Gearing (%)	(iii)	95	66	69	51	56
Profitability (%)						
Return on assets employed	(iv)	12	23	30	37	46
Return on shareholders' funds	(v)	22	29	38	45	51
Activity						
Stock days	(vi)	78	64	77	67	80
Debtor days	(vii)	82	72	112	119	116
Creditor days	(viii)	38	36	35	25	33
Fixed asset turn (times)	(ix)	1.5	2.0	2.0	2.2	2.7

*12 month period.
Stock days and creditor days for 1988 are based on the gross profit percentage for the 16 month period.
Source: Company Annual Reports.

The significance of the individual ratios shown in Example 8.3 could be explained as follows.

(i)   The current ratio represents current assets divided by current liabilities. Because the ratio has been consistently higher than 1.0, it suggests that the group should have little difficulty in settling its current liabilities out of the proceeds of its current assets.

(ii) The quick ratio is a conservative variation of (i) above because it excludes stock from the current assets figure. Even when measured on this conservative basis, the conclusion is similar: the group's current liabilities are adequately covered by its current assets.

(iii) The gearing ratio in Example 8.3 is the debt/equity ratio as shown in the Annual Report.[8] A high percentage is not unusual immediately after a major acquisition partly financed by borrowings (Del Monte). It is also consistent with a relatively large investment in working capital (stock days plus debtor days less creditor days) and the relatively low fixed asset turn common in manufacturing industries.

(iv) Return on assets employed represents trading profit (before interest receivable and payable) divided by net assets (excluding cash and bank balances and all borrowings). The denominator is an average of the positions at the beginning and end of the year. The ratio reveals that the group is positively geared. The return earned on its assets exceeds the cost of servicing its borrowings. In these circumstances, shareholders' returns are enhanced by the use of borrowings to finance the assets employed.

(v)   Return on shareholders' funds represents profit for the period after extraordinary items divided by capital and reserves. As with (iv) above, the denominator is an average figure. No adjustment has been made for preference shares as these are relatively insignificant. The outcome has been boosted by the effective use of gearing as explained in (iv) above.

(vi) Stock days represents the average stock figure divided by cost of sales per day (360 per year). It is an indicator of the time taken to convert stock into sales.

(vii) Debtor days represents the average trade debtors figure divided by turnover per day (360 per year). It is an indicator of the time taken to convert trade debtors into cash.

(viii) Creditor days represents the average trade creditors figure divided by cost of sales per day (360 per year). It is an indicator of the finance provided by trade creditors.

Ratios (vi), (vii) and (viii) reveal the existence of a large investment in working capital. The need to finance this contributes towards the relatively high gearing ratio.

(ix) Fixed asset turn represents turnover divided by average tangible fixed assets. It is an indicator of the utilisation of the tangible fixed assets employed in the business. A low ratio is relatively common in manufacturing industries with a large investment in fixed capacity.

151

The ratios for 1989 have to be interpreted in the context of the Del Monte acquisition. Because it was completed shortly before the company's year-end, it would have had a proportionally greater effect on the balance sheet than on the profit and loss account. The additional share capital and new borrowings used to finance this transaction would obviously not have made their full contribution to profit in 1989. Allowing for the distorting effect of the Del Monte transaction, users will probably draw the following conclusions from the table of ratios shown in Example 8.3:

Positive features

- The group is extremely profitable. Because the returns earned on its assets are high, it should have little difficulty in servicing its borrowings.
- The liquidity position is sound. The current and quick ratios suggest the group should be able to pay its current liabilities as and when they fall due.
- Gearing seems to be at a manageable level given the nature of the business and the large acquisition made towards the end of the 1989 year.
- Working capital is being managed effectively. The cycle has been reduced from 160 days in 1985/86 to 122 days in 1989.

Features requiring further investigation

- The profitability ratios show a declining trend.
- The fixed asset turn is also in a downward phase.

Explanations for these trends could be obtained by further scrutiny of the company's annual reports. The profitability ratios have been clouded by the revaluation of fixed assets in 1988 and the share issues made in 1988 and 1989. If the revaluation reserve is ignored, the return on shareholders' funds in 1988 would be 42 per cent compared with 56 per cent in 1985. At 42 per cent, the 1988 figure is highly satisfactory. It is not possible to calculate a meaningful figure for 1989 as the Del Monte acquisition took place shortly before the year end.

The fixed asset turn has also been affected by the revaluation reserve. Excluding it produces a figure of 2.7 for 1988 compared with 3.1 in 1985. This could be attributed to a change in the mix of the business. The timing of the Del Monte transaction means that the 1989 figure is meaningless.

DRAWING A CONCLUSION FROM THE ANALYSIS

Having followed some or all of the techniques outlined in the previous section, what conclusion are users likely to draw from the financial information contained in the 1989 Annual Report? How would it affect their decision-making?

The financial statements reveal a company committed to expanding its operations; a profitable company, but one experiencing some financial strain caused by its rapid rate of growth and its large investment in working capital; a company with a fair spread of activities serving a range of geographic markets. Allowing for the usual distortions caused by changes in the mix of activities and the timing of acquisitions, there is no suggestion in any of the group's financial ratios that a financial disaster could be imminent.

The validity of this conclusion seems to be borne out by the behaviour of the group's financiers. The Financial Review in the 1989 Annual Report commented that:

> At the time of the Rights Issue in 1988, we said that we had no intention of calling on our shareholders for funds in the foreseeable future. Nevertheless, the opportunity to acquire Del Monte and all this would mean for PPI were so important that, after careful consideration, we decided that we would be justified in making such a call. The resulting Issue of 115 million shares at 245 pence per share to raise £280 million was an outstanding success, at a time when other companies were not faring so well. This is an encouraging reflection of the views held by the investing public – and particularly by existing PPI shareholders – both of the deal itself and of PPI.
>
> The balance of the Del Monte acquisition was funded by term loans of $475 million (£303 million) and working capital facilities of $75 million (£47.8 million). It is equally satisfying to record that applications to participate in these issues exceeded requirements by almost 200%.
>
> The investment of Yen 15.6 billion (£68.7 million) in Sansui was funded by the issue of $110 million (£68.6 million) of $7^{1}/4\%$ Convertible Preference shares, which avoided any increase in debt or the necessity for a further call on existing shareholders.
>
> Other achievements over the year included the continuation of the process started in 1988 of widening the range of banks with whom we have strong commercial relationships. The breadth of these relationships means that we have constant access to funds, should they be required, at competitive rates.[9]

The faith of the company's shareholders and bankers extended into 1990. The Chairman's statement in the 1990 Interim Financial Statement pointed out that:

> Shareholders will be aware that the shares of Vestel AS were floated on the Istanbul Stock Exchange in June 1990, where it is now capitalised at approximately £385 million. Sansui is currently capitalised at approximately £475 million, and the combined market value of PPI's holdings in these two companies is approximately £660 million, the equivalent of £1.56 per PPI ordinary share.

As noted in Chapter 6, PPI's ordinary shares were trading at a significantly higher price than 156p. Figure 8.1 shows the company's share price at the end of each quarter during the period from December 1987 to June 1990.

THE LIMITATIONS OF ANALYSIS

The discussion in the previous two sections has suggested how some users might go about analysing and interpreting financial statements. It was not designed to be a comprehensive study of user behaviour in this regard. Instead, its purpose was to

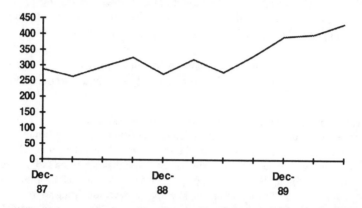

Figure 8.1. Polly Peck International PLC – quarterly share price in pence per share

highlight certain aspects of the methodology commonly used. Two observations are worth making:

- users seem to take the figures in the profit and loss account and the balance sheet for granted. The preparation of these documents is regulated by accounting standards. They are audited by independent, external auditors. They are assumed to be reliable;
- analytical review techniques can help to highlight anomalies in the financial statements. These techniques fail, however, to address the uncertainties inherent in the accounting allocation process that creates the profit and loss account and the balance sheet.

USING THE FUNDS STATEMENT AS A BACKDROP

Chapter 7 has suggested that there is another way of approaching the task of analysing financial statements. This method proceeds on the basis that the profit and loss account and the balance sheet are only as reliable as the accounting allocation process from which they are derived. Their integrity can never be guaranteed. There is a need for a backdrop against which to assess the predictions and estimates that have to be made to produce the profit and loss account and the balance sheet. This backdrop could take the form either of a funds statement or of a cash flow statement.

PPI's accountants had to deal with the same difficulties that always affect the preparation of a profit and loss account and a balance sheet. One of the issues which had to be addressed was the allocation to individual reporting periods of the £1 billion spent on the acquisition of the group's fixed assets . The following extracts show how they set about tackling this task:

Illustration 8.5: Polly Peck International PLC (1989)

ACCOUNTING POLICIES (extract)

DEPRECIATION AND AMORTISATION

Group freehold and long leasehold investment properties are not depreciated.

Provision for depreciation on freehold buildings where the remaining useful life exceeds 50 years is not considered to be necessary. It is the Group's policy to maintain its properties in good condition which prolongs their useful life and any depreciation involved would not be material. Depreciation is provided on a straight line basis on the cost or valuation of freehold buildings where the Directors consider that the remaining useful life is 50 years or less.
Short leasehold properties are amortised on a straight line basis over the periods of the leases.
Depreciation is provided on a straight line basis to write off the cost of other tangible fixed assets over their estimated useful lives at the following rates per annum

Plant and equipment	10-15%	Motor Vehicles	25%
Ships	7%	Aircraft	8%

ACQUIRED BRANDS

The fair value of businesses acquired includes a value, where appropriate, attributable to brands acquired with the business. These are recognised where a brand has a substantial long-term value, and earnings exceed those achieved by unbranded products. Amortisation will only be provided when the end of the useful economic life of the acquired brand can be foreseen. The useful economic life of brands and their carrying value will be subject to annual review and provision made against profits for any permanent impairment.

The company's Finance Director was sufficiently concerned about the appropriate accounting treatment of the acquired brands to include the following comments in his 1989 Financial Review:

> Brand management has become increasingly sophisticated, and brands themselves increasingly important in developing marketing strategies. This in turn has been reflected in high prices being paid to acquire companies with well-known brands. Currently accepted accounting principles suggest that costs of acquisitions in excess of the book value of tangible net assets should be written off against reserves. This implies that the cost of acquiring a brand is omitted from the acquirer's balance sheet. We, together with many other large companies and their auditors, believe this is wrong, as it understates the value of a company's assets and does not show a true and fair view of the state of its affairs.
>
> PPI wholeheartedly supports the inclusion of the cost of acquired brands in company balance sheets. Accordingly we have incorporated a value for the Del Monte brand name in these accounts, and will consider the valuation of the Sansui brand in 1990. We do not

believe that brands should automatically be depreciated, and it is therefore our intention that brand valuation will be reviewed annually, and a provision made against the value of acquired brands only if circumstances have led to a permanent decline in their value.[10]

Allocating the purchase price of fixed assets to individual reporting periods is a difficult process. One of the advantages of the funds statement is that it avoids having to wrestle with this problem. It allows the user to approach the subject from a different perspective. Instead of trying to allocate large sums of capital expenditure to individual reporting periods in a manner that requires predictions to be made about the timing and extent of future revenues, the funds statement concentrates on how the expenditure has been financed. It reveals whether the reporting entity has been able to re-invest surplus funds in the expansion of its business, or whether it is dependent on external funds provided by its financiers and shareholders.

To do this it is necessary to revise the layout of the funds statement. The version used by PPI is typical of many produced in response to the SSAP 10 requirement. It is cluttered with unnecessary detail. More importantly, the order in which the items are presented means that the statement does not lend itself to sensible analysis.

The source and application of funds statement in PPI's 1989 Annual Report has been reproduced in Illustration 8.6. Example 8.4 contains a revised layout of the statement similar to that used in Example 7.2 in the previous chapter. It should be noted that the statement presented in Example 8.4 suffers from the limitations outlined in that chapter. It is not a perfect document but it allows the user to view PPI's profit and loss account and balance sheet in a new light. To prepare it, certain additional information about the group's borrowings and share issues had to be obtained from the relevant notes to the 1988 and 1989 financial statements.

Illustration 8.6: *Polly Peck International PLC (1989)*

SOURCE AND APPLICATION OF FUNDS (extract)	12 months ended 31st December 1989 £m	16 months ended 31st December 1988 £m
SOURCE OF FUNDS		
Profit on ordinary activities before taxation	161.4	144.1
Adjustment for items not involving the movement of funds:–		
Depreciation and amortisation	28.9	19.2
Provision against other investments	0.8	–
Minority interest	0.9	–
Exchange variances:		
on results of overseas companies	(1.7)	(11.6)
on inter group funding	(19.3)	(98.9)
Related companies share of results less exchange variances	(0.6)	–
Loss on disposal of tangible fixed assets	1.6	0.2
	10.6	(91.1)
TOTAL GENERATED FROM OPERATIONS	172.0	53.0
FUNDS FROM OTHER SOURCES		
Bank loans (net)	686.9	76.2
Proceeds on sale of fixed assets	22.5	14.9
Divestments	51.8	–
Ordinary shares issued net of loan stock conversions and expenses	286.3	181.1
Guaranteed bond issues net of redemptions and expenses	37.3	116.0
	1,084.8	388.2
	1,256.8	441.2
APPLICATION OF FUNDS		
Acquisitions	582.6	74.6
Purchase of tangible assets	209.0	156.4
Purchase of other investments	17.8	9.9
Taxation paid	12.3	19.5
Dividends paid	18.7	14.4
	840.4	274.8
	416.4	166.4
INCREASE (DECREASE) IN WORKING CAPITAL		
Stocks and work in progress	77.4	60.6
Debtors	182.2	85.6
Creditors	28.8	(49.7)
	288.4	96.5
INCREASE IN LIQUID FUNDS	128.0	69.9

Revising the layout of the source and application of funds statement shown above along the lines suggested in Chapter 7, produces the following document:

Example 8.4: *Polly Peck International PLC*

REVISED FUNDS STATEMENTS

	12 months ended 31 December 1989 £m	16 months ended 31 December 1988 £m
Net borrowings*		
at beginning of the period	251.9	148.8
exchange restatement	19.1	(2.0)
at end of the period	803.8	251.9
Net increase during the period	532.8	105.1
Arising on acquisitions and disposals	45.5	17.2
Net increase attributable to business operations	578.3	122.3
Other sources of finance		
Share issues net of expenses	305.2	181.1
Business operations	(148.4)	(77.4)
Finance available for capital expenditure	735.1	226.0
Capital expenditure during the period		
Acquisitions	582.6	74.6
Divestments	(51.8)	–
Purchase of tangible assets	209.0	156.4
Proceeds on sale of fixed assets	(22.5)	(14.9)
Purchase of other investments	17.8	9.9
	735.1	226.0

*Excluding immaterial finance lease obligations

The information shown above could be further summarised as follows:

Example 8.5: *Polly Peck International PLC*

SUMMARISED FUNDS STATEMENTS

	1989 £m	1988 £m
Capital expenditure during the period	735.1	226.0
Financed by:		
Net borrowings	578.3	122.3
Share issues net of expenses	305.2	181.1
Business operations	(148.4)	(77.4)
	735.1	226.0

The picture that emerges from the funds statements is of an entity heavily reliant on the faith of its bankers and shareholders. In the 28-month period from the end of August 1987 to the end of December 1989, the group's business operations absorbed finance in excess of £220 million from these sources. Instead of being able to reinvest surplus finance in the expansion of its activities, the group was dependent on new finance to run its existing operations. Its ability to service its borrowing commitments and to make distributions to its shareholders was dependent on the proceeds of new loans and share issues. Being unable to generate surplus finance of its own, it would continue to exist only for as long as its bankers and shareholders were prepared to advance new finance. The news that its chairman had been interviewed by the Serious Fraud Office was probably sufficient for the group's financiers to lose faith in it. Without their support its chances of surviving were slim.

CONCLUSION

Under the existing accounting framework, it is beyond dispute that:

Historical cost accounting may be regarded as a modification of cash flow accounting. The historical cost profit and loss account seeks to provide a more useful statement than a receipts and payments account by reallocating transactions to different periods in accordance with the accruals and prudence concepts, so as to say in each year how much of the cumulative cash flow can sensibly be treated as a further instalment of cumulative profit earned to date. The balance sheet picks up the effects of that reallocation.[11]

Although users of financial statements are not provided with a receipts and payments account, it is possible to use the funds statement as a rough approximation. It provides a useful backdrop against which to assess the accounting allocations that give rise to the profit and loss account and the balance sheet. The funds statement is a simple, rather crude, document. Many users regarded it as a superfluous addition to the financial statements. It is worth remembering, however, that the profit and loss account and the balance sheet are only as good as the accounting allocation process which creates them. There is a clear need for a backdrop against which to assess the uncertainties, estimates and predictions that are inherently part of that process.

1   Polly Peck International PLC (1989), Annual Report, p. 3.
2   *Ibid.*, p. 6.
3   Polly Peck International PLC (1990), Interim Financial Statement, Chairman's Statement.
4   *Ibid.*
5   Polly Peck International PLC (1989), Annual Report, p. 1.
6   *Ibid.*, p. 24.
7   *Ibid.*, p. 4.
8   *Ibid.*, p. 56.
9   *Ibid.*, p. 24.
10 *Ibid.*, p. 25.
11 Paterson, Ron (1990) 'Primacy For The P&L Account', *Accountancy*, August, p. 80.

9:   Responding to the Crisis

'If seven maids with seven mops
Swept it for half a year,
Do you suppose,' the Walrus said,
'That they could get it clear?'
'I doubt it,' said the Carpenter,
And shed a bitter tear.

Lewis Carroll[1]

INTRODUCTION

The FRC's 1991 review of the State of Financial Reporting contained the following comment by the chairman of the ASB:

> The collapse of Polly Peck International has highlighted the treatment of certain foreign currency losses relating to investments and trading overseas, and posed the question whether SSAP 20 *Foreign currency translation* fails to specify with sufficient precision the nature of adjustments that should be made to the profit and loss account to take account of the loss in value of overseas assets that is caused by currency depreciation in a highly inflationary environment. Unless the results of foreign subsidiaries from such an environment are adjusted for inflation before their accounts are translated into sterling, there is a risk that the group's reported profit for the year may be inflated at the expense of currency translation losses which are deducted from reserves rather than shown in the profit and loss account.[2]

The extract provides a clue as to one of the consequences of the Polly Peck International disaster. The apparent failure of accounting standards to provide users with a reliable indicator of financial performance was clearly of concern to the body responsible for issuing them. On 29 October 1992, the ASB issued FRS 3 *Reporting Financial Performance*. As discussed in Chapter 4, greater prominence is now required to be given to gains and losses previously excluded from the profit and loss account. 'Accordingly, the FRS requires, as a primary statement, a statement of total recognised gains and losses to show the extent to which shareholders' funds have increased or decreased from all the various gains and losses recognised in the period.'[3]

It should be stressed that the FRC sees the need to improve accounting standards as part of a larger, more complex problem. Its *Second Annual Review* explains that:

160

At the heart of the whole system of financial reporting lie the company board and the board's relationship with the auditors appointed by shareholders to give assurance that the accounts presented to them give a true and fair view. In the competitive pressures of today's world, with the inherited weaknesses in accounting standards, and the pressures of innovation in financial techniques, the auditor's position as a champion of fairness has been eroded. That issue can only be fully addressed within the context of corporate governance. Accordingly, the Council was one of the sponsors of the Cadbury Committee, whose recommendations and code of practice are now on the table for action.[4]

The Report of the Committee on The Financial Aspects of Corporate Governance (the Cadbury Committee) was published on 1 December 1992. The Committee's purpose 'was to review those aspects of corporate governance specifically related to financial reporting and accountability.'[5] The Committee's Report notes that its 'proposals do, however, seek to contribute positively to the promotion of good corporate governance as a whole.'[6]

THE GOING CONCERN PROBLEM

Public criticism that the sudden collapse of Polly Peck International and certain other large public companies took place without adequate warning from the auditors, was one of the issues addressed by the Cadbury Committee. Its recommendations in this regard need to be seen in the context of the existing requirements.

In Chapter 1, reference was made to the *accounting principles* contained in Schedule 4 to the Companies Act 1985. One of these principles states that:

> The company shall be presumed to be carrying on business as a going concern.[7]

This requirement has given rise to considerable confusion. The Cadbury Committee has noted that 'under company law, accounts are prepared on the assumption that the company is a going concern. There is, however, no explicit requirement for directors to satisfy themselves that it is reasonable to make this assumption, for example by the preparation of an adequate cash flow forecast.'[8] The Committee's Report recognises the legislature's overriding requirement for accounts to give a 'true and fair' view. Section 226(5) of the Companies Act 1985 stipulates that:

> If in special circumstances compliance with any of those provisions [contained in Schedule 4 and elsewhere in the Act] is inconsistent with the requirement to give a true and fair view, the directors shall depart from that provision to the extent necessary to give a true and fair view.

If compliance with the going concern presumption contained in schedule 4 would result in the accounts not giving a 'true and fair' view, the directors are required to ignore that presumption. They would have to prepare the accounts on an alternative basis. Although the provisions contained in the Companies Act seem to be unambiguous, the Cadbury Committee concluded that:

> Whilst the requirement for directors to prepare financial statements giving a true and fair view creates a presumption that they will satisfy themselves that the company is not in financial difficulties and that the going concern basis is appropriate, there is no explicit obligation in company law that they should do so. There is similarly no requirement in law for the directors to report to shareholders that they have satisfied themselves about the going concern basis or the adequacy of financial resources.[9]

It is true that there is no requirement in the Companies Act 1985 to confirm that the going concern basis has been complied with. However, section 226(5) of the Act requires that 'particulars of any such departure (including those from the accounting principles in schedule 4), the reasons for it and its effect shall be given in a note to the accounts.' Instead of a confirmatory statement, the legislature requires departures from the going concern basis to be highlighted in a note.

A similar approach was adopted by the ASC in SSAP 2 *Disclosure of accounting policies*. The 'going concern' concept is one of four fundamental accounting concepts contained in that standard. The 'accruals' and 'prudence' concepts have been dealt with in an earlier chapter. Paragraph 14 of the standard describes the 'going concern' concept as follows:

> the enterprise will continue in operational existence for the foreseeable future. This means in particular that the profit and loss account and balance sheet assume no intention or necessity to liquidate or curtail significantly the scale of operation;

Paragraph 17 of the standard explains that compliance with this concept should be inferred by the absence of a negative statement:

> If accounts are prepared on the basis of assumptions which differ in material respects from any of the generally accepted fundamental concepts defined in paragraph 14 above, the facts should be explained. In the absence of a clear statement to the contrary, there is a presumption that the four fundamental concepts have been observed.

The Cadbury Committee's concern about the absence of explicit legislative provisions requiring directors to satisfy themselves about the going concern basis and to report this satisfaction to shareholders, is hard to understand. The provisions contained in the Companies Act 1985 and SSAP 2 seem to be clear enough. A possible explanation is that the Committee's approach originates from a desire to increase the role of the auditor.

Proposed solution

The background to the Cadbury Committee's recommendations on the going concern problem is explained by the following paragraph:

> In view of the understandable public criticism of the audit process when companies collapse without apparent warning, there are strong arguments for amending company law to place an explicit requirement on directors to satisfy themselves that the going

concern basis is appropriate, and to report accordingly to shareholders. There is also a strong case for extending the scope of the audit, to test going concern assumptions more specifically, and for requiring the auditors to give an opinion on the directors' report. Many proposals have been made to the Committee along these lines.[10]

The Committee has accordingly recommended that 'directors should state in the report and accounts that the business is a going concern, with supporting assumptions or qualifications as necessary' and that 'the auditors should report on this state-ment.'[11] It has also recommended that 'the accountancy profession in conjunction with representatives of preparers of accounts should take the lead in developing guidance for companies and auditors' and 'the question of legislation should be decided in the light of experience.'[12] The new guidelines should:

> ...strike a careful balance between drawing proper attention to the conditions on which the continuation of the business depends, and not requiring directors to express unnecessarily cautious reservations that could of themselves jeopardise the business. Directors should be required to satisfy themselves that the business is a going concern on the basis that they have a **reasonable expectation** that it will continue in operation for the time period which the guidelines define. Directors should not be expected to give a firm guarantee about their company's prospects because there can never be complete certainty about future trading. The guidelines should also recognise the position of smaller companies.[13]

Auditor involvement

It seems that the Auditing Practices Board (APB) is also keen to get involved in the business of making assessments about the future. In November 1992, it released 'a paper to promote public debate', titled 'The Future Development of Auditing'. The following two paragraphs are relevant to the going concern problem discussed in this chapter:

> As presently defined, the audit is essentially backward looking. Financial statements recording the past are a vital element of corporate governance. But at best they are an imperfect guide to the future. Even the requirement to consider whether a company is a 'going concern' has been met as an accounting concept, based on a statutory presumption that a company can normally be regarded as such, rather than being a serious assessment of the future of the enterprise concerned.
>
> The APB proposes that there should be a cultural shift in the audit so that it looks forward as well as backward. It is not realistic to suggest that annual reports should include, as a matter of course, financial forecasts and projections. Nevertheless it is reasonable to expect directors to respond to expectations that an unbiased commentary on future prospects is given, and auditors to take on some role in warning shareholders or other stakeholders of substantial future risks.[14]

The APB considers that these future risks fall into two categories. The company 'may not be able to sustain its core operations profitably or at all' and its 'style of management ... might facilitate imprudence or fraud.'[15] In proposing that the purpose of the audit be re-defined, the APB envisages that three specific matters would be covered. The third of these is that the audit would 'provide an independent opinion to those with an interest in a company that they have received from those responsible for its direction and management an adequate account of future risks attaching to the company.'[16]

An effective solution?

It is instructive to speculate how the recommendations of the Cadbury Committee and the proposals of the APB might have been applied to the Polly Peck International (PPI) disaster described in Chapter 8. Would they have added valuable information to the company's 1989 Annual Report?

The Cadbury Committee Recommendations

The Committee has recommended that 'directors should state in the report and accounts that the business is a going concern, with supporting assumptions or qualifications as necessary, and the auditors should report on this statement.'[17] How would PPI's directors have tackled the task of complying with this requirement? A good guide is provided by the following extract from the Chairman's Statement in the 1989 Annual Report:

> PPI intends to continue its unbroken record of growth and profitability into the 1990s and beyond. We will continually seek new sources for our existing product ranges, new products to expand those ranges and new markets into which to sell these products ... In conclusion, I am confident that 1990 will be an exciting start to a second decade of growth for the Group, and that the strategy we develop in the 1990s will be as successful as that implemented during the 1980s.[18]

It seems reasonable to conclude that the directors considered the company to be a going concern. The 1989 Annual Report would accordingly have included a statement to that effect.

What if the auditors had pressed the directors to provide supporting assumptions for their statement? The Finance Director's comments in the 1989 Financial Review provide a clue as to the likely response:

> Other achievements over the year included the continuation of the process started in 1988 of widening the range of banks with whom we have strong commercial relationships. The breadth of these relationships means that we have constant access to funds, should they be required, at competitive rates.[19]

The APB Proposals

These proposals require the auditor to give an independent opinion as to whether the company's management has provided an adequate account of the future risks attaching to the company. It seems appropriate to conclude that PPI's directors regarded these risks as being fairly remote. They were confident of being able to secure the funds needed to sustain the group's core operations. They would presumably also have been of the opinion that they were not guilty 'of a style of management which might facilitate imprudence or fraud.'[20]

Would the company's auditors have been in a position to disagree with them? They might have insisted on a statement outlining the risks of an aggressive growth strategy. How would this have been worded? Would it have been of any significance to readers of the Annual Report? Is it realistic to expect auditors to report the existence of risks arising from the style of a company's management? They would prefer not to deal with directors who managed their businesses in an imprudent or fraudulent manner. The issue is more likely to be addressed prior to accepting the audit engagement than when drafting the audit report.

Predicting the future?

The 'going concern' concept has given rise to a great deal of confusion. The Companies Act 1985 and SSAP 2 both require directors to form a judgement about the future in order to present historical information in a meaningful manner. They are, however, not being asked to predict the future viability of the company. What is expected of them is that they exercise informed judgement when allocating historical transactions to current and future reporting periods. The purchase of an item of plant is a good example. The estimation of its useful life for depreciation purposes is simply an attempt to present information about its purchase in a more meaningful manner. Directors also need to consider whether events that have already taken place are likely to result in future outflows of cash. They need to satisfy themselves that these liabilities have been adequately provided for. In exercising their judgement in this manner, they are not making a prediction that the entity will continue in existence. They have unfortunately not been blessed with this power. The 'going concern' concept has another purpose. It is to remind directors that financial statements will not give a 'true and fair' view if historical transactions are allocated to future reporting periods in circumstances where there is a serious threat to the company's continued existence.

Users need to make up their own minds about the future viability of the reporting entity. One of the purposes of financial reporting is to provide them with information that would be useful in this regard. The user's responsibility for making this assessment is incapable of being passed to the directors or auditors. They do not possess any special powers which enable them to make reliable predictions about the future.

There must be a danger that the Cadbury recommendations and the APB proposals could do more harm than good. If their purpose is simply to highlight the existence of the 'going concern' concept, they merely repeat what is already contained in the legislature and SSAP 2. If, however, they are designed to provide additional assurance about the future, they are fundamentally flawed. What does the Committee mean, for example, when it refers to the directors having to satisfy themselves about the going concern assumption 'by the preparation of an adequate cash flow forecast'? Can such a forecast ever be considered to be 'adequate'?

The Committee's proposals are likely to raise public expectations about the forecasting ability of directors and auditors, expectations that are incapable of being met. More importantly, they may deflect users from the task of making their own assessments about the future. The best guide to the future viability of the reporting entity is the information contained in its financial statements. The PPI 1989 Annual Report is a good example. A statement by the directors that the company is a going concern will never be an effective substitute for detailed analysis of the historical information contained elsewhere in the annual report.

WIDENING THE SCOPE OF THE AUDIT

The going concern problem was but one of several issues addressed by the Cadbury Committee. At the heart of its recommendations is a Code of Best Practice. The boards of all listed companies are expected to comply with the Code and to include a statement to that effect in their company's report and accounts. Reasons should be given for any areas of non-compliance. The Committee has also recommended that 'companies' statements of compliance should be reviewed by the auditors before publication. The review should cover only those parts of the compliance statement which relate to provisions of the Code where compliance can be objectively verified.'[21] The relevant parts of the Code are as follows:

- The board should have a formal schedule of matters specifically reserved to it for decision to ensure that the direction and control of the company is firmly in its hands.
- There should be an agreed procedure for directors in the furtherance of their duties to take independent professional advice if necessary, at the company's expense.
- Non-executive directors should be appointed for specified terms and reappointment should not be automatic.
- Non-executive directors should be selected through a formal process and both this process and their appointment should be a matter for the board as a whole.
- Directors' service contracts should not exceed three years without shareholders' approval.
- There should be full and clear disclosure of directors' total emoluments and those of the chairman and highest-paid UK director, including pension contributions and stock options. Separate figures should be given for salary and performance-related elements and the basis on which performance is measured should be explained.
- Executive directors' pay should be subject to the recommendations of a remuneration committee made up wholly or mainly of non-executive directors.

- The board should establish an audit committee of at least three non-executive directors with written terms of reference which deal clearly with its authority and duties.
- The directors should explain their responsibility for preparing the accounts next to a statement by the auditors about their reporting responsibilities.
- The directors should report on the effectiveness of the company's system of internal control.
- The directors should report that the business is a going concern, with supporting assumptions or qualifications as necessary.[22]

The Cadbury Committee's terms of reference required it to consider the responsibilities both of executive and of non-executive directors. This explains why non-executive directors feature prominently in the extracts from The Code of Best Practice reproduced above. The Code contains the following provisions on the composition of a company's board of directors:

- There should be a clearly accepted division of responsibilities at the head of a company, which will ensure a balance of power and authority, such that no one individual has unfettered powers of decision. Where the chairman is also the chief executive, it is essential that there should be a strong and independent element on the board, with a recognised senior member.
- The board should include non-executive directors of sufficient calibre and number for their views to carry significant weight in the board's decisions.[23]

As compliance with these two provisions cannot be objectively verified, they are not required to be reviewed by the auditor.

The auditors' response

Are auditors prepared to accept a wider responsibility of the kind envisaged by the Cadbury Committee? The following comments by John McFarlane, head of the working party responsible for 'The Future Development of Auditing', could be taken as a guide:

> Society is demanding more from auditors than the basic statutory audit. Their failure to respond to this has dented confidence in auditors. The role and scope of audit urgently needs to be extended to meet the revised needs of users of accounts.[24]

The paper produced by his working party notes that the culture of the auditing profession is essentially a function of a legislative requirement dating back nearly fifty years. The relevant legislation requires auditors to report on financial statements containing a record of past activity. The paper contains the following comment on this aspect of the auditors' role:

> Important though the role described above remains, it is clearly not enough to meet the present day requirements of many commentators. It does not encompass the way in which a company's affairs are generally conducted. It is not concerned with the future. And it

167

does not recognise a public interest beyond the needs of shareholders.[25]

'The Future Development of Auditing' accordingly contains proposals to redefine the role and scope of company audit. That the auditor should express an opinion as to whether management has given an adequate account of the future risks attaching to the company, has already been discussed. The other proposals require the audit to encompass:

- the proper conduct of the company's affairs; and
- the company's financial performance and position.[26]

The first of these proposals links in with the Cadbury Committee's recommendation that the auditors should review the directors' statement of compliance with The Code of Best Practice. 'The Future Development of Auditing' explains the background to one of the ways in which the auditor could report on the proper conduct of the company's affairs, as follows:

> An important facet of corporate governance is the maintenance of adequate internal controls, since weaknesses in this area open a company to additional financial and fiduciary risks, and inadequate controls are often an indicator of potential financial problems in the business. Accordingly, the APB considers that auditors should report to shareholders on whether the company has acceptable financial and other relevant risk management controls commensurate with the nature, scale and complexity of its business.[27]

This requirement is not dissimilar to one already contained in the Companies Act 1985. Section 221 requires a company to 'keep accounting records which are sufficient to show and explain the company's transactions' and to 'disclose with reasonable accuracy, at any time, the financial position of the company.' The auditors are, in turn, required by section 237 to investigate whether, in their opinion, proper accounting records have been kept. They are required to report failure to keep such records to the company's members.

The Cadbury Committee noted that the section 221 requirement means that the directors 'must in practice maintain some form of control system over the company's process of financial management.'[28] The Committee was, however, concerned that 'there is no explicit requirement in company law for them to maintain an effective system of internal control.'[29] It also noted that 'there is at present no Companies Act requirement for auditors to report on the adequacy of internal control systems.'[30]

It is difficult to envisage the Committee's recommendations and the APB's proposals having much impact in practice. For the financial statements to give a 'true and fair' view, the reporting entity's internal control systems have to be of a reasonably satisfactory standard. The directors will nearly always be of the view that the systems are satisfactory. They are, after all, responsible for installing them. They are also responsible for preparing financial statements that give a 'true and fair' view. Auditors are unlikely to be in a position to disagree with the directors on a matter of substance without simultaneously qualifying their opinion on the truth and fairness of the financial statements. Qualifications of this kind have been rare in the past and there is no reason to expect a sudden deterioration in the quality of record keeping. If weaknesses in internal control systems are going to be reported, it is unlikely that the reports will cover matters of great substance.

Expanding the audit function to include a report on the effectiveness of internal control systems is but one element of an apparent desire to install the auditor as a quality watchdog. The proposals in 'The Future Development of Auditing' go much further than reporting on the adequacy of financial and risk management controls. On the subject of fraud, the report notes that 'the APB intends to commission research into the way auditors can fulfil an extended detection role.' The Cadbury Committee expressed its opposition to the idea of a statutory duty to report fraud being applied to the generality of companies. 'The Committee does however see scope for extending to the auditors of all companies the statutory provisions applying to auditors in the regulated sector which enable them to report reasonable suspicion of fraud freely to the appropriate investigatory authorities.'[31] Existing practice in certain regulated industries prompted 'The Future Development of Auditing' paper to comment that 'it is realistic to expect auditors to respond to regulators' requests and to take on a role in relation to a potentially growing demand for monitoring basic ethical standards of corporate behaviour.'[32]

Increasing the responsibility of the auditor

Increasing the role of the auditor in the manner envisaged by the Cadbury Committee and the APB's proposals, requires consideration to be given to another issue:

> The cost and potential damages consequent on litigation are a major constraint on the development of a more responsive and effective audit service, and bear heavily on auditors irrespective of the degree of blame which attaches to them in a particular case. In addition, the litigious environment militates against the wider role and scope of audit set out earlier.[33]

In noting the existence of this constraint, 'The Future Development of Auditing' proposes that the litigation problem 'ought to be addressed again and urgently, if the progressive developments expounded in this paper are to be achieved.'[34]

CONCLUSION

This chapter has outlined certain aspects of the responses of the ASB, the FRC, the Cadbury Committee and the APB to public criticism in the wake of recent financial disasters like the Polly Peck International case. The perceived low level of public confidence in financial reporting and the audit function were matters of primary concern to the bodies concerned. Their proposals are characterised by a desire to tighten accounting standards, to improve the composition, operation and accountability of boards of directors, to strengthen the position of the auditor and to increase the scope of the audit function.

The chapter also contains comments on the limitations of certain of the recommendations and proposals made by the Cadbury Committee and the APB. Its primary purpose is, however, to highlight another more important issue.

> The formal relationship between the shareholders and the board of directors is that the shareholders elect the directors, the directors report on their stewardship to the shareholders and the shareholders appoint the auditors to provide an external check on the directors' financial statements. Thus the shareholders as owners of the company elect the directors to run the business on their behalf and hold them accountable for its progress. The issue for corporate governance is how to strengthen the accountability of boards of directors to shareholders.[35]

There is usually no need to strengthen the accountability of boards of directors appointed by the shareholders of small companies. These shareholders have little difficulty in exercising their power to control their companies. The accountability issue only arises because the shareholders of most large UK companies are incapable of exercising their rights of ownership. The Code of Best Practice bears testimony to this. It has become necessary to issue guidance as to:

- how boards of directors should be constituted;
- how they should operate;
- whether non-executive directors should serve on them;
- how their members should be remunerated;
- how they should liaise with the auditors;
- how they should report to the shareholders.

The rich man in the Parable of the Dishonest Steward had little difficulty making these decisions himself. He did not need a code of best practice to guide him. Shareholders in large listed companies are, by contrast, in a different position. They are incapable of making these decisions themselves and they are unable to determine whether they have been implemented properly. They need a code of best practice and auditors to assist them. They would also very much like to hold the auditors accountable for matters that could properly be considered to be their responsibility as owners, but which they are incapable of monitoring themselves.

No system of financial reporting can be expected to deliver a product of quality when the primary user group has been emasculated. It is for the users of financial statements to determine what information they need and to ensure that it is provided to them. No amount of legislation, no Code of Best Practice and no system of accounting standards can do it for them.

1 Carroll, Lewis ((1871),1872), 'The Walrus and the Carpenter', *Through the Looking-Glass* (London: Macmillan).
2 Financial Reporting Council, *The State of Financial Reporting – a review*, November 1991, para. 5.34.
3 Accounting Standards Board (1992), FRS 3, *Reporting Financial Performance* (London: ASB), October, para. 56.
4 Financial Reporting Council (1992), *The State of Financial Reporting – Second Annual Review*, November, para. 2.4.
5 The Committee on the Financial Aspects of Corporate Governance (1992), *Report of the Committee on the Financial Aspects of Corporate Governance* (London: Gee and Co. Ltd), para. 1.2.
6 *Ibid.*
7 Companies Act 1985, Schedule 4, para. 10.
8 *Report of the Committee on the Financial Aspects of Corporate Governance*, para. 5.18.
9 *Ibid.*, Appendix 5, para. 6.
10 *Ibid.*, para. 5.19.
11 *Ibid.*, para. 5.22.
12 *Ibid.*
13 *Ibid.*, para. 5.21.
14 Auditing Practices Board, 'The Future Development of Auditing' (1992), A paper to promote public debate (London: CCAB Ltd), November, paras 3.13 and 3.14.
15 *Ibid.*, para. 3.15.
16 *Ibid.*, para. 3.4.
17 *Report of the Committee on the Financial Aspects of Corporate Governance*, Summary of Recommendations, para. 11.
18 Polly Peck International PLC (1989), Annual Report, p. 6.
19 *Ibid.*, p. 24.
20 *The Future Development of Auditing*, para. 3.15.
21 *Report of the Committee on the Financial Aspects of Corporate Governance*, Summary of Recommendations, para. 3.
22 *Report of the Committee on the Financial Aspects of Corporate Governance*, The Code of Best Practice, paras. 1.4, 1.5, 2.3, 2.4, 3.1–3.3, 4.3–4.6.
23 *Ibid.*, paras. 1.2 and 1.3.
24 *Accountancy Age* (1992), 26 November, p. 5.
25 *The Future Development of Auditing*, para. 3.3.
26 *Ibid.*, para. 3.4.
27 *Ibid.*, para. 3.7.
28 *Report of the Committee on the Financial Aspects of Corporate Governance*, Appendix 5, para. 3.
29 *Ibid.*
30 *Ibid.*, para. 4.
31 *Report of the Committee on the Financial Aspects of Corporate Governance*, para. 5.28.
32 *The Future Development of Auditing*, para. 3.9.
33 *Ibid.*, para. 5.1.
34 *Ibid.*, para. 5.4.
35 *Report of the Committee on the Financial Aspects of Corporate Governance*, para. 6.1.

10: Achieving Utopia – Options for the Future

> *'The time has come,'* the Walrus said,
> *'To talk of many things:*
> *Of shoes – and ships – and sealing wax –*
> *Of cabbages – and kings –*
> *And why the sea is boiling hot –*
> *And whether pigs have wings.'*
>
> Lewis Carroll[1]

BACKGROUND

In April 1992, the ASB published a discussion paper which contained guidelines for the inclusion in company annual reports of an Operating and Financial Review (OFR). Although the document was issued by the body responsible for setting accounting standards in the UK, the OFR would not have the status of an accounting standard. The reason for this was explained in paragraph 3 of the discussion paper:

> The ASB believes that the desired standard of contents and drafting of such OFRs can only be achieved by general consensus rather than by regulation, but that the climate is now such that a consensus could be achieved by the issue of guidelines that are backed by influential bodies. The Financial Reporting Council (FRC) also took the view that a statement of best practice was the only feasible route.[2]

The approach outlined above contrasts with that adopted in North America. The Securities and Exchange Commission in the USA and the Ontario Securities Commission in Canada require a Management Discussion and Analysis report to be filed for all listed companies in their jurisdictions. The UK proposal does 'not provide any formal method of enforcing the preparation of OFRs of the desired quality.'[3] It hopes that 'the existence of the ASB Statement would establish a benchmark for disclosure which investors, analysts and financial journalists would treat as a reference point in their evaluation of the standards of reporting by large companies.'[4]

At first glance, the proposed OFR seems doomed to fail. The voluntary approach outlined above flies in the face of accepted wisdom. Compliance with accounting standards is backed by legislation and enforced by a Review Panel. What chance does a voluntary proposal have in an environment which has deteriorated to the point where 'the auditor's position as a champion of fairness has been eroded' by a combination of 'competitive pressures', 'inherited weaknesses in accounting standards' and 'the pressures of innovation in financial techniques' as noted in Chapter 9?[5]

NON-FINANCIAL ACCOUNTING STANDARDS?

There is an obvious reason why a voluntary approach has been proposed for the OFR referred to in the previous section. The nature of its contents is such that enforcement by regulation would be impracticable. As explained in its introductory paragraph, the OFR provides management with 'the opportunity to discuss in a structured way some of the main factors underlying the performance and financial position portrayed in the financial statements. By such means, users of the Annual Report would be given a fuller understanding of the business and the environment in which it operates.'[6] Being interpretative by nature, the OFR would not easily lend itself to detailed regulation.

The OFR would be an important contribution towards remedying an obvious defect in existing financial statements which 'provide information about the financial position, performance and financial adaptability'[7] of the reporting entity. The ASB's definition of the objective of financial statements notes that:

> Financial statements prepared for this purpose meet the common needs of most users. However, financial statements do not provide all the information that users may need to make economic decisions since they largely portray the financial effects of past events and do not necessarily provide non-financial information.[8]

One commentator has suggested that interpretation, discussion and analysis are an essential part of the 'true and fair' view. Writing in the July 1992 issue of *Accountancy* magazine, Professor David Hatherly commented that:

> No accounting policies or standards are capable by themselves of delivering a true and fair view without appropriate interpretation, discussion and analysis. Indeed I believe that the Accounting Standards Board will move on this, that the limits of promulgating standards and regulations will be recognised, and that emphasis will be placed instead on a much more fertile requirement for discussion and analysis. The ASB's recently issued discussion paper, proposing that management include an operating and finance review (OFR) in the annual report, is an important step forward.[9]

The provisions contained in the ASB's proposed OFR are worth examining in more detail, given their potential significance to the user of financial statements.

The proposed Operating and Financial Review

The ASB has recognised the need to provide guidelines as to the structure of the proposed OFR. It has accordingly suggested that management's interpretation and discussion of the financial statements should cover the following three main areas:

- a commentary on the operating results;
- a review of the financial needs and resources;
- a commentary on shareholders' return and value.[10]

The ASB's proposals stress that the 'OFR should build on the information given in the financial statements, it should not be a necessary guide to understanding them.'[11] The difficulty of regulating the preparation of a document like the OFR becomes apparent when the following proposals are considered:[12]

- The OFR should be fair, in the sense of being a balanced and objective statement of both good and bad news.
- A balance must be struck between, on the one hand, giving a too cursory (albeit accurate) overall impression, and, on the other, giving excessive detail on individual aspects of the enterprise's operations.
- What is intended is a discussion of the trends and changes, not merely an extraction of increases, decreases and percentages.

Although the discussion paper falls short of calling for the inclusion of profit forecasts and future projections, it emphasises the need for the review to be forward, as well as backward-looking. 'The OFR should, therefore, discuss those factors that have affected the results but that are not expected to continue in the future, and new factors that have not had an impact in the past but that are likely to be significant in the future.'[13] The discussion paper gives detailed guidance on the matters to be addressed under each of the three main areas listed at the start of this section.

Commentary on the operating results

The proposals state that 'the purpose of this aspect of the OFR would be to enable management to explain to the user of the financial statements the main influences and uncertainties affecting the enterprise's results and operating cash flows, by major segment, and thus assist the user in making his own assessment of likely future results.'[14]

To achieve this objective, the discussion paper lists a number of specific points which it envisages would be covered in this commentary. The following sample provides a good indication of the extent of the detail required:

- products or services designed to protect or enhance earnings or market share;
- sensitivity to the economic and business environment;
- dependence on major customers, suppliers or products;

- dependence on scarce raw materials or expertise of uncertain supply;
- termination or expiry of patents, licences or franchises;
- currency and commodity price risk and their day to day management;
- environmental protection costs and possible liabilities;
- the extent to which the growth in earnings has been affected by inflation;
- the influence of exchange rate changes on the results;
- the enterprise's expenditure on research and development and other revenue investment.[15]

Review of financial needs and resources

The discussion paper explains that this section would provide a discussion of the following aspects of the reporting entity's business:

- its current capital structure, the purpose and impact of financing transactions entered into during the period and major fixed asset or investment acquisitions and disposals;
- its approach to managing interest rate risk and foreign currency exchange rate risk;
- its current liquidity, peak borrowing requirements and borrowing facilities, confirmation that it can meet its short term requirements from existing borrowing facilities and details of any restrictions on its ability to transfer funds from one part of the enterprise to meet the cash needs of another;
- its fixed and working capital investment plans, distinguishing, if practicable, between expenditure intended to maintain existing businesses and that intended to expand existing businesses or develop new business areas;
- its internal and external sources of funds available to meet its capital expenditure plans, its working capital requirements and other financial commitments, and an assessment of its long term solvency.[16]

Commentary on shareholders' return and value

The final section of the OFR would 'enable management to explain to the user of the annual report the relationship between operating results and shareholders' earnings and dividend payments; and the relationship between the financial statements and the overall value of the enterprise.'[17]

This section should explain the relationship between the change in dividends and the change in operating profit, profit attributable to members, total gains and losses and earnings per share. It should also include a discussion of return on assets and return on equity. Provision is also made for 'a commentary on strengths and resources of the enterprise whose value is not, or not adequately, reflected in the balance sheet (such as brands and other similar items) and changes in such items over the period.'[18]

An option for the future?

Publication of the ASB's OFR proposals provoked a mixed response. Some companies expressed concern at the extent of detail required. Others were anxious about the disclosure of commercially sensitive information. The discussion paper's encouragement of comments on future prospects was seen by some observers to cause a potential problem with the Financial Services Act 1986.

As noted earlier in this chapter, Professor David Hatherly is a strong supporter of the proposals. His July 1992 article in *Accountancy* magazine continued in the following vein:

> If discussion and analysis is to be the centrepiece of the financial statements of the future, then what should the auditors' role be? My vision is that the audit report of the future will be a commentary on the operating and financial review, highlighting points of contention, uncertainty and difficulty.
>
> ...An audit report of this type would embrace: any going concern or cash flow difficulties; fraudulent activities of a magnitude or incidence likely to affect the business; any illegal acts which are giving a business advantage; any internal control or information-base deficiencies likely to affect implementation of business plans, policies or the recovery of assets; the impact of related party transactions on profit; the use of reserve accounting and other questionable accounting policies; highlighting of uncertainties and contingent liabilities; differences between cost and value; an assessment of the business segments; and the impact of price changes and currency movements.
>
> ...Investors and other user groups would find this type of report far more useful than the present one. It would therefore add considerable value to the present audit, not necessarily for management, but for those in whose name the audit is carried out.[19]

Professor Hatherly's vision of the future contrasts sharply with the corporate governance problem addressed by the Cadbury Committee. It seems difficult enough to increase the accountability of boards of directors to shareholders under the existing framework. His article nevertheless raises an important issue. Is the holder of 100 shares in a large public company entitled to unlimited information about the reporting entity? The Companies Act 1985 provides a mechanism for controlling shareholders to access detailed information through representation on the board of directors. Does the current system of public ownership require minority shareholders to sacrifice their right to unlimited information in return for the flexibility of buying and selling their ownership interests at will?

NON-MANDATORY ACCOUNTING STANDARDS?

The OFR discussion paper is significant for two reasons. First, its contents are a reminder to users of the extent of the information needed to make sensible economic decisions. Secondly, it raises an important point about the implementation of financial reporting requirements. The reasoning behind the voluntary approach proposed in the discussion paper is summarised in the following extract:

> In contrast to the regulatory approach adopted by the SEC [Securities and Exchange Commission] and OSC [Ontario Securities Commission], the ASB hopes that the voluntary approach proposed will enable preparers of OFRs to place less emphasis on precise interpretation of details of the recommendations and more emphasis on producing a coherent and readable discussion that concentrates on the more significant matters, but which remains fairly balanced between the favourable and unfavourable. Success or failure in this voluntary environment will depend on the willingness of commentators, analysts and institutional shareholders, as well as the business community itself, together with their representative bodies, to monitor the system and bring appropriate pressure to bear on companies that visibly fail to comply with the spirit of the recommendations.[20]

Further examination of the reasoning outlined above suggests that it could equally be applied to all accounting standards. The best way to get preparers to comply with the spirit of accounting regulations is to convince them that it is in their best interests to do so. If accounting information is important, failure to provide it should result in the reporting entity suffering an economic penalty. Compliance should increase its economic well-being.

CREATIVE ACCOUNTING IN THE UK: AN OVERALL CONCLUSION

It is not possible to provide a comprehensive examination of the current state of UK financial reporting in a short book. An attempt has nevertheless been made to highlight certain significant issues.

The underlying issues

Chapter 1 noted that the effectiveness of any system of financial reporting depended heavily on the knowledge, skills and abilities of the user. It concluded that legislation and regulation were unlikely to be effective substitutes for user ignorance.

Chapter 2 explored the attempts made in the last 20 years to secure an improvement in reporting practices by increasing the level of regulation. It doubted whether the ASC was successfully able to overcome many of the problems prevalent at the time of its establishment in 1970. It noted that the desire to secure improvements in financial reporting practices by increased regulation remained undiminished. It concluded that, although the latest financial reporting regime had many impressive features, there was a danger in expecting too much of it. The limitations of relying on any system of financial reporting to safeguard the quality of the information produced by it, were likely to be ever present.

Chapter 3 raised the issue of 'creative accounting': whether financial reporting could be used as a tool to distort the underlying reality. It noted the existence of a perception that it could be used in this manner. It suggested that this could influence the way in which certain preparers tackled the task of preparing their financial statements.

Chapter 4 addressed the calculation of an annual profit figure as a way of measuring financial performance. It concluded that the primary statements required by the existing accounting framework needed to be seen in their proper context. They could be regarded as crude attempts to deal with a complex present and an uncertain future.

Chapter 5 tried to understand the financial community's fascination with the gearing ratio. It concluded that the uncertainties and limitations affecting that ratio applied equally to the balance sheet. The latter's ability to be a satisfactory statement of financial position was undermined by its failure to represent either the value of the reporting entity's assets or the extent of all of its obligations. The chapter concluded that the balance sheet was a limited document, badly misunderstood by many preparers and users of financial statements.

Chapter 6 explored the relevance of financial statements to the investment decision-making process. It suggested that investors seemed to take the reliability of financial statements for granted. They also appeared to attach more importance to the reported earnings of companies than to changes in the level of their borrowings. It concluded that users needed a better understanding of the limitations inherent in the financial statements if they were to draw the right conclusions from the mass of information presented to them.

Chapter 7 sought salvation in statements showing the flow of funds and cash. It proposed that they could be used as a backdrop against which to assess the uncertainties, estimates and predictions that are inherently part of the process used to create the profit and loss account and the balance sheet. It suggested that users might have to make up their own minds about the wisdom of the reporting entity's capital expenditure. It doubted whether the existing accounting framework was capable of allocating this expenditure to individual reporting periods in a satisfactory manner.

Chapter 8 suggested that traditional forms of financial analysis placed excessive reliance on the information contained in the profit and loss account and the balance sheet. These documents were sometimes a poor guide to the viability of the reporting entity. It proposed that an alternative approach, one which placed more reliance on the financing of capital expenditure, could provide users with a valuable insight into the financial well-being of the reporting entity.

Chapter 9 dealt with recent proposals and recommendations designed to improve the public's confidence in financial reporting and the audit function. It outlined some of the measures designed to improve the accountability of boards of directors to shareholders. It expressed concern about the implications for financial reporting when the major user group seemed unable to exercise its rights of ownership.

A sensible conclusion?

Coverage of the release of the APB's recent paper on 'The Future Development of Auditing' included the following remark by the chairman of the working party responsible for that document:

> It is fundamental that the integrity of financial information can be relied upon by those who make decisions based upon it. Auditors have not demonstrated adequately that this is the case.[21]

It seems appropriate to conclude that the achievement of this happy state of affairs is dependent on many factors outside the control of auditors. It is doubtful whether any system of accounting standards is capable of producing consistently reliable measures of financial performance and financial position. Many users seem unaware of the uncertainties, estimates and predictions which are part of the process of drawing up financial statements. Accounting's ability to be 'creative' is more often than not a function of user ignorance. Educating the user would seem to be a more urgent priority than expanding the audit function.

Today's shareholders are unfortunately not in the same position as the rich man in the parable two thousand years ago. Unless they own a majority of the voting rights, they are unlikely to be able to control their stewards. The OFR discussion paper is a powerful reminder of the wide ranging nature of the information needed to make sensible economic decisions. The best way of providing this information is to convince preparers of financial statements of the economic consequences of their reporting practices. Failure to supply information to an informed user group should result in the errant preparer suffering an economic penalty. The successful development of suitable penalties may, however, prove to be elusive. If minority shareholders are unable to discipline their stewards, they do at least have the consolation of being able to dispose of their ownership interests relatively easily.

Financial statements prescribed by law will never be an effective substitute for the extensive information needed to make sensible economic decisions. Controlling shareholders have unlimited access to detailed information about the reporting entity. Minority shareholders, lenders and other investors have little alternative but to place their faith in the stewards chosen to manage their finances.

1   Carroll, Lewis ((1871),1872), 'The Walrus and the Carpenter', *Through the Looking-Glass* (London: Macmillan).
2   *Proposal for a Statement on Operating and Financial Review*, ASB, 1992, para. 3.
3   *Ibid.*, para. 20.
4   *Ibid.*
5   Financial Reporting Council (1992), *The State of Financial Reporting – Second Annual Review,* November, para. 2.4.
6   *Proposal for a Statement on Operating and Financial Review,* para. 1.
7   Accounting Standards Board (1991), 'The objective of financial statements', Exposure Draft of Chapter 1, *Statement of Principles* (London: ASB), July, para. 12.

8   *Ibid.*, para. 13.
9   Hatherly, David (1992), 'Company auditing: a vision of the future?', *Accountancy*, July, p. 75.
10   *Proposal for a Statement on Operating and Financial Review,* para. 5.
11   *Ibid.*, para. 6.
12   *Ibid.*, paras. 7–8.
13   *Ibid.*, para. 9.
14   *Ibid.*, para. 12.
15   *Ibid.*, extracted from para. 14.
16   *Ibid.*, extracted from para. 16.
17   *Ibid.*, para. 17.
18   *Ibid.*, para. 18.
19   Hatherly, David (1992), 'Company auditing: a vision of the future?', *Accountancy*, July, p. 75.
20   *Proposal for a Statement on Operating and Financial Review,* para. 23.
21   *Accountancy Age* (1992), 'APB unveils radical proposals for reform', 26 November.

Index